Glimpses of Eternity

Glimpses of Eternity

Arvin S. Gibson

Sixth Printing, September 2001

International Standard Book Number
0-88290-439-6

Horizon Publishers' Catalog and Order Number
1009

Printed and distributed
in the United States of America by

Horizon Publishers
& Distributors, Incorporated

Mailing Address:
P.O. Box 490
Bountiful, Utah 84011-0490

Street Address:
50 South 500 West
Bountiful, Utah 84010

Phone and Fax:
Local Phone: (801) 295-9451
WATS (toll free): 1 (866) 818-6277
FAX: (801) 295-0196

Internet:
E-mail: horizonp@burgoyne.com
Home Page: http://www.horizonpublishers.com

Acknowledgments

I wish to express appreciation to the many people who have assisted and encouraged me on this project. First among these is my wife, Carol Gibson, whose help during the interview phase was invaluable, and who made many useful suggestions during the entire project.

Duane Crowther rendered indispensable assistance throughout the project. He encouraged me, early in the work, to expand the investigative research areas; later he offered useful advice concerning the structure and organization of the book; he performed stellar editorial duties; and he managed the overall publication in an efficient manner. The personnel of Horizon Publishers and Distributors all helped to make the book a success.

I am indebted to Florence Susan Comish for her magnificent painting, *Ann's Angel*, which graces the jacket cover of this book. RoseMari Finter, Harry Blundell, Richard Sadler, Keith Warner, Marion Bergin, Pat Pexton, and Gary Gillum all provided useful help. Each of my children, Craig Gibson, Aaron Gibson, Dale Gibson and Leah Gibson made valuable comments.

The International Association for Near-Death Studies (IANDS) was a fertile source of research materials and references. Their perspective on the near-death experience was most useful.

This book would not exist except for the generosity of those whose stories reside within it. Their moving accounts of experiences, which in many cases were so sacred that they had rarely been told before, are the foundation for this book. I will never forget the feelings of love, wonder, and awe I underwent while these choice people attempted to explain, usually with great emotion, what they had experienced.

Fred Beckett, a Microbiologist working for the State of Utah, contacted me in the later research stages of the book. He was very familiar with the near-death literature and he helped me in that regard. In addition, he put me in touch with Professor Howard Storm from Northern Kentucky University. Professor Storm had an extensive out-of-body experience, and he kindly granted permission for us to use major portions of his experience in this book.

Many other individuals from different professional backgrounds reviewed an early version of this book. Their comments, from their various perspectives, were beneficial in contributing to the final published version.

Raymond A. Moody, Jr., in his pioneering work *Life After Life*, helped me to understand the significance of my father's account of his near-death experience. Many persons who have experienced near-death and many researchers owe Dr. Moody a debt of gratitude for disclosing the wide-spread nature of the phenomenon.

Glimpses of Eternity is solely the result of my work and my judgment. In exercising that judgment I attempted to do the research and to present the material in as accurate a manner as possible. It is my fervent desire that the material so presented will provide others with the same feelings of love, wonder, and hope which I felt as I listened to people tell of their experiences. I desire, also, as the readers explore Part II of the book, that they gain some of the peace and joy that I experienced upon discovering scriptures which related directly to many of the events described by those having gone through the experiences.

Arvin S. Gibson

Contents

Foreword

"Honey, the doctor says it's leukemia!" Those words changed my life. They came in a phone call from my wife, Jean. She had taken our four-year-old, Laura, to the doctor to find out why large bruises were suddenly appearing on her. It took weeks for us to wrestle with our emotions, to reconcile the nature of our faith in God, and to learn to accept His will concerning the imminent loss of the sweet young spirit whom we loved so deeply. We observed Laura's courage and inner strength as she, without complaint or fear, underwent chemotherapy, repeated blood transfusions, and frightening hospital stays.

She passed away in the car while we were traveling together. As we approached Cascade, Idaho, her spirit slipped from her body. She had been lying in a makeshift bed on the back seat. Shortly before she left us she sat up, looked at me and said, "Daddy, I'm going to wake up soon." At that moment I lacked the eternal perspective to fully grasp what she was saying to me.

A kind physician at the small Cascade hospital could only say, "She's gone—there's nothing I can do for her." We were told there were no mortician's facilities there, so we took her small body and headed back to McCall.

As we drove northward, Laura suddenly appeared to my wife. I didn't see her—but Jean did, and that was enough. Jean said, "She's not a little girl now." She described her as being tall and slender, with long blond hair, and dressed in white. She appeared as if in her mid-twenties. Laura didn't speak. She didn't need to. Jean could see from the serene expression on her face that all was well with her, and she was given to understand that Laura had successfully entered the next phase of her eternal progress. With this knowledge we were buoyed up, strengthened, and able to respond to the emotional demands of her funeral and burial.

But I'm a curious person. I wanted to know exactly where she was, what she was doing, what life was like in the Spirit World, and how she was allowed to appear to Jean. Oh, I had lots of questions. Out of that intense curiosity my book, *Life Everlasting* as born. I gathered the accounts of about 150 individuals who had gone beyond the veil of death and then returned, in some way, to communicate their experiences to loved ones still on earth. Much of my research was drawn from diaries and personal historical accounts. I found dozens of individuals who underwent the same types of experiences. Their isolated accounts, often not shared with others until long after the individuals' deaths, substantiated other records, and a vast network of facts and patterns about the next phase of eternal existence emerged.

In my research, I had focused primarily on experiences of individuals who had entered into Paradise—the spirit world abode of the righteous. I knew there was much more research to be done on near-death experiences, as scientists now call them. I knew relatively little, for instance, about what happens at the moment of death.

That's why I was thrilled when Arvin Gibson showed me his manuscript. He told me of his carefully controlled interviews with dozens of individuals who have had near-death experiences and ventured into the future life. My research was historical—his was based on oral interviews with living people. He has supplied a whole new level of evidence and opened areas of inquiry which I had not pursued.

I've worked with Arvin Gibson on a previous book-publishing project and know him well. He's precise, detail-oriented, careful to document his findings, unwilling to overstate his conclusions, and focused on accurate, unbiased reporting.

Glimpses of Eternity is the result of disciplined research. Arvin has interviewed a large number of people of diverse backgrounds; reported their near-death experiences in a factual, non-editorialized manner; and then examined the meanings of those experiences in the light of other NDE literature and from the perspective of Latter-day Saint scriptures and teachings. His new insights constitute a significant contribution to current understanding.

I learned from him. Many thousands of readers will also learn from him. Those who feel the same insatiable longing for understanding concerning man's future life which I experienced will find knowledge, new meanings and comfort from his research and writing.

Of all the insights he documented which add to the base laid in *Life Everlasting*, the most important to me is the increased understanding of the vast love of God which encompassed them as they met the Lord Jesus Christ. Many of those whom he interviewed experienced it, though they couldn't describe its magnitude, depth and all-encompasing grandeur. Certainly, that experience is to be a focal point in man's eternal growth. I anticipate that encounter with tremendous excitement and joy!

I deeply appreciate the significant contribution to knowledge which Arvin Gibson has made in his great book, *Glimpses of Eternity.* May all who read it experience the same excitement I experienced as I edited it and prepared it for publication.

Sincerely,
Duane S. Crowther
Editor and Publisher

Introduction

A Marvelous Experience

. . . I found myself walking . . . in a completely different sphere. It was beautiful beyond description and we were walking on a path. . . . It was a different world than this one. . . . As we walked along the path I noticed a profusion of flowers and trees. They were of a wider variety, and they had many more colors than on earth—or maybe it was that I could see more colors than on earth, I'm not sure.

. . . I noticed someone on the path ahead of us. As we got closer to the individual I could see and feel that he was a magnificent person. I felt overwhelmed as I looked at him. He was bathed in light. [My guide] asked if I knew who that was, and I answered yes. It was Jesus Christ.

When we got close to the Savior, I felt a tremendous love emanating from him. It's hard to describe, but you could feel it all around him. And I felt a similar enormous love for him. I fell at his feet—not because I thought about it, but I couldn't stand. I felt an overpowering urge to fall at his feet and worship him.

. . . As I knelt there at the feet of this marvelous being I became conscious of my past life being reviewed for me. It seemed to occur in a short period, and I felt the Savior's love during the entire process. That love was . . . well, it was everywhere. And it was as if we could communicate with each other without speaking. After a period the Savior reached down and I knew I should stand. As soon as I stood, he left.

[My guide] next led me to a city. It was a city of light. It was similar to cities on earth in that there were buildings and paths, but the buildings and paths appeared to be built of materials which we consider precious on earth. They looked like marble, and gold, and silver, and other bright materials, only they were different. The buildings and streets seemed to have a sheen and to glow. The entire scene was one of indescribable beauty.

> *. . . There was a feeling of love and peace. On earth there always seems to be something . . . you know how things bother you here. There's always some problem troubling you—either it's health, or money, or people, or war—or something. That was missing there. I felt completely at peace, as if there were no problems which were of concern. It wasn't that there were no challenges. It's just that everything seemed to be under control. It was such a wonderful feeling that I never wanted to lose it.*
>
> *And there was the feeling of love. Love from . . . from Jesus Christ. It emanated from him, and it was all around; it was everywhere . . .*

This astonishing personal experience was related to me by my father, Marshall Stuart Gibson, when I was a young man. He only told the experience a few times in his lifetime; each time was a spiritual event.[1]

The experience related by my father occurred in 1922 while he was working in Bingham, Utah for Western Union, and was the result of a massive heart attack. My mother, my grandmother, and my aunt were present during the attack. They got the bishop of the local LDS ward to give him a blessing and he returned to life.

Dad recounted this experience when I was a young man attending the University of California at Berkeley, during a period when I was struggling with some of my beliefs. I was profoundly affected by his, and my mother's, descriptions of what had happened. I knew that my parents never lied, and it was obvious that they were convinced the experience had been real.

Why This Book?

Numerous books have been written about individuals who have had Near Death Experiences (NDEs) in which they apparently left their body or had some other unusual experience related to approaching death. The sheer volume of such books, as partially delineated in the bibliography, attest to popular interest in the subject. My own interest stemmed from my father's description of what had happened to him, and from the corollary description of the event from the point-of-view of my mother.

My father died in 1963, and in 1978 I read Dr. Raymond Moody's book *Life After Life*.[2] Later, I read Dr. George Ritchie's *Return from Tomorrow*.[3] Both books detailed experiences of people who had supposedly died, left their bodies, and later returned to life. Some of the accounts were remarkably similar to what my father had, years before, told me. In later years I read most of the books listed in the bibliography.

In reading the literature on NDEs, I felt that Dr. Raymond Moody and Dr. George Ritchie provided a significant service—through their pioneering work on NDEs, and through the publication of these experiences. By announcing to the world the existence of the NDE phenomenon, and by showing that different events had many elements in common and were not as rare as previously supposed, they caused the scientific community to treat the subject with the serious attention that it previously lacked.

Other investigators quickly followed the lead of Dr. Moody and expanded upon his work. The resultant investigations included studies from other countries,[4] critical analyses of the recorded events,[5] statistical studies,[6] historical studies,[7] semi-successful attempts to recreate NDEs through hypnosis,[8] and even application of experimental drugs to determine whether NDEs could be duplicated in the laboratory environment.[9] The Gallup organization, based on a survey, estimated that there are eight million Americans who have undergone NDEs.[6]

Most of the studies were conducted in such a way as to enhance their credibility in the scientific world. One book, in fact, used the word *scientific* six times in the first two pages as if, in so doing, the author could assure others of his objectivity.

Interestingly, despite the fact that NDEs are spiritual by their very nature, few authors have attempted to correlate the experiences with Christian and Jewish religious teachings and literature. Raymond Moody and George Ritchie, both religious men, acknowledged the spiritual nature of the experiences. Dr. Maurice Rawlings in his book *Beyond Death's Door* showed the coorelation between Christian Biblical scriptures and NDEs,[10] but most investigators do not follow his example.

A few LDS authors have attempted to relate the events to LDS scriptures and studies.[11] One of the best books in this regard is *Life Everlasting* by Duane S. Crowther.[12] As an indication of its worth it is still being published after many printings since its introduction in 1967. It was published, in fact, before Raymond Moody's book *Life After Life*, which was first published in 1975. Mr. Crowther documents many of NDEs recorded in the early and recent history (up to 1967) of The Church of Jesus Christ of Latter-day Saints and describes what they mean in the context of LDS teachings.

As an active member of The Church of Jesus Christ of Latter-day Saints I was, of course, familiar with the teachings of that church and of the LDS scriptures relating to life after death. Those teachings and scriptures are, for the most part, in harmony with what people having NDEs said they had experienced. Indeed, many of the teachings of the Prophet Joseph Smith, writings from the Book of Mormon, and writings from the Doctrine and Covenants give details that parallel some of the NDEs to a remarkable extent—and usually these teachings and writings provide additional information as to causes, effects, and ultimate outcomes.

I wrote this book, then, to fulfill a perceived need by relating *new* NDEs to the available LDS scriptures and literature. In so doing I hasten to explain that I do not, and cannot speak for The Church of Jesus Christ of Latter-day Saints—that privilege is reserved for the Prophet and other General Authorities. Rather, I speak as a person who has spent a lifetime as a member of the Church, and I speak as one who is convinced that the LDS Church is true in all of its claims. Any analysis of the data which I present is made in that context.

The book has two major objectives:

1. To offer new accounts of NDEs, and other analogous experiences, and to present the data as completely as it was received during interviews with the people who had these unusual experiences.

2. To attempt to provide meaning and understanding of the new experiences detailed in this book, and some others from the literature, by reviewing the events in the light of available LDS scriptures and teachings.

How the Research was Conducted

Three types of research were conducted for the book: 1) seeking and obtaining first-hand (and in some instances second-hand) accounts from individuals who had undergone NDEs or analogous experiences; 2) reviewing much of the available literature on NDEs; and 3) reviewing and comparing events from NDEs with LDS scriptures and teachings.

Since others have performed statistical work on the fraction of individuals undergoing NDEs who proceeded into out-of-body situations, or "core experiences" as they have been defined in some books,[13] no attempt was made to repeat those analyses. Rather, I screened out, ahead of time, those individuals who did not proceed from an NDE into an out-of-body, or as a minimum, an unusual spiritual experience.

To find suitable candidates I used two methods: referrals from friends, relatives, and associates; and advertisements in local papers and publications. Both methods were fruitful. Indeed, the respondents could have been multiplied many times simply by continuing the effort for a longer period.

During the period from December 1990 through June 1991 we interviewed 45 respondents, of whom I included 38 first-hand experiences in this book. There were also four second-party experiences which I incorporated. Two first-hand experiences from other sources were included, bringing the total of first-hand accounts to 40. Numerous others were rejected because they didn't meet the previously established criteria for the book.

In soliciting candidates to interview, no attempt was made to screen for religious or non-religious beliefs. The only criterion that had to be met was that the candidate had undergone some type of NDE, or other incident, which led to an out-of-body or related spiritual event. By reason of the location of the interviews, in the greater Salt Lake City region, most of those interviewed (71%) professed allegiance to The Church of Jesus Christ of Latter-day Saints (Mormon Church).

The interviews were conducted in my home or in the home of the respondent, except for one which was conducted by telephone. Where women were involved, my wife, Carol Gibson, was usually present and she assisted in the interviews.

All the interviews were taped, later typed, and then forwarded in draft form to the respondent. The respondents then made any corrections that they felt were appropriate to make the written accounts correspond precisely to their memory of what happened.

Some of those interviewed preferred to be recognized with their true identity; others preferred a pseudonym. For those desiring complete identification we used their full names; others desiring anonymity were assigned a pseudonym for a given name, with no surname.

To assure complete coverage of the subject, those interviewed were first asked to give background information about themselves and the incident. Then they were asked to tell, as completely as possible, what had happened to them. We had previously prepared a check sheet with pertinent questions that were to be covered before the interview was complete. By reviewing the check sheet as the interview proceeded we were able to ascertain when desired topics had not been covered. We then asked questions, in as open-ended a manner as possible, to cover the desired issues.

I have frequently been asked two questions concerning the interview phase of the research. These are: "What was the motivation of those responding to your advertisements?" and, "How do you know they were telling the truth?"

Regarding the first question, of all those responding, only two individuals asked if there was a fee involved. When I explained that we couldn't pay a fee, otherwise people might be accused of fabricating a story for money, the individuals quickly understood. The primary motivations that people had for responding to our queries were threefold: to talk to someone who was sympathetic to what they had to say; to find out about others who had had similar experiences; and to help others by sharing what the respondent knew about death.

One lady put it this way: "For many years I thought I was the only one who had experienced anything like this." Another said: "When I first tried to explain what had happened, my doctor, my friends, and even my husband, implied that it was a dream, a hallucination, or I was crazy. I stopped telling others until recently."

The second question, concerning whether or not the individuals were telling the truth, is interesting. The very nature of the experiences was such that they were anecdotal and unique to the individuals involved. We, of course, observed the individuals during the interviews, and in essentially all the cases they were emotionally moved when they reached certain points in the interviews. Some could hardly continue as they relived the experience in their minds.

The demeanor of the people during the interviews was that of persons who had undergone a profound experience, one that affected their understanding of who and what they were, and one in which there was no need to embellish the reality or truth of what they had experienced. They knew what they had experienced and they could not, or would not alter the facts to suit other people's preconceived notions of what might have happened. For this, and other reasons discussed in Part II of the book, I became fully convinced that the individuals, whose experiences are included in this book, were telling the truth and their experiences were real and were accurately related and recorded.

The other phases of research for this book involved reading the available literature on NDEs, marking appropriate sections of books for later reference; and searching the appropriate scriptures and other LDS recorded teachings by the Prophets, and marking them for reference.

In the latter phases of the research I received a copy of a tape covering the experience of Howard Storm, a Professor of Art from Northern Kentucky University.[14] The taped experience was so unusual and so extensive that I transcribed it into a written experience. With Professor Storm's kind permission I have included much of his experience in different chapters of Part II of this book.

How this Book is Organized

Part I, which follows this Introduction, includes printed accounts of the interviews of respondents largely as they were recorded on tape. The interviews are reported, including background information, in their totality and with as much detail as practical. In some instances, considerable background information is given, either because the information is directly pertinent to the experience, or, equally important, because it adds to a better understanding of the individual. The reader can review the interviews without the interjection of editorial comment and can thus obtain a better feeling for what the respondent was saying in the setting of the total experience.

Part II provides an analysis of the Part I data in the context of LDS scriptures and teachings. References from other NDE books are also cited where appropriate. Part II also contains some observations and speculations, by me, which are the results of observing the respondents during the interview process and of studying the detailed accounts of their experiences.

Part I

The Experiences

Could you gaze into heaven five minutes, you would know more than you would by reading all that ever was written on the subject.

Joseph Smith
(History of the Church,
Vol. VI, p. 50)

Chapter One

A Hunter and a German Soldier

Derald Evans

Hunting for Bighorn Sheep

I first met Derald Evans in early December, 1990. He was a tall man dressed in running clothes. He had an easy smile and soft-spoken manner which quickly put me at ease. His graceful movements, typical of one who spent much of his time outdoors, belied his sixty years. Derald said that he had run a race that morning and was, therefore, still in his running clothes.

As background to his story, Derald explained that he was a hunter. In mid September of 1968 he had drawn a Desert Bighorn Sheep tag for the San Juan area of Utah. Only eight or nine tags a year are given out, and Derald was excited to get it, because if successful in his hunt he would have a "grand slam," to represent the four types of bighorn sheep—he already had the others.

He drove into the remote area of Utah where the sheep were, near Blanding, in his four-wheel drive truck. It was a hot time of the year, 98 degrees Fahrenheit, and he had to carry a lot of water with him because there was none available where he was going. He put food supplies, bedding, tent, and ammunition in his pack and set out to climb the Mancos Mesa, one of the largest mesas in the world. Upon reaching the top, he pitched his tent and settled in for the night. Having seen some rams before he began his climb, he intended to track them the next morning.

Derald woke early, had a quick breakfast and put on his day pack with about a gallon of water. He got his rifle and started tracking the rams. By late afternoon he had covered fifteen miles on the top of the mesa, when he spotted one of the rams. He started jogging, and after about two miles, suddenly, the ram appeared fifty yards ahead of him. He raised his rifle, almost automatically, and got the ram with one shot.

As he went to cape the ram—skin it and remove the horns—he noticed large clouds gathering in the south. They appeared ominous and black, so he worked rapidly, caping the ram and packing the meat in his pack. By the time he finished it had begun to snow. The temperature dropped from the 90s to the 30s within about fifteen minutes—and Derald was dressed in a T-shirt and light trousers. There was no shelter and no firewood.

Derald began to run towards his camp, which was seventeen miles away. By this time it was snowing heavily, thunder and lightning were crashing all around him, and the wind was gusting to eighty miles an hour. He could see where he was going only by the lightning flashes.

It was about eight o'clock at night and he began to shiver uncontrollably from hypothermia. In one of the lightning flashes he saw a place where the ground dropped off near a ledge. Upon examining it close-up he found a crevice that he crawled into, and he covered himself with sand, which was still warm. It saved his life, and he spent the night under the sand.

Struggling to the Truck

The next day it had stopped snowing and Derald started for his camp, which was still about eight miles away. His food and water were gone, and he was extremely weak. He ate snow to quench his thirst as he traveled. It took him all day to reach the camp, which, when he arrived, had blown over the cliff from the previous night's storm. He despairingly spent another night, without food, buried in the sand.

Derald tells his own story from this point. I asked him how he made it down the cliff in his weakened condition.

"With great difficulty. It took all the energy I had to get down, and I still had five or six miles ahead of me. Also, by now it was dark again. It had taken most of the day to climb down the cliff. There was a partial moon so I could see, and it had warmed up so there was no longer the danger of freezing, but my energy was almost gone.

"I rested for a short while; then I started towards the truck. I could picture a jar of peaches in the cooler, and the thought of that peach juice kept me going. I staggered along for a time until my energy level got so low that I could only walk for ten steps, then lie down—then stagger for another ten steps and lie down again. Each time I could barely make the ten steps. Finally,

I could see the white truck ahead of me. By now, though, my energy level was so low I could only crawl.

"I crawled up to the truck, and let the tail gate down. I lay on the tail gate for awhile. Then I got the jar of peaches from the cooler. I was so weak I couldn't open the jar. I got a jug of water and tried to drink it, but my throat wouldn't swallow. I massaged my throat and washed my face until I felt a little better. Then I took off my boots and was astonished to see that my socks were completely gone on the bottom; I had worn them out.

"I stood in my bare feet on the sand beside the truck, and many little sand burrs, which were all around, hurt my feet; I had to climb back into the truck. My energy was still gone, though. I felt that if I could lie down on my bed in the back of the truck for a short period I would be all right. I managed to get into the bed with my clothes on—I was completely exhausted."

Life or Death—An Argument

"The next thing I knew I was standing beside the truck and wondering how I got there. I thought to myself: *How did I get here? That's foolish to come out here again. Why don't my feet hurt from the burrs?*

"The moon was up and I could see in the back of the truck, and I saw myself lying there. As I looked in the truck I said to myself: *I look like I'm dead. I've never seen anyone look so bad. What in the world is going on? This must be a bad dream from which I will soon wake up. How can I be standing here in the sand and see myself lying in the truck? This doesn't make sense.*

"I kept looking in the truck and wondering about the strangeness of the scene. Suddenly everything started getting bright."

"It was still dark outside, wasn't it?" I asked Derald.

"Yes, except for the moon, it was dark. But the back of the truck and the surrounding area started to get bright. My first thought was: *Terrific. Someone is coming with their car and he will be able to help me.*

"I turned around to look at the source of the light. It was a white light. As it came closer I put my arm up to shield my eyes. It was bright . . . no, it was white—so white. I had never seen anything like it. It was brilliant.

"I was absorbed in watching the light—the beautiful bright white light. It gave me a feeling like . . . almost like soft music, or something that was one-hundred percent pure. It's hard to describe in words. I had never seen nor heard anything like it before. It was not frightening, though. More softening. And it kept coming closer . . . getting brighter and brighter. I had to keep my arm over my eyes to shield them; I couldn't look directly into the light. I will never forget the feeling I got from the light.

"Next, I became conscious that there was a male individual standing in the light. I was aware that I knew him but have subsequently been unable to remember who he was. I am sure, though, that I knew him from somewhere."

"Did he communicate with you?"

"Yes, he said, 'You know why I'm here—we've got to go.' "

"What was your reaction?"

"I told him that I couldn't go. He responded that I didn't have anything to say about it. He said I had to go with him and it would be all right."

"You disagreed with him?"

"I argued as strongly as I had about anything in my life. I told him that there were children that I had to care for. I mentioned my two daughters and I told him that there were other children that I couldn't explain to him right then, those other children also would need my care.

"For some reason I seemed to know that there would be more children in the future that would be dependent upon me. It puzzled me, that I would know about some, as yet, unknown children, but I did. I continued to argue for some time and the individual in the light listened."

"When the individual talked to you, was it as if you were speaking, or was it more a transference of thought?"

"It was as if I were talking to you."

"Why did you argue so hard to come back? Didn't you like it where you were?"

"Yes, I liked it. In fact, there was no pain, I wasn't hungry and thirsty anymore, and I wasn't exhausted from the ordeal I had been through. I wanted to come back, though, because I felt I hadn't lived my life through yet. For some reason I knew that I would be needed. I wanted to do more hunting, and I knew I had more children that I would be responsible for. I was disturbed over the thought of not being able to complete living my life to its fullest, as I saw it. I knew I was arguing for my life."

"And you explained this to the individual?"

"I sure did—and he was sympathetic and seemed to understand. He was calm during the entire discussion."

"So the decision to come back was yours?"

"Most certainly."

"What happened next?"

"As suddenly as it had come, the light began to diminish. It disappeared towards the east."

"Did the individual go with it?"

"Yes, he had been standing in the light; when the light disappeared, he disappeared. I was left alone in the night, standing outside the truck wondering about the whole experience.

"When he left I knew that I had to get back into my body so I tried to enter it. I found that I had to go in through the head. It was a strange feeling—like trying to get into a tight-fitting shoe, trying to squeeze into it. I struggled as if I couldn't easily fit into my body. Suddenly I was back."

"How did you know that you should enter your body through your head?"

"I have no idea, but that's where I went. It was from the head down, and I can remember how difficult it was. I struggled and struggled to get in. Once I started entering it went fairly easy."

"When you first left your body, were you aware of passing through a dark hole or seeing darkness before you saw the light?"

"There was no special darkness that I remember, other than the night."

"Okay, so you were back in your body then?"

"Yes, I was in my body lying on the bed. As I lay there I could see my heart beating in my chest. It was palpitating and I was sweating. I was almost afraid to breathe. I thought: *I'm not going to move. If I move I'll die again.* "

Returning Home—Aftereffects

"I stayed in my bed, afraid to move, until morning. With the morning light I got enough courage to sit up. Still being extremely weak, I drank some water, and I managed to get the peach jar open and drink some of the peach juice.

"Carefully getting up, I stood in the sand; the burrs hurt my feet again. I put on my boots and walked around the truck looking for tracks in the sand. I couldn't get over the marvel of the experience I had had and I wanted to see if some human had brought the light and left tracks in the sand. I circled the truck several times but I found nothing."

"Did you realize what had happened to you?"

"I wasn't sure. I was still weak, though, so I rested for the remainder of the day and took nourishment. Gradually my strength returned and I felt well enough to drive.

"When I got back home and my wife saw me she remarked: 'You are the walking dead—you look like you died.' I was astonished. What a strange statement for her to make. Still, for some time I didn't tell her or anyone else what had happened. Ultimately, I told her and she was shocked.

"My life continued normally from that point until one year later at my daughter's wedding my wife died. She had an aneurysm and died on the spot. Prior to the wedding my wife and I had expressed concern that the man my daughter was marrying was unsuitable. My wife felt some distress because of this disagreement but we had no warning of her impending death.

"My daughter had three little boys from the marriage, and then her husband left her. She returned home and I helped raise the boys—in fact, they think of me as their father. They are now ten, nine, and eight years old, and my daughter has never remarried.

"I married again, and my second wife had two children whom I have also helped to raise. As you can see my life has been involved in caring for children. How I knew that during the time when I saw the light, I don't know."

"Has your experience changed you?"

"It has made me softer—more patient in dealing with others. My frustrations used to be expressed with outbursts of anger; that is no longer true."

"Did your religious beliefs change before and after the experience?"

Derald looked thoughtful and was silent for a moment. Tears came to his eyes. Finally, he said: "Not really. I am a member of the LDS church, and I love nature. Sometimes when I am out with nature I get a spiritual feeling. Once when I was lying looking at the stars with one of my hunting buddies he asked me who my hero was. Without hesitation I told him it was . . . " Derald choked back some tears, ". . . it was Jesus Christ."

Karl P. Muecke

Early Life in Germany

I interviewed Karl P. Muecke at his home in Sandy, Utah on January 2, 1991. When we met he shook hands with an iron grip; his broad smile and ready welcome showed his love even before I got to know him. His lovely wife, Gertrude, was present and we visited briefly while we became acquainted. Then I asked Karl to tell me something of his background before he disclosed the nature of his unusual experience.

Karl explained that he was born in Hamburg, Germany in 1919. His family were members of the Church of Jesus Christ of Latter-day Saints, and they took their faith seriously. When war came to Germany in 1939 Karl was inducted into the Army; he prayed that he might never have to take a life.

Karl's prayer was answered, although he had to suffer through much of the war on the Russian front, where, on two occasions, his position was overrun by the Russians. On one of these occasions his division of 450 men had to march for twenty-one days, in the winter, without food. Karl was one of fifteen men who survived. All of the survivors had frostbitten faces, hands and feet—and Karl had frozen feet and legs.

On at least two occasions after that his life was spared in a near miraculous manner, once by some Russian civilians who took pity on him. The war ended in 1945; Karl begins his story at that point.

"I was in Flensburg, Germany when the war ended in May, 1945. Then I went home to my family in Hamburg. Things were hard in Germany at the time. There wasn't much food, and many houses had been destroyed. Despite these difficulties I was reunited with my wife and my children. It was a joyous reunion and we took up life as best we could. Some weeks after returning to Hamburg I was released by the English commander and was given three month's wages and papers to be a civilian.

"I wanted to go to America to go through the temple, but in 1946 I was called on a mission for the Church. My wife worked and supported me. It was hard; things were still difficult. I served my mission in West Germany from 1946 through 1949, and, despite the hard times, it was a spiritual experience."

"After your mission, then, did you come to America?" I asked Karl.

"Yes, I worked two jobs for awhile to get the money for passage, and then in 1950 we came to America.

Shortly after we arrived my wife, my two children, and I went through the Salt Lake Temple and were sealed."

"Did you speak English?"

"No, but I found a job working in interior decorating, and I learned English there and in church. Also, I attended classes at the University of Utah. We lived happily in Salt Lake City until 1971."

"What happened in 1971?"

"My wife got cancer and died. I lived for two years as a single widower. Then I met this lovely lady who had lost her husband," Karl smiled at Gertrude, "and we were married in the Salt Lake Temple. Gertrude had four children from her previous marriage."

A Medical Operation with Complications

"I was happy for the opportunity to help raise my new children. Everything in my life was going well again, but I had a problem with the muscles in my shoulder. In 1978 I decided to have it operated on.

"I went to the LDS Hospital in November for what I thought would be a routine operation. They wanted to put me in a private room, because my insurance would pay for it, but I preferred a room where I could be around other people. They put me in a ward with three other men. I was scheduled to be in the hospital for three days. They checked me physically before the operation and found that all of my vital signs were normal—there were no complications, and the operation could proceed as planned.

"The operation itself took one and one-half hours. They brought me to Recovery where Gertrude met me. I felt very tired, so I encouraged my wife to leave and do some Christmas shopping with her mother. Gertrude left, and the nurse came and gave me some medicine; I fell asleep shortly thereafter.

"When I fell asleep, there was a lady visiting her husband in the same room I was in. After awhile she told her husband that something didn't seem right. She walked over to my bed and, after looking at me, said, 'He's not breathing—he is dead.' "

"It's fortunate that she was prompted to look at you."

"Yes, and also that I didn't get put in a private room. If I had been, I wouldn't be here now. Anyway, the lady ran into the hall and shouted for help. A heart doctor was nearby, and he came into the room and began beating on my chest. Later, it was black and blue from where he beat my chest. He also used electrical paddles to shock my heart back into regular motion."

"Did that get your heart going again?"

"Yes, and they put me in Intensive Care. They estimated that I had stopped breathing for two and one-half minutes, and they were worried that there would be brain damage. Later tests showed that my brain was okay."

"Did they ever determine why your heart stopped?"

"When I had recovered enough, several weeks later, the nurse who gave me the medicine after my operation came into my room and apologized. She said that the medicine was wrong and could have killed me. She wasn't sure who had marked up my chart to take the medicine."

"What about your wife? Was she aware of your crisis?"

"They called her; she called my Bishop and told him to come quickly. On the way to the hospital the Bishop drove as rapidly as he could, honking his horn as he went through traffic lights. Both my wife and my Bishop arrived soon after they got my heart going again. The Bishop found an LDS doctor, and they gave me a blessing in which I was told that I would have a beautiful and a long life."

The Colorful Spirit World

"During the period when my heart stopped, I had a beautiful experience. After I went asleep, when the nurse had given me the medicine, I found myself in the spirit world. It wasn't this world—it was beautiful. It's hard to describe . . . the colors, they were clear colors. I was walking in a field, and there were trees and flowers like I had never seen in this life. Everything was bright, and the flowers and trees . . . I had seen some of the trees in this life but many were different from this world. It was very colorful, more so than in this life."

"Do you have any memory of passing through something black before you got to the spirit world?"

"No, I just remember walking in this beautiful area; then I knelt down and prayed. I prayed for peace."

"Did you get it?"

"It was all around me, the most peaceful, the most beautiful feeling—it's hard to describe.

Instructed by a Voice

I felt a presence, and I heard a voice. The voice spoke twice, and I didn't understand it. Then it spoke a third time, and I understood.

"The voice called me by my holy name."

"You mean the name you got in the Temple?"

"Yes, and then it told me that I was to return to this life. I had a special mission to perform—my life was not yet through."

"How did you feel about coming back?"

"I was happy, and I was sad."

"Why were you happy, and why were you sad?"

"I had mixed emotions. I loved the feeling that I enjoyed in the spirit world, but I also wanted to return to my family. And I understood that I had more work to do."

"While you were communicating with this voice did you see anyone?"

"No, it was more like feeling a presence. It was a beautiful feeling, a spiritual feeling."

Afterthoughts

"After the experience, I found myself back in my bed at the hospital looking into the faces of my Bishop and my sweet wife. I felt very tired and went back to sleep."

"So you didn't tell anyone about your experience right away?"

"No, I was too sick. I told Gertrude a little bit, and the next day my Stake President visited me and wanted to know all about it. I was too tired. He said that when I got well I should come to the High Council and bear testimony to them."

"Were you in the hospital long?"

Gertrude interjected, "It was supposed to be a three-day hospital stay. He was three weeks in the hospital—then he was recovering at home for two more months."

I asked, "While you were having this spiritual experience, Karl, did it seem real to you, or was it like a dream?"

"It wasn't a dream. It was real."

"What was your body like? Was it a physical body?"

"No, it wasn't like our body here. It had arms and legs, though, I remember kneeling. It was . . . sort of light. I didn't feel any gravity."

"Has the experience changed you in any way?"

"I'm more outgoing than I was, and I love people, all people, and . . . and I love Christ. Also, I'm not afraid to die."

"Do you have anything else you'd like to say?"

"Well, as I told you, years ago when I was called on my mission as a Priest, there were six of us in the West German Mission, and we were called home to a conference. I was ordained an Elder by a Swiss fellow, Max Zimmer. Then President Benson, who was the European Mission President, gave me my mission blessing. In that blessing he promised me that I would be protected from the evil influences of Lucifer, and I would have knowledge and power to love all people . . . all people."

"And you feel that your experience when you met with the Presence in the spirit world included the charge to love all people?"

"Yes, that was part of my mission."

"Thank you, Karl."

"Thank you, Arvin." His eyes and handshake smiled back to me the love he felt . . .

Chapter Two

A Critical-Care Nurse

Janet McClellan

Identified from Another World

The snow had stopped falling when Janet McClellan drove up, but it was one of those cold, foggy nights which are typical of Utah in January. She was dressed in a khaki uniform suitable for helicopter duty on a cold night. She was a young (31 years old), attractive woman with dark hair and a ready smile.

She indicated that she was on night helicopter duty and didn't have much time, so, after introducing her to my wife, we went to my study and began taping her experiences. I asked her to tell me something of her background. I already knew that she was married, had two children, was an active Latter-day Saint in my son's ward, and lived in West Jordan, Utah.

She began, "I am a critical-care specialist and I have worked in the intensive care unit of many hospitals for the last ten years."

"You're a Registered Nurse?"

"Yes, and all of my experience has been in the critical-care area."

"Why don't you begin by explaining some of the experiences of patients who have had near-death experiences?"

She laughed. "I've thought about this for some time since you called. Most of my patients are intubated—they can't speak because of tubes in their throat—but the one who really began it all was a lady who could speak.

"I was working in the intensive care unit side at Utah Valley Hospital, and I went to the coronary care side to relieve for lunch. I walked in, got a report of the patients I was to care for, and sat down to review them. One report was of a fifty-, or so, year-old lady who had suffered a cardiac arrest. She appeared to be doing fine; she was awake and alert and seemed able to leave the hospital soon.

"After reading the report I sat there watching the monitors, but the fifty-year-old lady kept motioning me to come over to her bed. I walked over, thinking I would get her a drink . . . whatever. Maybe she was having chest pains.

"As I walked up to her and asked what I could do to help her she said, 'Pull the curtain.' After I pulled the curtain she told me to get a chair and sit down. Then she said, 'I have something I need to tell *you.*'

"I pulled up a chair and she said, 'Now don't be shocked. I need to tell *you* this—I was shown you, and I have seen you, and I need to tell you what I'm about to say. I don't know why I'm going to tell you, but I'm going to tell it . . . because that is why I was allowed to return to this world.'

"She then proceeded to say that this was her second out-of-body experience. She further told me that this experience paralleled, almost exactly, her first experience. She said that after she suffered a cardiac arrest she left her body. She could see the paramedics working on her."

"This happened on the way to the hospital, then?"

"I didn't go back in her medical history record, but I assume that's true.

"She traversed up the tunnel, and she said she was familiar with the tunnel because she had been through this before."

"How did she describe the tunnel?"

"She said it was misty-dark."

"Had she read any of the literature on . . ."

"No, she hadn't read any books. She said that the only people she had talked to about this were her children."

"Okay, it was misty-dark, and there was a tunnel. What next?"

"There was a light at the end."

"She saw the light?"

"Yes, she said because she had been through this before she knew exactly what to do. She went to the light and entered a garden area with a bench, and many of her family members were there.

"Then she said, 'I need to describe for you the feelings I had there.' She proceeded to tell of feelings of peace, of love, and . . . happiness—that the pain was gone. She said, 'I had no pain.'

"She told me that she then walked down the path and was met by a man, who she described as Christ, and she was asked a question, 'How have you loved your fellow man?'

"She had been through this before, so she expected it, she said. For the second time her life rolled before her as if on a movie screen, and she was able to see and comprehend all of her acts.

"After this confrontation she walked back to her family, and she didn't know exactly who it was who spoke to her, but someone said to her, 'You must go back.' And she told me it was at this point that she was shown me, in my capacity as a nurse, and that she needed to relay this experience to me.

"After that she remembers waking up with all the doctors and nurses in the hospital. She said that she had been waiting for three days for me to walk in—that's about how long she had been in the hospital."

There was a long pause as Janet considered what she had told me. Then I asked, "Had she described the circumstances behind her previous experience?"

"She had suffered another cardiac arrest."

"Do you recall how long ago it was?"

"Well, as I remember, the experience I just described was in '81 or '82, and the previous experience was two or three years before that."

"When she saw the person she described as Christ, did she actually see a person, or did she feel just a presence?"

"She saw a person—and she talked with him."

"When you say she talked . . ."

"She didn't go into that. Now I know . . . I've read enough to know that you don't always speak. She just said, 'I talked with the person.' "

"Was it before or after she went through the tunnel when she saw her body with people working on it?"

"Before."

"So she was present and could see the paramedics working on her. What was your feeling after you heard the story?"

Janet laughed. "I was pretty shocked, especially about her telling me that she watched me from the other side."

"That's interesting. Did she indicate how she felt about coming back?"

"Yes, she said that the first time she had to come back because of her children. This time she had to come back, for only a very short time, to talk to me, and to say goodby to a daughter whom she had not spoken with for a short period of time. After she accomplished these acts, she said, 'Then my time will be done, and I will be allowed to go back.' She didn't say I will die—she used the words, 'I will get to go back, and I have no fear of that.' "

"Did she say anything about how real her experience was, whether it was like a dream, or real?"

"Oh, she was adamant . . . very adamant that it was real."

A Spirit Guide

"The next experience must have been about eight months later. I was taking care of an elderly gentleman who had suffered cardiac arrest, and we had resuscitated him. He was not doing well and they decided to let the gentleman die."

"Who decided?"

"The family and the doctors. He was in his eighties and he was comatose.

"You know—you work twelve hour shifts. For six hours I beat my brains out trying to save him, and for the last six hours I sat by his bed holding his hand while he died. My feeling is nobody should die alone."

"That's a good sentiment."

"I think so; so I always sit and hold my patients' hands and talk to them while they die. Comatose or awake, I know that they probably can hear me.

"I had pulled my chair next to his bed and I was holding his hand. The door to the room was behind me. I felt someone walk into the room. Thinking it was a fellow nurse I turned around to . . ."

"Was it something you heard?"

"No, I felt this presence walk into the room, and I turned around to ask what he needed, but nobody was there. And I could still feel the presence.

"This person walked up to the side of me, looked over my shoulder, and read my notes. He walked over to the other side of the bed and looked at the patient. And then he walked back here," Janet pointed behind her, over her right shoulder, "and he just stayed there.

"I couldn't figure out what I was feeling. I kept looking over my shoulder . . . I mean, I felt I should see somebody, and there was no one there. There was just me and the patient.

"I got up to do some mouth care on the patient, and this person followed me. He went to the other side of the bed to observe me as I cared for my patient."

Janet began to cry and I reassured her, "That's all right. Most people cry when they tell of these experiences."

"It was so real. I knew somebody else was in that room, and . . ." she had difficulty speaking, "it lasted for *five* hours."

"Until he died?"

"When his heart stopped . . . two people left that room. There were two people there and . . . and they looked at me and I could feel them leave the room. So I'm pretty convinced that there are people watching us.

"It was kind of scary at first until I realized that the person was there to help—I think my patient's name was Stanley—to help Stanley along. The person was just waiting until it was the right time for Stanley to go."

Janet laughed with a slightly embarrassed laugh. "I even started talking to the person for awhile."

"What did you say?"

"I said, 'I know why you're here. I know you are here. I can feel you, and I feel like I can reach out and touch you. I think you're here to help Stanley along, and I appreciate that; I'm sure Stanley is grateful for your help. I'm trying to make Stanley as comfortable as I can.' "

An Atheist Changes His Mind

"The next experience involved a call from Radiology for a cardiac arrest emergency. We resuscitated the patient—who had previously indicated that he was an adamant atheist—and we got him up to the intensive care unit. He was awake and alert and he was very angry, especially with me."

"How old was he?"

"He was in his late sixties."

"Why was he angry?"

"He told me . . . and he swore like a sailor while he did. He said, 'Why did you bring me back? I was, for once, out of pain. I was at peace. WHY did you do this to me? It is my time.' Oh, but he was angry.

"I asked him what I did, and he said, 'Well you were pumping on my chest, and you gave me some medicine in my veins.'

"I told him that was my job, to try and save people from death."

"Was he unconscious during the period that you worked on him, and did he correctly describe what you did?"

"Yes, he was unconscious. And it was clear from his comments that he had seen the whole resuscitation effort."

"As he talked to us, there were present in the room a nurse, me, two doctors, and another nurse. Then he said, 'My time has come. Jesus has come for me and he's standing right there.' And he pointed between the nurse and the doctor."

"Did either of the doctors say anything at that point?"

"No, they just sort of stood there and listened."

"He repeated, 'Jesus is here—I am leaving now.' and he cursed again and told us not to bring him back. At that point he went into ventricular fibrillation and died."

"What was the reaction of the nurses and doctors?"

"When we saw that he was dying we all went to pounce on him again. But we were physically unable to get to that bedside."

"What do you mean you were physically unable to get to the bed?"

"There was a barrier. All five of us could not get within two feet of that bed."

"Did you all try?"

"Yes."

"What was the reaction of the others?"

"One of the nurses broke down in tears, ran out, and went home. I stood there somewhat stunned. The Doc, who was an active Latter-day Saint, said, 'Well, I guess he was pretty serious, wasn't he?' "

"What was the nature of the barrier as you tried . . . explain it as best you can."

Janet sighed and seemed at a loss for words. I asked, "Was it something solid, or was it that you couldn't move?"

In exasperation she responded, "I don't know, we could not get . . . we could move up to two feet. We could move, we just couldn't pass through this barrier to get to the patient."

"Fair enough. What was your reaction to all of this?"

"Well, after all that I've been through, I figured it was this man's time and don't mess with God. Leave well enough alone," she said with a slight laugh.

"And this man had previously told you that he was an atheist—he didn't believe in God?"

"That's correct. He didn't believe in life after death or in God. But he stated, when he was yelling at me, that he was wrong and he wanted to go back."

Other Experiences and a Personal Perspective

"Since the experience with the atheist, most of my patients have been on a ventilator, with a tube in them, and they can't talk. Just two weeks ago I had a gentleman who, as he woke up, I asked him, 'Joe, do you recognize me?' He nodded his head vigorously that he did. I had been one of the nurses that resuscitated him.

"I asked him if he was angry with me and he nodded his head affirmatively. I said, 'Joe, I understand where you have been. You've been to the other world, am I correct?' The patient nodded his head 'yes.' This man was a Catholic."

"What was his illness?"

"He had suffered a cardiac dysrhythmia and had gone into heart standstill."

"I then asked him, 'Joe, were you at peace there?' and he nodded his head positively. Then I asked, 'Joe, can you understand what I am asking you?' again he indicated that he did. 'Do you want to go back?' I asked, and he again was affirmative. Next I asked him, 'Do you want to stay here?' and he shook his head negatively. I asked him, 'Joe, did you meet your Christ there?' and he nodded that he had.

"Then he tried to mouth to me words I couldn't understand, and he wrote me a note which asked, 'How did you know?' I told him that I had talked to a lot of people, and I understood. I also told him that there was a purpose behind his resuscitation, and if Christ had not wanted him to come back we would have been unsuccessful in the resuscitation effort. I explained that there was a purpose, and that he should work with us and with God to fulfill that purpose.

"He indicated that he understood. I explained that it might even be for a short period, like twenty-four hours, to give his family time to say goodby, but that was still something that he must work with."

"How old was Joe?"

"He was, maybe, seventy-two."

"So, in general, you work with older people?"

"Yes, that's true. And the children I've worked with—I've not had occasion to talk to, or they've been so ill that it wouldn't have been appropriate."

"What is your feeling, Janet, after having seen these different individuals, or . . . whatever else you'd like to express?"

"I know it's real."

"Do you mean they believe their experiences were real, or is it that *you* feel their experiences were real?"

"Well, when I was having my last baby, in July of 1987, I ruptured my uterus and nearly hemorrhaged to death. During this trauma they put me to sleep, if you will, but I didn't go to sleep. I was very much aware of what was happening, and . . . and I was given a choice.

"Now I didn't leave my body, or anything, but I was very much aware of what was happening. And a voice said, 'It's okay if you want to die.'

"Because I had really wanted to die—I was in so much pain. And I was dying, I *knew* I was dying. The voice also said, 'It's okay, there's work for you to do if you choose to stay.'"

"You mean in this life?"

"Yes, but if I chose to die it was okay also."

"How many children did you have then?"

"This was my second child.

"As I lay there, all of a sudden I really wanted to live. As soon as I made that decision I went to sleep, and I went out. But it wasn't until I made that really conscious decision.

"During this experience I was very aware of what was going on. I could feel them cut my abdomen, and I felt the tube going down into my lungs. I also knew, before I went to sleep, how near death I was—I mean, I work in the stuff all the time. And I knew it would just be minutes, or seconds, before I died. At the time I didn't care. I was in so much pain I was begging to die. And then . . . there was no pain."

"You suffered pain even though they were giving you pain killers?"

"They really couldn't give me pain killers, as such, because they were afraid my baby was dead. I was bleeding inside and they had to get me cut open to stop the hemorrhaging."

"I understand. How many children do you have now?"

"I have two. They were able to save that child, he's a little boy."

"So, then, you believe there is a life after death?"

"I know there's a life after death."

"Have your religious feelings changed as a result of these experiences?"

"Yes. I was sort of a Sunday Mormon. I went to church on Sunday, but I rebelled much of my childhood. At one point I even asked for my name to be taken off the records of the church. I didn't have a testimony, I realize now. I had judged the whole church on the way certain people lived.

"I had lived in California and Minnesota, and it wasn't until I moved back to Utah that I realized that there was a God, and there is life after death. Just because some Mormons don't practice their religion doesn't mean that the teachings put forth by Christ are wrong. It's up to me to live my life the way the Lord wants me to."

Chapter Three

Unusual Healings

Ruth

Some Near-Fatal Medication

Ruth was waiting for us as my wife and I drove up the snowy street on a gray day in January. She motioned us into the warmth of her lovely home. She explained that her husband was a nuclear engineer, with a PhD in that field, and she had traveled to various places with him. They had moved from California to Utah because of a job opportunity for her husband.

I asked Ruth to tell us a little of the background leading up to her experience, and she began: "I had a lukewarm Catholic background. My mother was not Catholic, and my father was a Catholic who never went to church. We lived in a small town in New Hampshire, and the church there was extremely small; it was a reconverted restaurant. So we went to church weekly, but there wasn't much real spirituality.

"In 1963, when I was in my middle thirties, I had a thyroidectomy. Then, a couple of years later, it seemed that my left lung was deteriorating. I used to smoke, not very much, but apparently it was too much for me.

"I didn't have a church—I wasn't a spiritually organized person. But I was always kind of interested, on the edges. My husband was not. He's an engineer and he is not interested in religion at all."

"Where did you meet your husband?"

"I met him in Boston at an intercollegiate club. He was doing his graduate work at M.I.T.

"In 1964 my health was bad. I had started having these, sort of, nervous tizzies. They were not too bad; I'm normally a stable sort of person. But I figured it was the result of the medication that was responsible for my out-of-body experience."

"Was the medication for the problem in your lung?" I asked.

"No, the lung problem was later. This medication was . . . we were going to go to Europe and the doctor gave me birth control pills. I would take the medication in the morning, and ten minutes after I had taken the pills it would seem that my breath had stopped. I would, by instinct, breathe in and out and the breath would start again, like a motor. It would just catch, and then I would be okay—until the next time I took the medication.

"I normally took the medication in the morning but one day I took it at night. And that was a mistake because I was always a sound sleeper."

A Tunnel and Beings of Light

"I had taken the medication, and as soon as my head hit the pillow I was out. The next thing I knew . . . I knew it was too late. I knew that I was dying. I felt a little bit curious but very apprehensive. And I knew it was too late.

"It was as if I were proceeding down a tunnel of light. Then I came to the end, and there were three beings of light. They were waiting to greet me, and they were so filled with love. It was the most pure, unselfconscious, beautiful experience of my life . . . ." Ruth began to cry.

"They didn't look like anybody. They were composed of, let's say, tissues of light. I recognized them, I knew them, yet they didn't have faces, or names that I know now, but I knew them, and they knew me. We knew each other very well and it was like . . . like a reunion.

"They didn't say a word, and then . . . then I thought of my young ones. My children were still young, very young, and . . . and I snapped right back into my body. And I was wide awake and I knew that something important had happened.

"I later told my doctor about my experience. He told me to never take that medication again. He knew that there was a connection between the medication and the experience. I didn't take it again, but I read in the newspaper a couple of weeks later that some woman had taken that same medication and she had died. She was not as lucky as I was."

"Where were you living at the time?"

"That was in 1964 and we were living in San Diego. The experience was so . . . so real, it's just as though it happened last week."

"As you were with the three beings of light do you remember if they communicated any special messages?"

"Nothing specific—it was just love."

"Why did you leave that wonderful place?"

"Because of my loved ones—I had two small children."

"You were aware that that was the case?"

"Oh yes. I knew it . . . I knew it, that was the answer."

"What did your body feel like when you were in the spiritual world?"

"Peaceful, very peaceful. Yes, as soon as I reached the three beings I felt fine. The fear had gone, totally; there was no apprehension. I was where I was supposed to be. That was the feeling I had."

"Did you notice whether you had any form? Could you feel gravity?"

"I felt exactly like *myself*. I had not lost my identity—I was still me."

"Did it feel like a dream?"

"I would say it was like a dream, only more so. It was an intense experience but very natural. It was vivid, unforgettable . . . so it must have been in my highest consciousness."

"When you first were aware that you were dying did you have any cognizance of seeing your body lying there?"

"No. I've read about that type of thing but I didn't experience it."

"You mentioned seeing a tunnel. What sort of a tunnel was it—can you describe it?"

"It was large, not cramping at all. But I've thought about it later. Maybe . . . maybe actually it was movement, you know, spinning out, whirling out. I'm sure my soul had left . . . on a journey. And maybe that's why it looked like a tunnel.

"Every time I drive through a tunnel, now, that experience comes back. We went to Italy a few years ago, where there are many tunnels, and they reminded me of my experience."

"What was the light like which you saw at the end of the tunnel?"

"It was an opalescent blue. And each being had a somewhat different color. One was golden, one was kind of pinkish, and the other was a blue-blue.

Lung Problems and a Healing

"About a year after this experience my left lung started giving me trouble again. I mentioned that I smoked—not much, maybe ten or twelve cigarettes a day, but it was too much. I went to a doctor and he did a number of tests including an x-ray. I had had flu, pneumonia, pleurisy, and other related problems. His x-ray showed that I had a spot on my lung.

"I went to another doctor and he told me that eventually the lung would have to come out. He asked me if I smoked, and when I told him I did he told me to quit. The doctors had scared me enough that I stopped instantly.

"Anyway, during this period I went to a church in San Diego that someone had recommended. It was the Self Realization Church, and it was based on spiritual precepts. I was sitting in the back of the church and I felt this tremendous peace, and . . . and I had a spontaneous healing. I didn't know it was a spontaneous healing—it felt like electricity, and it came from my neck and spread down over my back. It was so powerful that inside I was thinking that I wasn't ready for this, whatever it was. In fact, I hoped it would stop." Ruth laughed as she thought back.

"I went in for a chest x-ray, a month later, and I didn't expect anything different. The doctor came out; he was just beaming, and he said, 'This is perfect, your lung is completely healed.'"

DeAnne Anderson Shelley

A Remarkable Woman

I first met DeAnne Anderson Shelley in 1970 when I was bishop of the San Jose 12th Ward in California. She was a dynamic, attractive, ebullient young woman with a choice family. She had an optimistic view of life; indeed, she reflected this optimism in everything that she did. She had three choice children, Jan, Joyce and Raymond, and a tall, successful businessman husband, Fred Anderson.

DeAnne was then thirty-eight years old. She looked younger, and she had a zest for life that attracted people to her. As I got better acquainted with her and Fred, she told me of an amazing series of physical crises in her life. I later met her physician who confirmed the medical problems she had undergone.

The complete story of DeAnne's unusual experiences is told in the book *In Search of Angels.*[1] I shall include a portion of her experiences here because of their pertinence to this book, and because of the remarkable similarity of her description of a healing experience to that described by Ruth.

DeAnne and Fred had attended a Presbyterian church in Hayward, California, and were living a busy life, when, in 1961, she came down with Bulbar Polio. She was put in a local hospital for awhile, in an iron lung, and she was partially paralyzed for a time. After five months in various hospitals and rehabilitation centers she recovered.

Then, in 1964, after moving to Vacaville, California, she became ill again. Thinking it was a recurrence of polio, she was put in a hospital; there they diagnosed her illness as acute multiple sclerosis. The disease attacked her muscles and central nervous system, and she quickly deteriorated. She became largely paralyzed, she could only breathe with the aid of a tracheotomy, and within a short period she lost her sight.

Her doctor, John E. Parkinson, used the best medical techniques available but she continued to decline. After about five months of crisis, on one particularly critical night, Doctor Parkinson informed her husband that DeAnne couldn't last through the night.

After giving Fred the distressing news, the Doctor, who was an active member of The Church of Jesus Christ of Latter-day Saints, left for home. He later told Fred and DeAnne that, as he was preparing for bed, he had a strong feeling he should return and give DeAnne a blessing even though Fred and DeAnne were not members of his church.

The Doctor called the local Stake President of the LDS Church and the two of them returned to the hospital. When asked if he would allow them to give DeAnne a blessing Fred readily agreed. In the blessing DeAnne was promised that she would live and that the medicines would be effective. She was also told that she had more purpose in life that was yet to be fulfilled.

The Doctor and the Stake President returned to their homes after the blessing. When Doctor Parkinson returned the next morning Fred was present. DeAnne awoke, and although unable to see, she began crying. When asked why she was crying DeAnne explained that she had just had a gorgeous experience and she didn't want it to quit. She told the doctor and Fred that she had been in this beautiful place, with brightness all around, where she could see again, and where there was no anguish or pain. She met her father there, who had previously died, and he looked wonderful. He was wearing a long white robe and he was not as wrinkled as she remembered him in life. He told her that he was thrilled she didn't have to suffer so much anymore.

After seeing her father she became aware that she had to return. She awoke to find that she was back in the hospital, blind again, and in terrible pain. That was why she was crying.

In a short period she recovered her sight. Over the next several months, with the aid of extensive physical therapy, she reached the point where she could ride in a wheelchair. She could also walk, with some difficulty, with the aid of braces and crutches. Her limbs were atrophied from the effects of the disease, which was still with her, and from lack of use.

As a result of discussions with the doctor and others, and following much study and prayer, Fred and DeAnne joined The Church of Jesus Christ of

Latter-day Saints. A few months after joining the church DeAnne asked for and received a special blessing from Patriarch John L. Murdock in Napa, California. In the blessing she was promised that one day she would lay her crutches and braces aside and would be made whole. She was also told that she would become involved in genealogy.

In February, 1965, DeAnne and Fred traveled to Oakland to go through the Mormon Temple there. She used the wheelchair in going through the temple.

Walking Away From a Wheelchair

The next portion of DeAnne's experience is reproduced from the book *In Search of Angels*, exactly as DeAnne related her experience.

"Were you excited [to go to the temple]?"

"I'll say I was. They put me in the wheelchair so that I could move around in the temple. Everything went well until after they had started the endowment session, then I became ill."

"What do you mean you became ill?"

"There was this vibration in my body. It was as if electricity was going through it."

"Did you feel sick?"

"Yes, I felt as though I couldn't catch my breath, and that I might faint. The electricity was so strong."

"Did anyone else notice?"

"Maxine felt the vibration, and she noticed that something was wrong with me. She raised her hand and they stopped the session. One of the matrons wheeled me out and Doctor Parky followed me."

"So you went out into the hall?"

"Yes, and Doctor Parky helped me to lie down on a bench. He took my pulse and said that I seemed to be excited. He told me to lie still for a period and I'd probably be all right."

"Did you tell him how you felt?"

"I tried to but I'm not sure he understood at first. As I lay there my arms and legs began to feel . . . they felt light. They always felt so heavy after I got MS. Even to move my ankle was a big deal. If I wanted to move my legs I had to pick them up with my hands; they wouldn't move by themselves. Now, all of a sudden . . . it must have been over in five minutes: I felt like I could use my legs. My neck and back felt better too."

"Did you tell your doctor that you could move your legs?"

"Yes, and I *showed* him that I could lift my left leg. Maybe he understood then that I'd been healed, I'm not sure. In any event he put me in the wheelchair, and we went back into the session."

"How long were you in the hall?"

"It couldn't have been more than ten or fifteen minutes."

"They started the session up then?"

"Yes, and they came to the part where they invite some couples to come up front. I stood and walked up, Fred saw me, and he came up."

"What was his reaction?"

"He stood with me and tears were streaming down his face. I was just happy—happy—happy!"

DeAnne never used crutches again. In subsequent years her children grew up, and married. Fred was killed in an airplane accident and DeAnne married another wonderful man, Melvin Shelley. They are living today in Arizona, and DeAnne is active in performing genealogy work—indeed, she has become an expert in that field.

Lois Clark

A Car Crash

Lois Clark was living with her mother when Carol and I visited her in her home in West Valley, Utah during the winter of 1991. She had been married but was presently single. She proudly described her five children and one stepdaughter who lived in other places around the country. She was born in El Paso, Texas, in 1934, but her parents had moved around considerably, in the summer each year, due to her father's occupation as a railroader for the Southern Pacific. The family belonged to The Church of Jesus Christ of Latter-day Saints.

Lois began her story: "In 1965 my husband and I had been Christmas shopping and we ran out of gas. He parked the car alongside the road and went for gas. I stayed with the car with the children in the back seat, including my baby girl. As we sat there a drunken driver hit us and knocked us into the median; I was thrown out of the car. Then the car rolled backwards over me. The children were relatively unhurt in the back seat.

"I was unconscious for a period. When I came to my oldest son was standing over me and he said, 'I'm going to lay over you, Mommy, in case the car blows up.' Shortly after that I became aware of the pain. When they got me to the hospital they found that I had massive injuries. One kidney was messed up, I had a broken jaw, and my teeth were all knocked loose.

"I kept going in and out of consciousness, so they didn't have to use as much anesthetic as they otherwise would have. They were using a syringe to try and extract a sample from my kidney—they wanted to determine the damage to it before they operated, or to see if they needed to operate. I had so many broken bones they weren't sure I could stand the operation. I heard them say, 'You'd better do something, she's flattening out.'

A Bright Light, Forms, and Beautiful Music

"I didn't hear anything else for awhile—and I'm floating up here—and I'm looking down at this woman on a table, and . . . and I realize it's me. There were all these people working around the table, and there was this form lying there.

"I thought, *What's going on?* and all of a sudden I saw this bright light. I've never seen anything like it as long as I've lived, since. It was just beautiful. So I started walking towards this light to see what was beyond it, but . . . but every time I started to take a step towards it I was told, 'No, go back.'

"I didn't want to go back to all that pain. But finally I went back, I guess, because I kept hearing the doctors say, 'Okay, okay, she's starting to get stabled out.'

"When I woke up the next time I was in my hospital bed with all this paraphernalia around and on me. And I felt a little bit at peace, but I was angry."

"Why were you angry?"

"Because they wouldn't let me just die, I guess, 'cause I kept praying to die. I hurt so badly . . . well my whole body was just a torment of pain."

"What happened next?"

"I talked to some people who helped me to realize that I should pray to be relieved of the pain, and to get better, rather than to die. I did this and things started to get better."

"While you had this experience did you see anybody or anything?"

"I saw forms. I didn't see recognizable faces or anything, just forms . . . and the one was brighter than the others. But they just all kept telling me to go back, and I didn't want to. I wanted to stay."

"Okay, so you saw some forms that you didn't recognize. And one seemed brighter than the others, you say?"

"Yes. One seemed to just shine with brightness. The others seemed at peace—sort of idyllic. It was really strange, because I thought, *Well they should know the pain I'm going to have. Why are they making me go back into something I don't want to?* Afterwards I talked to a friend of mine in the church, and she suggested that perhaps they knew I had something more to do."

"Did you have a feeling yourself of why they wanted you to come back?"

"Not until ten or fifteen years ago when my mother and I started living together, and we realized that we were here to take care of each other. That brought it home more than anything else. I knew that I had the children to raise, but that didn't bother me so much as to be . . . as to be in a place so beautiful."

"How many children did you have then?"

"The four—my baby girl was not quite two."

"Have you felt since, that one of the reasons you had to come back was because of the children?"

"Yes, in fact there have been incidents since then when I have been close to death—not as bad as with the automobile accident—but each time it has been the children who drew me back. The children have always been my life."

"When you saw this light, did you see anything dark ahead of time?"

"The only dark I saw was to the side. I saw that light and wanted to go towards it, that's all my mind would hold."

"What did the light look like?"

"It was kind of a . . . a yellow, mellow, bright, white light."

"Was it hard to look at?"

"Yes. It was so bright to begin with that I had to, sort of, look down, then up, and then blink my eyes down again."

"Did you feel as if it was real, or a dream?"

"At the time that I was in the place to see the light I thought it was real. The whole thing . . . oh, there was the light, and there seemed to be soft, soft, soft . . . you couldn't really hear it, you more felt this music. It . . . it was soft, and immaculately beautiful. There was, I guess there's no way to really describe it. There was a feeling of peace, beauty, love, and . . . it just felt like this is what I want. This is the ultimate. You're so at peace within your whole being that you just seem to float, like . . ."

"Could you see the doctors working on you?"

"Yes, when I wanted I could look down and see, there I am . . . ." Lois laughed as she described the situation. "I thought, *Okay, I've left that there, now, and I can go on—it's marvelous*. And then to be told that I had to go back, I fought the thought."

Breast Cancer and a Remarkable Healing

"I had another experience about three years ago that helped me a great deal."

"What was that?"

"I had cancer of the breast and they told me that if they couldn't get it all when they did surgery they wouldn't give me very long. It was that bad already. My husband was retired military and we had been using K.I. Sawyer, a small military hospital. They transferred me to the better-equipped military hospital at Wright Patterson for the surgery.

"There was a young LDS missionary whom we had previously known in Texas, and who now lived in Cincinnati. I called him. He came to the hospital and gave me a blessing in which he asked Heavenly Father to please let me be rid of the cancer so that I might continue to be able to raise my children and grandchildren. After he left I told my daughter, Trisa, who had been with me in the hospital that something was wrong."

"What was wrong?"

"I didn't feel the same way as I had before—the pain had been terrible, almost unbearable at times. Now I felt different and I couldn't explain why."

"My daughter said that maybe I was just excited and tired. She suggested that I go to bed and rest some before the operation. So I went to bed, although I still felt different, and I went to sleep with the help of a sleeping pill.

"The next morning I woke up, and I . . . I had no pain. The nurse had me take a shower and use medication to prepare for surgery. As I walked back to my room I understood, all of a sudden, why there was no pain. The cancer . . ." Lois had difficulty continuing. "The cancer had been taken away. I was overjoyed.

"The Doctors came in and told me to go get the final x-ray for the surgery. My daughter joined us and we went downstairs where the x-ray machine was. They took a mammogram and then they came in and said: 'There's something wrong with this machine. We're going to have to take you to another machine because this one doesn't show us what we know is there.'

"I just smiled because I already knew what was going on. I told my daughter, she was kind of teary too, and we went to the other machine where they took a second mammogram. The doctors came in and the surgeon said: 'I don't know what's wrong. I'm sure with two machines we should have gotten a true reading, but there is no cancer showing. Yet we know there was cancer, because we have the original set of x-rays right here. We won't cut into someone, though, where there's no reason to cut.' "

"How did you feel about it?"

"I was happy but I didn't understand it. As lowly a person as I am, I still don't understand. Why me?" Lois began to cry.

"When you got your blessing you said that you knew something had happened to you. What did it feel like?"

"During the blessing, and when he was saying let me be rid of the cancer, I felt, from the tip of my head to the end of my toes, I felt . . . it felt like a washing through process. Like little waves going through my body. Afterwards, it felt kind of like, you know, when your hands are asleep and they come awake again. It felt like that down through my chest. It was mostly my chest but also the rest of my body. Like I'd been asleep for a long time, and I was waking up."

"Did you tell the missionary what had happened?"

"Oh, yes, and he was ecstatic."

"Has there been any recurrence of the cancer?"

"None."

Chapter Four

A Majestic Being

Ann

A Child with Leukemia

Ann was a lovely lady, forty-two years of age but looking much younger, who came to our home in Bountiful on a clear January day in 1991. She had been trained as a medical technician, and although previously married, she was presently single. She had four children who were dependent upon her.

She had been raised as a child in Southern California. Her parents were Protestants who converted, with her, to The Church of Jesus Christ of Latter-day Saints.

She began: "My first experience happened when I was four years old. My parents moved to a new home in Glendale, California, and I had my own room. I had been ill several times and my parents knew that I wasn't feeling well but apparently were unaware of how very sick I was. I had been hospitalized several times as they attempted to find out what was wrong with me. The Doctors knew it was some type of blood disease—later identified as leukemia. The hospital had sent me home to be with my parents; my mother couldn't be with me in the hospital all the time.

"I was tired, listless, and generally sad of heart. My parents loved and cared for me, but I couldn't seem to communicate to them how badly I felt on this particular occasion. My father was having severe back problems and this may have accounted for their seeming indifference.

"Anyway, on this one night my mother put me to bed and tucked me in. She was worried about my Dad and didn't seem to notice that I had a hard time climbing into bed. I felt so tired that . . . that I simply wanted to get to sleep. I lay there for a moment waiting to go to sleep when I noticed a light coming into the room. It was a beautiful golden-white light which seemed to appear in the wall to the left of my bed."

"Did you notice anything besides the light?"

"Not at first. And I wasn't afraid, just curious about the light. It was about three feet up from the floor and mid-length of the bed, which was located near the wall. As the ball of light grew the pain and feeling of illness suddenly left me. I had no idea what was happening, but I felt at peace."

A Beautiful Lady of Light* and a New World

"I sat up and watched the light grow. It grew rapidly in both size and brightness. In fact the light got so bright that it seemed to me that the whole world was lit by it. I could see someone inside the light. There was this beautiful woman, and she was part of the light; in fact she glowed."

"Did the light hurt your eyes?"

"No, even though it was bright by mortal standards."

"Tell me more about the lady in the light."

"Her body was lit from inside in a way . . . it's very hard to explain what she looked like. It seemed as if she were a pure crystal filled with light. Even her robe glowed with light as if by itself. The robe was white, long-sleeved, and full length. She had a golden belt around her waist and her feet were bare. Not that she needed anything on her feet since she stood a couple of feet off the floor."

"Were you frightened by her?"

"No, just the opposite. I had never seen such kindness and gentle love on anyone's face such as I saw in this person. She called me by name and held out her hand to me. She told me to come with her—her voice was soft and gentle but . . . but it was more in my mind. Communication was easier than when you verbalize thoughts. At the time I thought of it as 'mind talk.'

"I asked her who she was and she explained that she was my guardian and had been sent to take me to a place where I could rest in peace. The love emanating from her washed over me so that I didn't hesitate to put my hand in hers.

"As soon as I was standing beside her we moved through a short darkness to a beautiful, even brighter, light. And then I saw . . . there was this astonishingly beautiful world before me. It was like nothing else I have since seen on earth. Somehow I knew, inside of me, that the earth had been left behind. I had no idea where I was, and I didn't care. I felt a deep, profound peace . . . no, it was more than that. It was a world of peace and love.

* This event is depicted on the cover of the book. The scene, entitled "Ann's Angel," is from an oil painting by Florence Susan Comish of Provo, Utah.

"The new world looked sort of like the world I had left behind, but it was also very different. Everything glowed from the inside with its own light. The colors were beyond anything on earth—they were more vibrant, brilliant, and intense. And there were colors I had never seen before—don't ask me what they were. There were shrubs, trees and flowers, some of which I had seen on earth, like evergreens, and others which I hadn't seen before, and I haven't seen since. They were beautiful, beautiful.

"I asked my guardian why she took me to this place. She said that I needed the rest because life had become too hard for me to live.

"There was also grass all around, and a little hill with sand at the base in a sort of play area where several other children were playing. My guardian took me to the area and left without my knowing it. I immediately joined the children in play. There were toys in the sand and we built castles and roads and played with the toys. I was totally immersed in this new world of love, peace and play."

"Did you stay with the children very long?"

"It seemed long in one sense; in another, it seemed timeless. I felt thoroughly refreshed, enlivened and spiritually rejuvenated. I was filled with a zest for life. It is impossible to explain what it felt like to be lighter than air, with no pain, and totally at peace with everyone and everything around. I simply accepted my existence in the new world and lived.

"When my guardian returned I thought we were going to another part of this fascinating and wonderful world. Calling to me, she gently took me by the hand and said that I had to leave. When we started back the way we came I realized that we were returning to the earth, and I asked her why I had to go back. She told me it was time to return, and it would be easier for me to live on the earth now.

"We came back through the darkness, as before, with the surrounding light making a sort of tunnel through it. The peace followed me and I was content. We emerged back in my bedroom. My guardian smiled at me, and suddenly I was back in bed without the slightest idea of how I got there."

"Could you still see your guardian?"

"Yes, but the light was diminishing. I waved at her, and she smiled and waved back. Then the light sort of gathered around her and she was gone. I went into a peaceful sleep, content in the knowledge that someone loved and watched over me."

"Did you tell your parents?"

"Not until years later when I told my mother. I didn't think they would believe me. The next time they took me to the hospital for a checkup my blood tests showed that I was normal."

"So you must have been healed during or after your experience?"

"I think it was during the experience."

"During your experience did you feel like you had a body like the one on this earth?"

"No, it was lighter."

"But you had arms and legs?"

"Sure, I could touch the other children, and I could feel and smell. I played in the sand and made sand castles with my hands. As we were playing, sometimes I would walk, and other times, when we went as a group, we just floated."

"It's amazing that you remember all those details after so many years."

"It's because it was so real. I still remember it as one of the more realistic events in my life. I was able to do things that I never did in any dream. It was real."

Spinal Meningitis and a Wonderful Experience

"I was approximately twenty-eight when I had my next experience, and I was living in a trailer in Southern Utah in the Skull Valley area. My husband was a physician, and I was working to help in a construction project in the area, as well as caring for my two children.

"One day I felt quite ill but I was cleaning up the trailer, because I knew I had to or I would be in trouble."

"In trouble with whom?"

"My husband—he was having emotional problems, and he took some of his problems out on me."

"Okay, so you were feeling ill. What seemed to be the trouble?"

"Well, when I first got up I felt just fine. Just a little while later, though, I suddenly got this fever and a really weird headache. I didn't know what it was but I thought it might be the flu so I kept going. In about three hours my head felt awful and my back hurt; my whole spine ached. I also noticed that I had these spasms going up and down my spine, and they would pull me backwards. The spasms got stronger and stronger as time passed, and I knew something was wrong. My temperature had climbed to over 105 degrees in less than three hours.

"I didn't realize how sick I was. I figured I could keep working and it would go away. At one point I fell down and couldn't get up, but I kept working on the floor. By this time I couldn't think properly. While I was on the floor one of the workers from the project came in and found me on the floor. He took one look at me and left—he rushed to a phone and called my husband. He told my husband that I appeared to be seriously ill. In fact, he said I looked like I might be dying.

"My husband came and looked in on me, but by then I had managed to get on my feet. I didn't want him to see me when I was sick because I was afraid of what he would do. He was abusive to me. He asked me how I was and I told him I was just a little tired. He said he had to see some other patients and would be back to check on me.

"When my husband came back he made me lie down on the couch, and one of those terrible spasms bent me backward. He took my temperature and checked my other vital signs. Then he took me into the bedroom and put me in bed—he had to lift me onto the bed. He got his hypodermic needles and gave me a couple of shots to control the spasms. He also took some blood for a blood test.

"I drifted in and out of consciousness and sleep for the next several hours. I remember my husband coming in and going to bed, but it was mostly a haze for those hours, until I awoke and found that I could hardly breathe. I was just breathing these little gasps. I tried to lift my arm but it fell back. I knew I was in desperate trouble, and I was kind of afraid. All of a sudden I wasn't there, I was . . . I was floating. It was so fast I didn't realize what had happened. And the pain—it was gone. There was this tremendous relief. It was, I don't know, just suddenly—WOW!

"I was floating, I was floating, and there was no pain. I looked up and noticed that I was coming up to the ceiling. I remember wondering what was on the other side of the ceiling, and then I went right through. I found myself standing, and still moving up, and I went into this blackness. I traveled in the blackness—sort of like a tunnel—until I came to this person who blocked the way."

A Beautiful Man

"There was this person standing in the way, and I couldn't go around so I stopped. The person was in a brilliant, brilliant light. I was fascinated. Even the hair was lit up, it was beautiful. In fact the person was beautiful, it was a man, he had this . . . oh, I didn't know that men could be that beautiful.

"I wondered who he was and he identified himself as my Savior, Jesus Christ. And I thought, WONDERFUL. I had this joy, that was, you know, welling up inside of me. It was like an explosion going on in me.

"Then he said, almost immediately, that I had to go back." Ann covered her face and began to sob as the memory of that event flooded back. Carol and I waited for several minutes while she regained her composure. I asked her, gently, "You didn't want to come back, I take it?"

With great difficulty Ann continued, "No, I cried to him: 'No, please. I don't . . .' "

"You had children then, didn't you?"

"Yes, I had two."

"Did you know why you had to come back, was that explained?"

"At first I cried out, I . . . I pleaded with him. I didn't want to go back. There was the pain I had just been in, the pain . . . it was far beyond anything I could handle."

"And that's why you didn't want to come back, right?"

"Yes, and the other reason was that life had become just plain hell for me."

"Because of your husband?"

"Yes."

"Did you get back all of a sudden, or was it . . .?"

"No, I pled with him and he held me for a while. I don't know how long I pleaded and begged, it was a little bit of time, then . . . then I knew that he was feeling my sorrow and pain.

"Suddenly I felt this tremendously powerful . . . it's beyond the words of powerful, it's . . . I was suddenly enveloped in this deep, deep peace. It surrounded me, enveloped me, and he said: 'If you will go back I will put you immediately to sleep and when you awake you will be completely healed. And the pain will be gone.'

"Well I stopped crying, and I thought for a few moments. I looked at him and I knew that this was an absolute promise if I did what he said. I knew this was my Savior, and he was asking me . . . he was giving me the choice. I bowed my head and said that I would, and that very powerful peace stayed with me. It finally penetrated into my heart. I relaxed and turned around."

Return to This Life

"I went, again, into the darkness, and I came out under the ceiling of my room. I stopped and looked and I could see the whole room; it was almost as if the moonlight was in there. I could see my husband sleeping and my own body next to him. My husband was breathing but my body was motionless. I didn't look at my face because I was afraid that the agony of the pain would be on it. I instinctively knew that if I looked at the face I would not go back.

"I knew that was my body, yet the real me was up near the ceiling. That thing down on the bed, it . . . it repulsed me. But I could feel the presence of my Savior, so I went over to my body and turned around. Then I settled down into it, sitting up. I hesitated in this position because I really didn't want to complete it. I was afraid I would feel that awful pain again—yet I felt reassurance from Him. I could feel that it would be all right.

"I lay back and . . . and that terrible pain hit. I gasped because of the awful severity of the pain. Then instantly I was out; before I could take another breath I was unconscious. It was so fast that the next morning when I woke I realized I hadn't even had a chance to think.

"I awakened the next morning with a feeling of complete peace. The fever was broken, my body was covered with sweat, and there was no pain. I was kind of weak, but nothing like I had been, and I knew what had happened. I remembered back—and I prayed—and gave thanks to my Heavenly Father and to my Savior.

"In my prayer I promised to do what I had to in order to live on, because there had to be a purpose. He had told me, and I remembered, that my missions were not finished. I remember wondering about *missions*. Why not *mission?* And I remembered that when I had gone to the other side I was pregnant with another child. I had to return for that purpose as well as my other children."

"Did you find out what had made you ill?"

"Yes. Three days later the test results came back. It was a very deadly form of spinal meningitis—one that normally kills. My husband tried to make me think that it was his shots that made me well, but I knew better.

"My husband died about one-and-one-half years after this experience."

"What is your feeling now about your experience? Did it feel real also?"

"Very real, even more so than the other one; because in the other one I was so young. There was no way to deny what I had seen. That much pain, and then being released from it, there was no way. . . ."

"You subsequently read some of the books on life after life, and . . ."

"Yes, my mother brought me some last year. When I talked to her I explained that I didn't know what to call what had happened to me. She told me that she had read a book which told about others having similar experiences. She thought it would help me, and it did."

"But you hadn't read any books when you had . . ."

"I'd never heard of it. I thought I was the only one who had gone through something like this."

"What is your feeling about death, now?"

"Because of my experience when I was very young my feeling hasn't changed much. When people talked about death I thought it was something else. When I was an adult, and after I put two and two together, it was hard for me to go on living. I remembered this beautiful place without pain."

"So, again, what is death to you?"

"Death is totally irrelevant from the point of view of the individual experiencing it. There is no death, there is no such thing, at least as most people think of it. It's simply a change. That's all it is."

"Do you have any messages you'd like to leave others?"

"I'd tell them that this fear about death which people have is a falsehood; it's a lie. If we have loved ones, and it's their time to go, let them go. If it isn't their time to go, because they have more work to do, they should complete their mission."

Lucy

A Jewish Background

Carol and I visited Lucy and her husband shortly after they moved into a home in a small town in Northern Utah. Lucy admired some sewing my wife was working on and we chatted for awhile; then I asked Lucy to tell us a little of her background. She began:

"I was born in Long Island, New York, on Aug 7, 1957. My father was military. He was a German emigrant who came to America when he was eight. He and my mother were Jewish, and when I was six years old my father died—after a strange dream."

"What was the dream?"

"I was just a little child so I don't remember all the details, except he dreamt that he was going to meet two men, and after that he would die. My father had been ill because of injuries he got in World War II. He told my mother about it and he was convinced that it would happen."

"Where were you living when he had the dream?"

"In Virginia. The next day after the dream we were walking in a field, and my father saw two men ahead of us. He ran to catch up with them; they turned out to be Mormon missionaries. Two days later he told my mother he was going to be baptized into the Mormon Church."

"Did the missionaries teach him in that period?"

"I don't think they did. It was something he knew that he had to do. My grandmother and others were yelling at him, they were Jewish, and told him that he shouldn't do it. He couldn't be submerged in water, because of his injuries, or he would die. He insisted, despite their protestations—he said he had to. He was baptized two days after that, and two days after the baptism he died."

"How did he die?"

"He was on the grounds of the VA hospital in Virginia. He'd had chest pains, and when he got to the hospital he just dropped. They rushed and put equipment on his chest, and everything else, and he came back to life. When he came to he ripped the medical equipment off himself and told them to leave him alone, to trust him, he knew what he was doing. Then he died."

"You weren't baptized at the same time as your father, were you?"

"No, it was only my father. But before he died he made us promise that we would all be baptized; my mother, and all my brothers and sisters. He also insisted that the temple work be done to seal my mother to him."

"How did your mother feel about it?"

"She blamed the LDS Church for his death. She had us all baptized, later, because she promised my father, but none of the others stayed in the Church—only me. My grandfather on my father's side joined the Church years later. My mother, still, will hardly speak to me because I stayed active in the Church, and because I married a Mormon."

"What happened after your father died? Were you raised in the east?"

"No, we moved to Southern California, and my mother remarried. I grew up in Southern California and became involved in the entertainment industry—movies and TV."

Hit by an Automobile—Return from Death

"My first experience was in the State of Washington. I had been visiting some of my brothers, my sisters, and my mother who had moved to Washington. I was only there a week when I was hit by a car. I was walking on a crosswalk going across the street, and there was a woman ahead of me, an older woman. I don't know what happened but I felt that something was wrong and I pushed the older lady; then I was hit by a car. I was thrown into the side of a building.

"Much of my body was fractured. One leg was broken, my thyroid was badly damaged, and—they told me this happened, I have no recollection—I got up from the accident, and the emergency crews had to chase me up a hill. They caught me and took me to the hospital. I don't remember that either. When I got there, apparently I went into cardiac arrest."

"When was this?"

"Let's see, my baby daughter had just been born, she was born in 1981—the accident was in 1982. Anyway, I had died, and I remember seeing myself hurt on the table. I could hear them saying, wake-up, wake-up, wake-up. I don't remember where I was in the room, I just saw it. Then I was in a hallway looking for somebody. I don't remember who I was looking for but I was searching for someone.

"I saw someone beckoning to me, but I didn't want to go. I wanted to stay. The next thing I knew I heard the doctor say, she's okay, she's okay. He was yelling at me. He said, 'Are you here, can you hear me, do you understand what I am saying?' And that's how I knew that I was no longer dead.

"They said I was dead for a minute-and-a-half. It all happened very quickly. After that, when I had been in the hospital for about three days, I had a dream. In the dream I was looking at a house that was split in half. In one side of the house were people I knew who were dead. In the other side were all the people I knew who were alive. I was in a car between both places. It was very intense, and I had that dream continuously for about a month."

"Did you ever get a feeling for what the dream meant?"

"I always took it to mean that I had been between life and death. Shortly after that I was sent home. I was an invalid and couldn't walk. My mother took care of me in her house. I had been in her house about six months, and I was angry because of my invalid status."

A Prayer for Help

"As I lay at home I blamed God for my troubles. I went through a lot of prayer searching and, being Jewish by birth, I didn't just pray to God, I yelled at God." Lucy laughed through her tears as she thought about it.

"Anyway, He kept telling me it would be all right. I heard him . . . ." she continued with difficulty. I heard him talk to me—he told me to have faith, to have trust. But when you're in that state you don't believe anything. You know, you start thinking you're going crazy."

"Were you having other problems?"

"It was just everything. I was recovering from a divorce, I was having trouble with my girls, the doctors said I had cancer in my leg, and they told me I had diabetes—I couldn't walk. My leg was so bad they decided to amputate it. The day before the operation was to take place I took extensive time for prayer. As I prayed I was told to have faith and to believe."

"Was it the voice you heard before?"

"No, I . . . I have seen Christ." Lucy struggled with her emotions. "He put his hands out to me and he told me to believe. And, you know, you try to, but you're going through so much, you . . . you want to believe but you don't. You do and you don't."

"What were the circumstances when you saw Christ?"

"I was praying, asking why. You know, there's got to be a reason. 'Cause I believed myself always to be a very good person. And I was asking, why? . . ."

A View of the Savior

"While I was praying, instead of the voice I saw Christ. I saw him, like you, and he put his hands out to me and told me to trust, to have faith, and to believe."

"Were you in your bedroom?"

"Yes. I was on the floor, because . . . you know, I couldn't pray on my knees, so I was on the floor. And He was above me. It seemed that he was towering but it might not have been that. He was a being of light, mostly. And his robes were of a blue-tinted light. He seemed to be a very strong man, very gentle, but very strong.

"It was a very calming feeling. He kept saying, have faith—he never said anything with his mouth. I just knew he was talking to me."

"Did you see light around him?"

"Oh yes, but most of Him was light."

"Was there light in the room?"

"My, yes."

"Did the light come first, and then him, or what?"

"No, it wasn't gradual. He was there . . . he was not there, and then he was there. And the light sort of encompassed the room."

A Leg that Wasn't Removed

"After this experience I prepared to have my leg removed. I started to go to the doctor's office for preliminary tests before surgery. On the way to the doctor's office there was another building, and something beckoned me to it. I had my mother push me up there. There was a Naturopath—a natural doctor. When I was in there, the doctor was in back . . . he was in back. He said that he felt he had to come forward, he didn't know why. I had just come in the door.

"He rushed me into a room, and he told me that something was stuck in my leg. He told me to wait a moment, and he called another doctor. Another doctor came over, a woman, and they removed something from my leg. Anyway, I *walked* out. . . . I had not been able to walk for two years. I walked for the first time in two years." Lucy wiped away the tears.

"Did you see what they removed from your leg?"

"It was cement, a piece of bricking, that was stuck in there from my accident. I had been through sixteen surgeons—the finest surgeons in the State of Washington. They all said it was hopeless. There was nothing they could do to restore the use of my leg. It turned out they were wrong. But it was the Spirit that brought me to the other doctors."

"Did you ever determine why your initial doctors didn't see the cement in your leg on an x-ray?"

"I don't know for sure. I asked them later when I showed them how it had been removed. They said that it didn't look like a piece of cement in the x-rays. They thought it was bone marrow."

"Have you read any materials about other people who had experiences like yours?"

"No—I've been too busy working and taking care of my kids. Oh, I've heard of some of them on TV but I haven't read anything."

Chapter Five

Fear Not Death

Jennette

Heart Operation

Jennette was at her home in Salt Lake City when Carol and I met her. We admired her beautiful art, ceramic and other pieces. She had a delightful sense of humor despite numerous health problems. She explained that she was forty-nine years old, and that she had lost her husband the previous spring. From her demeanor it was clear that she missed her husband sorely.

"Okay Jennette, why don't you tell us a little of your background so that we can understand you better?"

"Well, I come from a background of English and German hard-heads. I was born in Pasadena, California, and I came to Salt Lake City about twenty-two years ago."

"Where did you meet your husband?"

"I met my husband in Salt Lake City when I was working in a machine shop during the day and in a tavern on weekends."

"Were your parents here in Salt Lake City?"

"My parents were divorced when I was quite young, and I was raised by the strong arm and hammer of my grandmother, who is now deceased."

"Do you have children?"

"I have four living children—two boys and two girls. My daughters are both in the Salt Lake valley, one son is in Las Vegas, and the other lives in Denver. I also have three grandsons."

"It sounds as if you have a fine family. Perhaps you can tell us, now, what happened to you and under what circumstances."

"Three years ago I was on disability for asthma and depression. That summer I was doing a lot of fishing and camping, and I found that I always got out of breath and couldn't get far from the camper. Thinking that it was the high altitude and my asthma, I ignored it. Then, while I was baking a birthday cake for my daughter, I had such an attack that I thought I would go get a shot and finish the cake later.

"I went to the hospital and instead of giving me a shot they said, 'Honey, this is your heart, and we're putting you in intensive care.' I was flabbergasted. After a week of various tests they put me in surgery."

"Which hospital was this?"

"Holy Cross in Salt Lake . . . My Doctors decided I needed a mitral valve replacement and a double bypass. The mitral valve had gone sour, because as an infant I had had scarlet fever.

"The original surgery was scheduled for early in the morning of February 28, 1988. And I wasn't fearful at all. After the surgery I went into Intensive Care where they determined that bleeding was occurring. They rushed me back into surgery to find the source of the bleeding. That was at five P.M. on the same day."

"This was bleeding in the heart?"

"Yes—it turned out my heart was misshapen and in the wrong place. Instead of a normal heart's shape, my heart looks like a mushroom. So the bleeder was on the back side of the mushroom instead of where they expected to find it. There was a vein towards my back rib leading to the valve and that's where the bleeding was coming from.

"The original team of surgeons tried to correct the problem on the second, afternoon surgery. They thought they had it corrected and put me back in Intensive Care. Eight to ten hours later I was still hemorrhaging. So for the third time in twenty-two hours, on February 29th, I went back into surgery, this time with a new team of surgeons. And this time they found the problem, but it was during this third surgery that I had my experience.

"I was on the operating table and I could see the doctors' faces, and I could hear a few words of what they were saying. I could see inside myself where the problem was. I tried to tell them, 'Look under that lip edge.' Of course, being anesthetized I couldn't tell them anything, but mentally I was trying to tell them, 'That's where the bleeder is, that's where the bleeding is coming from.' "

"Could you see them as this was going on?"

"I could see them—it's like I came out of my body and was two feet above them. And I could see what they were doing, and I could see the heart, and I could . . . I just knew where the bleeder was before I even rose up from my body. It just came to my mind . . . I just knew where it was.

"I wanted to explain where the bleeder was, but I couldn't, and in my anxiety to express it I came out of my body. I tried to communicate to the doctors, but I couldn't communicate, and I could see what they were doing. There were three surgeons and four nurses all working together.

"I finally decided that there was no use, the doctors weren't hearing me. And I kind of floated up to the top of the room. Like I was looking down from a distance, and still more distance, at them."

A Bright Light and a Marvelous Being

"Then the scene changed and I was surrounded by a greatness of light. Like a beautiful summer day with warm sun on the beach. Then I saw what appeared to be a great pipeline, like . . . something like a pipeline you might find buried alongside the road for sewage or something, you know, a great pipe.

"I walked into that, and there was the brightest light at the end. It took a long time to get to the end where the brightness was greatest, and . . . and a figure stood there in a white robe with hands outstretched. In my heart I know it was my Christ. It was . . . it was the form of Jesus Christ. I felt a lightness of heart and easiness—it was as if in a dream state but more real. There was no pain, or anxiousness, just serenity and peace.

"There were no vocal words, but there was no need for them. It was like my words were through my mind into the spiritual mind of my Christ and back to me, without hearing. There was no need to hear. So, definitely no need to speak, and yet a communion was there.

"I was so happy to be in that place, so close to my Savior, and feeling such warmth and comfort, as . . . as I'd never known on earth. And my Christ spoke to me and told me that I must go back, my work was not yet done. I had more work yet to do. I felt sad, and I knew that I had to follow the direction."

"Why did you feel sad?"

"Because I really wanted to enter . . . I truly wanted to enter. I didn't want to leave that glorious peace. The serenity . . . there are no words that can explain . . . " Jennette began to cry but managed to continue, "the peace, the calm . . . " she struggled for words.

"Love, I guess?" I added.

"Oh my, well you hear talk of angels. But it's like you *are* an angel. It's like you can perceive and all is so unnecessary. It's like a free spirit, a knowing being, I mean . . . I can see why they use sheep as an image of the Savior's pasture, because . . . things are so sublime—like sheep, so unobtrusive, so sublime. And I really think there's a connection.

"Well, then I closed my eyes on my Savior, and my youngest daughter was standing over my face weeping. When she saw me open my eyes she said, 'Mamma, mamma you're with us, you're going to be all right, I know you are.' "

"How old was your daughter at the time?"

"She was twenty-five, or thereabouts. So then it was in and out for three to five days. I believe I was five days in Intensive Care. Then they moved me to another hospital room and I was there for another ten or twelve days before I came home."

"When you were undergoing this experience, did your body feel like it was a body, or what was it like?"

"No, it was just something lying there, like another patient I was looking at."

"No, I mean your spirit body . . . "

"Myself?"

"Yes, yourself. What was it like?"

"It was an amazing thing, it was . . . there was no weight of a body. It was like floating on water, only there was no water around."

"Did you have arms and legs?"

"Oh, as far as I know I did. I really didn't look at myself. I was getting places somehow; now whether I was floating, or walking, I'm not sure. I don't understand how I did it, and I didn't question it before now. It's not in my nature to question things like that."

A New Direction

"After I came home I took my rest, of course, and took it easy, and . . . and I didn't mention this to anyone right away."

"You didn't mention this to your family?"

"No . . . no, it was something I wanted to hold inside myself. About seven months after the surgery, though, I had such a pressure inside myself, that . . . that things weren't right, things were incomplete. And I knew that I had to go to church, because I hadn't gone to church since that time.

"So I went to a Four Square Gospel Assembly in Salt Lake, and I stood up before the congregation and gave my testimony of the beautiful light, and the wonderment of being that close to my God. And the true knowledge and glory of what it would be like to walk hand-in-hand with him . . . and how he had given me that wonderful opportunity, and then how he told me that my work was not done."

"Did you understand from that what your work was?"

"No sir, I still didn't know what my work was. Now I believe I do."

"Okay, what do you believe it is?"

"Well, He has pointed it out in funny ways, or . . . rather in ways you wouldn't think of. A family, in Salt Lake City with nine children . . . and somebody calls me. 'Where will we go? We need food, we need clothing, we need a house. What will we do? One child has no arms.' And I go, whoa. And I jump in my car, and I spend four days running to get things like welfare assistance, social security changeovers, Shriner's Hospital appointments for the girl with no arms, housing, food stamps, food banks, clothing, and all those other things."

"So you sort of felt you were to help people, and perform . . . ."

"Yes, those things kept happening. And then a job opened up, through Valley Mental Health, where I began to get paid for helping people. In that position I was doing the paper work: of social security, to apply for needs that the State pays for, food stamps, Medicaid program, to help them with clothing, with financial help, knowing where to go to get their needs filled—and I was being paid for that. And I loved the work. I finally had to give it up, though, because my health deteriorated."

"So as a result of your experience you feel compelled to help people?"

"Yes. My daughter has remarked how I am more giving than I was before, to everybody."

"Is there any final message you'd like to leave?"

"For those who haven't had the experience I have, I'd like to tell them to fear not death. Fear not death!"

Pauline

A Swimming Accident

Carol and I met Pauline at our house in January 1991. She was fifty-one at the time and had an abiding interest in horses. She raised Arabians and a variety of other breeds and spent much of her time with her horses. She was a Licensed Practical Nurse by occupation, and had spent much of her professional life in the military. She was born in the eastern part of the country but had traveled throughout the U.S. During her travels she had joined The Church of Jesus Christ of Latter-day Saints.

Pauline explained that she had undergone two near-death experiences. She began her story:

"The first experience I had, where I was aware of this sort of thing happening, was in 1969 when I was in Long Beach California where I was attending Long Beach State College. I had gotten this idea that I wanted to go scuba diving—I heard that Catalina Island had excellent locations for diving. I was also going to physical therapy school at the time, and I needed a break and a diversion, so I enrolled in a scuba diving class.

"I got through the class and the final test was that we had to put on all the scuba gear and do a lot of swimming under water in the pool. The last thing we had to do, and it all took about an hour, was tread water for fifteen minutes with our shoulders out of the water.

"I remember I was really anxious to pass this test, because I wanted so badly to go out and scuba dive. I was treading water for about, I guess, ten minutes. Suddenly I got this horrible, horrible cramp in my lower abdomen, and I doubled up. I couldn't straighten out no matter what I tried to do.

"There were two life guards, it was a big olympic sized pool, but I don't remember ever calling for help. I kept splashing around and trying to get my head out of water. Every time I took a breath . . . I found out that you don't breathe in water, you swallow it if you're conscious. It's just sort of a reflex, and I swallowed all this water. I ended up starting to sink—you cannot float when you're drowning. You absolutely cannot float.

"Everything was happening at once. I was scared and yet I didn't want to call for help. My pride, I guess, stopped me until it was too late. I kept thinking I could get out of the trouble I was in. All of a sudden I could feel myself sinking, and there was this pain in my chest. It was a hot searing pain, and it was unbearable. I remember my toes touching the bottom of the pool, and I just stayed there.

"Within seconds I felt really warm. I had been very cold—and I was without pain. I couldn't believe it. And then, the peace, unbelievable peace."

"Do you remember seeing anything special during this period?"

"No, it was just a short period, and then I was aware of people grabbing me, and I felt roughed up as they pulled at me. I started to come to as they threw me over the edge of the pool. Then I was conscious of people screaming at me. They asked me why I was fighting so hard."

"Were you fighting?"

"I guess I was. I was very angry because I really didn't want to wake up. I felt as if I were in a vacuum, and I knew I was dying. It felt familiar, as if I had been in that state before—longer than the one I am now in—and I didn't want to come back. It was such a peaceful feeling, and I felt as though I had been robbed."

An Out-of-Body Experience

"My next experinece was in 1983; I was living in Salt Lake City. It was winter and I was working at a nursing home. I rode my bike until I got to 5th East and 30th South, and I was tired. My feet were cold and I needed a rest. I didn't have really warm clothes because I couldn't afford them. I parked my bike and sat down under a huge oak tree. I was so tired, I knew I couldn't stay awake, and I was shaking from being so cold. I thought I would just rest there for awhile, and I would be okay.

"I went to sleep, and all of a sudden I was warm. My mind was clear too, more so than when I had been awake. Then I remember seeing myself, and I wasn't very far away, maybe three feet. I could see my body lying under the tree, and I knew that I wasn't going to wake up. It was early dawn and it started to get light. I remember thinking: *somebody is going to see my bike and find me here*."

"Were you afraid of that?"

"Yes, because I knew that people who had been frozen and brought back suffered severe pain. I didn't want that to happen, so I fought and fought to wake up. I finally did, but it was really hard. My feet felt like stumps. I got to my bike with great difficulty."

"Do you remember how you got back into your body?"

"I was standing up and I just sort of lay down in it; then I was able to start getting my eyes open. My mind was sluggish, more so than when I had been out of my body."

"Is there anything else you'd like to say."

"Yes, there was a third, different kind of experience."

"What happened?"

"A few years ago I was trying out a horse I was thinking of buying, and it ran away with me. It only stopped when it crashed into a fence and threw me off. I was knocked unconscious. When I came to I felt pretty awful, but I managed to get up and get to my truck. I went to the VA Hospital and they checked me out and sent me home. My roommate put me in bed, and she said I stayed there without moving for two days.

"While I was lying unconscious, or asleep, I dreamed that I had died, and I was brought to this kindly man in a great hall. He asked me how I had spent my time on earth. In response I thought: *well I never went to church because I was too busy taking care of the sick and the dying*. Then I remember thinking that I had to wake up. I forced myself to come awake."

Chapter Six

A Strange Journey

Forrest Hansen

Forrest Hansen was an affable young man who came to my home in late February, 1991. He explained that he had been born in 1956, in Atlanta, Georgia, to LDS parents, but that he had not been active in the church since he was eleven. As an adult he had rejected religious affiliation with any church; he currently considered himself an agnostic Humanist.

Forrest had come to Salt Lake City when his mother moved here, and he graduated from Highland High School. He was presently single; he remodeled apartment buildings for an occupation.

After having had three unusual experiences Forrest began to read substantially from books on near death experiences and from other related texts. His speech verified his interest in books—he was articulate.

A Childhood Illness

"The first experience was when I was about six years old. I had an extreme illness, with a temperature over 106 degrees fahrenheit, and I came close to dying."

"What was the illness, do you remember?"

"I don't. It was a common childhood illness complicated by some other factors."

"Where were you living?"

"It was Atlanta."

"Okay, so you were very ill. What happened?"

"There wasn't much of a visual experience. It was more one of sensation."

"What did you feel?"

"It was an out-of-body feeling."

"What do you mean by out-of-body feeling?"

"I have to relate it to later experiences. It was like them."

"And how did that feel?"

"Great—there was no pain."

"So during your illness you had pain and then it was relieved?"

"Yes, there was severe pain before the experience. It disappeared during the experience. That's what I mean by an out-of-body feeling."

"When you finished this experience did you feel better, or were you still ill?"

"I felt better because the experience terminated at roughly the same time that my extreme fever broke. Whether I felt better because of the experience or because of the break in the fever, I'm not sure."

"And you don't know which was cause and which was effect?"

"Not really, I couldn't separate them."

A Journey to the Stars

"In the next experience I was eighteen years old, and I had another severe illness. It was a stomach ailment. I can't . . . there was a medical term for the illness but I don't remember what it was. I was in the hospital."

"Where was this?"

"It was Salt Lake, I was living here then. To lead up to this experience I should tell you that I've always been interested in studying various religions, part of which led me into studying meditation techniques. But the experience itself was very different from the usual meditative experience, and that's why it stands out to me. Having practiced meditation, I'm usually able to analyze, even in a dream state, what has happened to me. My memory is retained of the events, even after dreams. Also, in a meditative state I can direct what is happening, whereas in the event I'm about to describe I was just along for the ride.

"In this particular incident I'd been ill for a few days with a high fever. I began getting the same feeling as when I was young—the out-of-body feeling. At which time I found my physical sensations beginning to fall away. It was almost step by step. I began to lose feeling from my skin, various things like that. Until I reached the point that I was very much aware of my heart beating, and of breathing—to the point where I felt like I was thinking in order to breathe.

"Then I seemed to cross into another area, where even those sensations were left behind, and it became strictly a mental sensation. My visual experience then went to where I . . . I left my body. I was able to see my body and I went . . . ." Forrest laughed briefly. "This almost sounds silly to me.

I then went through the ceiling of the room, into the attic, and through the roof. I was able to see the neighborhood."

"This was in the hospital?"

"No, this was at home. All of this occurred before I went to the hospital. I was home alone at the time, and I was too sick to do anything about it. After all of this happened my sister came over and hauled me off to the hospital."

"All right, so you were seeing the neighborhood. What happened next?"

"Then we went through the clouds and up into the stars."

"We?"

"Well, me."

"There was nobody with you—you didn't see anyone else?"

"No it was just me. Now this was a . . . I wasn't aware of any body whatsoever. It was strictly a mental experience. Even the sensation of motion was not one you'd have where you could feel wind or something like that. It was only motion that you'd feel, like . . . like your equilibrium, or something. Only a mental experience.

"Then, traveling through the stars, I went farther, even to the point of seeing the earth falling behind."

"Did it look like pictures you've seen from satellites?"

"As I recall it seemed as though it were quite a bit darker. I was aware of the light curving around the edges, I guess from the sun.

"This all happened rapidly; it sped up even more as I traveled through the stars at a phenomenal rate. All this felt really comfortable and didn't seem especially unusual."

"Were you aware of any other sensations of darkness or lightness?"

"No, not at that time. From there it seemed to me that I traveled through the stars at a rate . . . and it occurred to me while I was doing it, that this speed could only happen in thought rather than in a physical sense."

"Why is that?"

"Well, I didn't know at the time. I have since analyzed it. At any rate this seemed as though it went on for a long time. The next change in the experience was the realization that the stars were starting to fall off to one side as well.

"This continued for a long time until the area in front of me was becoming dark; the area in back of me was the only source of light as the stars kept falling away. The stars began to shrink away into a smaller space until they became a single point of light. Then that disappeared and there was nothing but total darkness.

"The sensation, at that point, was of no motion because there was no point of reference. This didn't seem particularly uncomfortable either. Looking back on it, it seems as though it should have been unpleasant, but it wasn't."

A Being of Light

"The next thing that happened was that I was aware of something moving into my range of vision. This was a being, or an image of a being, constructed completely of light. It was not focused enough to make out distinct details, but it was obviously a human-type image.

"Upon confronting this image, I recall vividly the ideas exchanged between me and it. The specific exchange didn't seem spoken, but was understood. The image asked, 'Do you want to terminate your physical existence?' I recall pausing long enough to consider it and I said, 'No, I can't do that yet.' That was the end of the experience—I woke up."

"When you said that you couldn't do that yet, at the time, did you have any emotional feelings about why you said that?"

"No. At the time I felt that it was a physical consideration, that I couldn't do that yet. It seemed to me that the image was asking if I wanted to terminate my physical existence and become a mental entity like it was. And it just occurred to me that I couldn't do that yet—I wasn't to a point that I could do that in my development."

"So you felt that there were other things that you had to do for your development to proceed?"

"Yes, but . . . it even occurred to me that it wasn't something that I was going to be able to do in my lifetime."

"Tell me what you remember about the appearance of the image."

"When I say constructed of light, I also mean that it was semi-transparent and had depth. The light seemed to be particles of light, of which there were an innumerable quantity."

"Fair enough. Then the next thing you knew you were back . . . ."

"I woke up and I was still sick. I was throwing up blood. I literally couldn't move, I was doubled up. My sister came home, managed to get me into a car, and took me to the hospital. They took care of my emergency and released me within a day or so."

A Giant Geometric Shape in Space

"Not long after that illness and out-of-body experience I was in a car accident in which my spine was damaged. The spine damage resulted in a diminished liver and kidney function. Since that time I've been chemically sensitive. I assume the kidney and liver don't extract the amount of toxins that normally build up in the blood stream.

"So, if I'm unusually tired and happen to get around something toxic, which happens at work sometimes when I get around an oil-based paint, or any other chemical, I'll get extremely ill. Usually the illness is accompanied by a high fever. One of these episodes, about two years later, was bad enough that I was having heart problems.

"Was it heart irregularity or pain?"

"It was pain, and it was serious enough that I lay down on the couch at home, and I went to sleep. When I awoke I found I had been asleep for twenty-six hours, during which time I had another experience. The experience itself (I don't think it took very long chronologically, maybe a few moments) occurred sometime during the twenty-six hour period.

"The imagery of the experience was in a blank area, just blackness. I became aware of a point of light, and the blank area was cut in half by a plane that this point of light was on. The plane looked sort of like a piece of glass, only it didn't seem to be solid. The next image, as this image grew, was the sight of two cone shapes that emanated from either side of the point of light. The apexes of the cones were located at the light and their two axes were congruent and perpendicular to the plane. The cones appeared to be constructed of light particles.

"The next addition to the image—and I was just sort of watching this, I didn't seem to have any particular say or determination of what was occurring—was another form, at the center of which was the point of light. This other form was a sphere, and there was a larger sphere around the smaller one. The two cones came out of the spheres at opposite sides.

"The final image of this sequence was another, larger cone, that was off in the distance. It came and enveloped the entire geometry. The cones themselves seemed to have this light substance that filled them. So they weren't just hollow images.

"The next thing that happened was . . . I was traveling—and this thing was huge from my perspective, as large as anything I've ever seen. I would describe it as analogous to being in the mountains and looking at the Milky Way, or something like that. It had that type of gigantic proportion."

A Tunnel and Images of the Past

"Next, I was looking at the side of the geometry and I traveled to the end of the largest cone, and then traveled through it into one of the smaller cones. I looked down the center of this cone. The image was that of a tunnel with a light at the end of the tunnel."

"Would you describe it as a tunnel of light?"

"Yes, and the walls had considerable depth to them. As I traveled down the tunnel toward the point of light I became aware that if I stopped it produced the image of a memory."

"Could you stop at will?"

"I seemed to be able to. The memories were specific images of people or places. And each memory wasn't just an image, it was a sequence of a memory."

"And these were images rather than thoughts?"

"Yes, not a complete image in a physical sense, more a—I hate to use the word—ghost image."

"Were they images from your past, or what?"

"Yes, they were from my past. For some reason I got the idea that I should check and see if they were correct. I also observed that they weren't necessarily in chronological order. They were more in a meritorious order."

"What do you mean by meritorious?"

"They were more by the impact they had on me during my life. The ones that had more impact were easier to access, and . . . and so on.

"I looked toward the light but that was it. I didn't make it there. At least not that I recall. It was my intent to go to the light, but for some reason I didn't finish the trip.

"What did you recall next?"

"Waking up and being disoriented about time."

"Did you go to the hospital?"

"No. Except for the time confusion I felt great."

"Did you tell anyone else about this experience or the previous ones?"

"Only recently, in the last year-and-a-half. And then only because I came across some of the books describing analogous experiences."

Thoughts About the Experiences

"These experiences have affected the way I think and live in every way; partly because I think of them a lot and have analyzed and researched them to death. The resulting conclusions, and the philosophy I've developed from those conclusions, have had a profound effect on my personal character."

"In what sense was your personal character changed?"

"I used to be . . . ." Forrest laughed with a somewhat embarrassed demeanor. "I was a less than desirable character—I don't think I am anymore."

"Why did these experiences change the way you dealt with others or whatever it is that you say profoundly changed?"

"The philosophy is pretty involved. If I were to say something about being near death, just that in itself, would affect your attitude. It's like anything else—if you lose something you learn to appreciate it."

"That's true. What is your attitude about death? Is it different from before?"

"Ever since I was young I haven't had any belief in an afterlife. I still don't, so in that sense my attitude hasn't changed. And . . . and at the same time I carry a belief that there might be . . . ."

"That sounds like a contradiction."

"Well, it isn't in the sense that . . . a lot of people who have had near-death experiences look on it as an after-death experience. I don't. So I don't see it as a reinforcement of that belief. I try to keep an open mind, though, and I realize there are a lot of things that people don't know yet. So I have to leave some possibility that there may be . . . I don't see it as proof though."

"Do you think the experiences were related to your background, or to your culture, or to how you were raised, or were they independent of those effects?"

"They were related to issues and ideas that I was thinking about—that most people think about."

"How do you know what most people think about?"

"Well I would think that anybody who was dying, and was aware that he was dying, would have some thoughts about death. As to the content of the experiences being related to anything I was familiar with, no they weren't. They were new ideas."

"Did you, during the experience, or later as you thought about it, get a feeling as to what the geometric shapes meant?"

Forrest grinned and pulled a sheet of paper from his briefcase. It was a drawing of the geometric shapes as he had previously described them. "Okay, remember that the images took place in a blank field. The plane seemed to be in motion in a direction perpendicular to itself, and I was represented by the point of light on the plane. This point of light corresponded to my place in space and time. The two small cones seemed to represent past and future, with the cone extending to the left of the point of light being the past and the one to the right being the future. The rest of the experience went on like a video, and I wasn't able to analyze what it meant at the time."

"Did the other geometries mean anything to you later?"

"Yes, it occurred to me that this was more of a symbolic image than I had thought at first. The cones were . . . I knew that if I were to move forward or backward in time there was only a certain distance that I could travel within a particular instance of time. This was the construction of the cone, similar to a graph. That is, if I were to move forward one second, the farthest I could move would be this distance. The cone seemed to represent the outside perimeter of the set of experiences I could have—not necessarily that I could experience everything in the cone, but that was the limit.

"What did the spheres represent?"

"The smaller sphere corresponded to the distance I could travel in an entire lifetime. The larger sphere was a representation of the entire universe. The larger cone corresponded to the limits of the entire universe.

"So basically, what we have here is the beginning of the universe, its expansion, my place in it, possible realms of my existence, and the things that could affect me prior to my existence and after my existence."

"By your existence do you mean your existence on this earth at that point in time?"

"Yes."

Chapter Seven

The Importance of Children

Bob Amodt

Bob and Margaret Amodt visited Carol and me at our home in March 1991. They were a couple, in their late twenties to early thirties, who appeared to have a close-knit relationship. They explained that they had been together about ten years and had four children.

Bob was born in Salt Lake City where he graduated from high school. He currently was attending Salt Lake Community College, studying auto collision repair, in anticipation of opening his own shop.

Margaret was born in Salt Lake City and was raised in West Bountiful, Utah. As a girl, Margaret had a horse and was interested in rodeos.

Bob's Experience

Bob began his story: "On a beautiful day, April 10, 1980, I was riding my motorcycle south, approaching 9th West and 7th South in Salt Lake City. I saw a school bus in the turn lane. I almost got to it, and it suddenly turned across the street in front of me. I thought: *I can't make it—I'm going to be dead.*

"I remember seeing the stripe on the side of the bus just before I hit. The next thing I knew I was looking down on top of the bus. It was like . . . it was like in slow motion. That was the first time I knew that there was a number on top of buses. I didn't know that, but there was a great big number on top of this bus.

"I was looking down and I saw my motorcycle come falling out from the back wheel of the school bus. It was still moving."

"As you were looking down did you see your body down below?" I asked.

"No, it was like in slow motion. Everything was quiet, I didn't feel anything."

"There was no pain?"

"I didn't feel any pain. It was really peaceful. The next thing I knew I was rolling on the ground on the other side of the bus. I stood up and walked away from it."

"Did anyone call an ambulance or the police?"

"Yes, the paramedics showed up and they said they didn't see any way that I should be alive. I was supposed to have hit the bus at 66 miles-an-hour."

"Let's see now, Bob, as you hit the one side of the bus did . . .?"

"I didn't feel myself hit, or anything."

"Now your physical body wound up on the other side of the bus?"

"Yes."

"How did you get to the other side?"

"I don't know. It's a blank when I hit. I remember seeing the one side of the bus, I remember looking down, and the next I knew I could see everything spinning around. Then I got up and walked away."

"When you looked down, could you have been in your physical body, just flipped over the bus?"

"No way."

"Did the medics take you to the hospital?"

"No, I was in pretty good shape and they told me I could go home if I wanted to. I had a little road rash they had to scrub out of my knees and my elbows."

"Did you have a helmet on?"

"No, and I didn't even get my clothes dirty."

"Has that particular experience affected the way you think and believe?"

"No. I just wonder about the missing time between the one side of the bus and the other side. There's a blank there. And I wonder how I was able to see the top of the bus."

"Have your religious feelings changed as a result of this?"

"Yes, I'm a strong believer in God. There's got to be a God or I wouldn't be alive today, I don't think. Just before I hit I prayed to God and begged forgiveness, because I thought I was going to be dead."

"So you believed in God before your accident?"

"Yes."

"What religious faith did you follow then?"

"I was Catholic."

"Do you still follow your faith?"

"No, not a whole lot. I believe in God, though. Religion is more what you've got inside of you."

Margaret Amodt

Her Children Ran Through Her

Margaret began: "In 1983, I didn't know I was pregnant, I had an ectopic pregnancy."

"What is that?"

"It means the baby was in the tube. The fetus exploded the end of my tube. I was bleeding internally."

"Were you in the hospital?"

"I spent the whole weekend, and I thought . . . you know, I thought it was just stomach cramps. Monday it was getting worse so I called my grandmother to come and take me to the doctor."

"Did you know you were pregnant?"

"No. She took me to the doctor and he sent me to Emergency at Holy Cross Hospital. The pain kept getting worse . . . in my shoulder; I couldn't lift my arm. And I hurt all over, there was a lot of pain."

"Did your husband know what had happened?"

"Yes. He was called, and he came to the hospital. He was with me when I had to go to the bathroom. He helped me, and when I stood up the blood must have gone to my legs. He said I took two steps, and then I was gone. I don't remember passing out but he told me about it later."

Bob interjected, "When she fell down I caught her, and she was pale and cold; she was really limp. I yelled for the nurses to come, and they brought the thing to start her heart. Margaret was out for, I'd say, seven or eight minutes."

"What do you remember next, Margaret?"

"I knew I was . . . I felt so good. And I thought: *Wow, this is beautiful.* I really liked it, the feeling I had."

"The pain was gone?"

"Yes, the pain was gone."

"Did you see yourself—your body?"

"No, the first thing I saw was my kids. They had been taken to my parents' house. They were running around, laughing."

"How many children did you have?"

"Two little girls. They were playing and I was in my parents' house. I remember, I wasn't standing, I was, like, floating. And then my oldest daughter ran right through me."

"Did that surprise you?"

"Yes. I tried to hold her and I couldn't. And she started screaming . . . I could hear her scream, 'Mamma.' Shortly after that I was back in the hospital and I felt pain. It was awful."

"When your daughter was screaming your name, was that just a normal reaction of your daughter, or . . .?"

"No, I think that she knew I was there. That's how I felt, and later we talked about it."

"How old was she?"

"She was almost three years old."

"Was your mother present?"

"No I didn't see my mother, or my father. I saw my brother playing with the kids, but I was more focused on them. And then I knew that . . . that I had to come back."

"How did you know that you had to come back?"

"I don't remember anyone saying anything to me, but I just . . . I just knew it."

"Did you have any consciousness of how you got back?"

"I was just, all of a sudden, back, and I was yelling and . . . I don't remember yelling. I remember the pain, and I wanted to go back where I was before the pain."

"When you came to, and the pain hit, were you in bed or were you on the floor?"

"I was with my husband on the floor. The nurse was there sticking some stuff up my nose. I think that's what brought me back, because I didn't want to face the pain again."

"Did you see a bright light or anything of that sort?"

"There was, I would say, a bright glow around me. Not my body, it was around me when I was gone."

"You could see a glow?"

"Yes, it was bright, and it was around me. Kind of like a bubble. It was peaceful."

"When you were in your parents' home did your body feel like a body?"

"No."

"What did it feel like?"

Margaret thought for a moment. "It didn't feel like air either . . . energy!"

"Did this energy have arms and legs?"

"Just like me."

"As far as you can tell it was just like your present body?"

"Well, okay, I didn't look down. It was as if I were hovering, and I could see my children."

"And you actually tried to embrace your child?"

"Yes, my daughter. She was running and I reached out to hold her, and she ran through me. I saw her just run through me."

"Did the experience change the way you felt about religion?"

"I was raised LDS but I wasn't active, and I'm still not. But I've heard a lot of things said—that there's no such thing as life after death. After my experience I *knew* that there was something else. And it's a lot more beautiful than here."

"Why do you say it's more beautiful than here?"

"I just felt good."

"How do you feel about death?"

"I can hardly wait," Margaret laughed, and continued, "when it's my time."

Norma

Watched her Baby Delivered from Out-of-Body

Norma was at her sister's home in Salt Lake City when Carol and I visited her in mid-March, 1991. She was staying with her sister for awhile in order to get assistance while she recovered from an illness. She was a lovely blonde lady with an enthusiastic manner.

Norma explained that she had been born in Salt Lake City in 1954 to an LDS mother and a Catholic father. Her early family life was not particularly a religious one, although her mother stressed the importance of a belief in God.

Norma was married at a young age to a man who, ultimately, physically abused her. She lived in Kearns, Utah, after she was married, and she later moved to Wendover, Nevada, where she trained and worked as an emergency medical technician. She had seven children from this first marriage.

When she discovered she was pregnant with the fifth child, while living in Kearns in 1980, she was fearful that her husband would become violent and beat her as he had in the past. She felt overwhelmed by this prospect and believed, in her despair, that she couldn't face it. Her story follows:

"I took a thirty-eight revolver and put it against my head, solid against my head. It had bullets and I pulled the trigger. The revolver bounced off my head, I do not know how. I was sitting on the tub so my body would fall into it, and I shot the toilet.

"The water went rushing from the toilet, but I was so stunned, so in a daze, all I could hear was the ringing from the gun, that I left. I went outside and started walking, barefoot, with a pair of Levis and a T-shirt, and it was snowing outside. Somebody saw me and brought me back home. I did get in trouble for being pregnant and for breaking the toilet.

"When it came time for me to have my baby, Bobbie, I had been in labor and was at the hospital, but the baby wouldn't come. The doctor told me that I would have to bear down and force him out or he would die. I did what he told me, and when I did, I left."

"What do you mean, you left?" I asked.

"I was above my body. I could see my body, I could see the doctor, I could see the nurse, I could see the lights over the table, and there was something behind me—something I saw out of the corner of my eye. But I was so concerned with what was happening . . . I was seeing myself like looking in a mirror, but I was looking down.

"It felt like it was just seconds that I was out there, but it was long enough for the doctor to deliver the baby. I saw that it was a baby boy. The baby was a little bluish. I watched the doctor cut the cord.

"They were worried about me; the doctor called for a crash-cart; the nurse was running around. The nursery lady, the one that takes the babies to the nursery, she took the baby right from the doctor—without him cleaning the baby's nose or anything else. They were concerned that I was dying. I saw them put the baby in the warmer.

"I was out there for . . . it must have been just seconds, but I felt nothing. I didn't feel myself deliver that baby. I did not feel cold, I did not feel warm. I did not hear anything, I was just calm. It was dark around me except for those lights over the table. I was watching the doctor work fast, and the nurse was doing something with me.

"And then there was something behind me, sort of a light behind my head. I went to turn towards the light, but before I could get to it I felt this vacuum. It grabbed me and pulled me back into my body. I wanted to stay where I was, but it was like I wasn't supposed to be there. It just sort of sucked me back in."

"Why did you want to stay where you were?"

"Because it felt so good, but I knew I had to come back."

"How did it feel?"

"Serene, calm, everything was okay. There was no real feeling. Now, here on earth you can feel cold, you can feel warm, you can feel anxiety, you can feel sad, you can feel happy. There, there was no special feeling, except an . . . an awe. I don't know how else to explain it."

"Okay, you were sucked back into your body. What happened next?"

"I was in convulsions, and the nurse was slapping me and calling my name. I then started to respond and breathe again. I felt my lungs fill in a gasp of air as if someone had just opened my lungs. I must have blinked, or something, because they knew I was there. The doctor said: 'Do you know what you have?' I told him I knew it was a boy. He then asked me where I had been, and I told him I didn't know. He said that he would come and talk to me in the recovery room.

"He came into the recovery room, he brought me a flower, and he said: 'Where did you go?' I told him, and he said that I was the second person that had done that to him.

"After the experience I knew that it was not my time to go. There would have been no family or anyone to greet me. I'm not afraid to die, but it was not my time."

"Do you have any feeling for why it wasn't your time?"

"Yes, I was to have more children, especially Jonathan, my youngest child—and then there was Amanda."

Amanda and Jonathan

Some Special Children

"At the time of my experience I was married to an abusive husband. I had three more children by him. The last one by him, the seventh, was Amanda. When I was three months pregnant with her, my husband was mad because I wouldn't give him gambling and drinking money. I wanted to use the money for baby things and other things for the kids. He stomped on my back. He stomped right on me.

"I had started to bleed a little, so I went to the clinic in Wendover. They felt for fetal heart tone and couldn't find any. They told me that there was no life, and they would have to give me some medicine to abort the dead fetus. I objected and went to my regular doctor in Salt Lake. All the way in from Wendover I prayed that I had a live child in my stomach and not something else.

"My doctor in Salt Lake also said there was no life. He told me they would have to do a D and C. When we went into the operating room, I was all prepped and ready for the operation, he said: 'I'm going to do an ultrasound just to be sure I know the position of the fetus, so I'm not blindly searching.' There was still no heartbeat or movement of any kind.

"After the ultrasound the doctor told me that they weren't going to do an operation. He said that the baby would be out on its own in five months. The ultrasound showed I was four months along and everything was okay. Also, they were now getting heartbeats."

"All right, Norma, now tell me why Jonathan was so special."

"After I had Amanda my husband decided to get himself fixed. I told him that I was to have one more male child—I had seen him, in a dream."

"Did you have Jonathan by that husband?"

"No, I found that I didn't have to take his abuse, so I divorced him. Later I found this wonderful man I'm now married to. Jonathan was born to us."

"Is that what makes him so special?"

"Partly, but there are other things too."

"What other things?"

"During his birth we almost lost him. The line on the monitor, which showed the baby's heartbeat, went flat. I pled with them to save my baby. Because of the difficulty during birth they were going to do a C-Section, but there wasn't time. The doctor grabbed him by the head with a forceps and pulled him out. He was gray-blue when he came out.

"Later, in the hospital room, I was lying in bed with Jonathan, crying and praying. I was telling my baby that we almost lost him, and he didn't even have a name. I prayed to know what to name him.

"A lady, whom I'd never seen before, came into my room. She said: 'I've been inspired to tell you that you'll find your baby's name in the Bible. Then she left. I wasn't religious at the time, and I was skeptical, but I picked up the Bible. It fell open to the name of Jonathan and then to the name of Daniel, so I named him Jonathan Daniel. Those names mean 'gift from God,' and that's what I think he was.

"Then one day when Jonathan and I were in the car, he was about a-year-and-a-half old, he said: 'I miss my Father.' I told him that his Daddy would be home before we got home. He said: 'No, my Father in Heaven. I used to sit and talk with Jesus.' It frightened me. I didn't know what to do with this child. I hadn't taught him such things.

"When he was about two, he said: 'I talked to my grandfather and my uncle, and they told me I had to wait a very long time to come and be with you.' I talked to my husband, Kerry, and told him what Jonathan had said. Kerry asked me if Jonathan had said what they looked like. We brought Jonathan in to tell us. I had never seen pictures of my husband's dead relatives, nor had I talked about them to Jonathan.

"Jonathan described my husband's father and uncle who had died when Kerry was four years old."

Choosing a Church

"These experiences have affected the way I think about religion. I told you my father was Catholic and my mother was LDS. I went to the Baptist, the Episcopal, and lots of other churches, but I really wasn't religious. My mother said she believed in the LDS church, but I should choose for myself. Someday, she said, I would know which was the right one."

"Do you?"

"Yes. When Jonathan started talking about these things, my husband and I talked about it. Kerry had been raised LDS, and he believed in the church—he was active, except for one period in his life when he had a bad experience.

"Anyway, things started falling into place; my husband adopted my children, he baptized them, and we were sealed in the temple last September. Our children were sealed to us, including five by my previous husband.

"Those are interesting experiences, Norma. Is there any last message you would like to leave?"

"Yes. There really is a God and there is a place for everyone. This is just one stage, there are other stages, maybe many stages, for us to go through. I know I really was there—and you don't have to be afraid of death. There is a place to go."

"One last question, Norma. How do you feel, now, about suicide?"

"I'd never try again because I know it's wrong, and because I want to be with Jesus when I die. I wouldn't be with him if I commited suicide. But before, I didn't know that, and things were so bad that . . ."

As we finished Norma's interview her husband, Kerry, phoned and she told him of the interview. He said he would drop by and meet us. When she explained that Kerry had also had an unusual experience as a boy, I asked if he would tell us about it. When he arrived he agreed to tell us what happened.

Kerry

A Mountain Fall

Kerry was a large, strong, but gentle appearing man with a ready smile. He began his story:

"I was born in 1950 here in Salt Lake City. I've been a member of the LDS church all of my life and have been active except for one period a few years ago. I went to high school in Richfield in southern Utah.

"When I was four years old, my father was killed in an automobile accident in Oregon, along with two uncles and an aunt. It was Thanksgiving day of 1954. One aunt survived, along with my mother and myself. I had a broken pelvis."

"All right. Will you tell us, now, about the particular experience that you had?"

"In 1963 or 1964, I, and five of my younger companions went hiking in the mountains west of Richfield. We were up on a rock known as *Bull's Head*. It's approximately a thousand feet from the valley floor.

"Does it look like a bull?"

"Yes, and I was in the eye, a little wind cavern, on the head. I was climbing out over the top when a rock broke, and I fell 65 feet and landed on a 15-foot ledge."

"Did your companions see you?"

"They saw me climb over the side, and they came around the back way and found me. The oldest kid was ten except for me, I was fourteen.

"I broke both of my wrists, my left leg, and I had a concussion. It took the Sheriff's posse about five hours to get me off the mountain.

"During the fall . . . I remember falling, and I remember blacking out about ten feet before I hit. I also remember counting to at least four before I blacked out, so it was a long drop.

"While I was unconscious, or whatever, I came out of the dark into the light. I'm not sure where I was . . . ."

"Did you see your body separate from yourself?"

"No, I was walking along and I looked up and saw two men approaching. As they got closer I recognized one as my father and the other as his brother, both of whom were killed in the car accident in 1954."

"How did they look?"

"They looked the same as the picture which was on my mother's piano, at the age when they died. I ran up to my father and . . . and I'm trying to remember if I hugged him or not. I either hugged him or shook his hand. I knew who the people were, and they said: 'It's not time for you to come yet, you still have something to do.' And then I woke up."

"How were your father and uncle dressed?"

"They were dressed in suits. I imagine it was the suits they were buried in."

"When you saw them did you see bright lights or anything of that sort?"

"It was at least as light, or lighter, than it is outside during the daytime. Kind of white-light."

"How did you feel?"

"I wanted to be with my Dad. I hadn't gotten to know him at all. But I felt at peace after that—I wasn't allowed to see him when he died in the hospital. My injuries were too severe."

"Did your body feel different during the experience? Did you have pain, or not?"

"No I didn't have any pain at all. When I came back to consciousness, then I had pain, but I was also in quite a bit of shock at the time."

Chapter Eight

A Vietnam Experience

David Herard

Background and Initial Combat

I first talked to David Herard on the telephone in Bangor Maine, where he was remodeling an old farm house, in late March, 1991. Later I met him at my home in Bountiful, Utah, where he and his former wife, Peggy Cassidy, came to meet Carol and me.

David was relatively small in stature (5'-6" tall) but large in spirit. He was dark-complexioned, of French Canadian heritage, with a mustache and a large smile. He explained that he was born in 1946 and grew up in Waterville, Maine. He said that he grew up on the tough side of town, but that he had fun with his two older brothers and an older sister. He began by telling of his military experience:

"In 1965, three months before I graduated from High School, I enlisted in the Marine Corps. I enlisted specifically to go to Vietnam."

"Oh you did? Good for you," I commented, "not many people would say that, I guess."

David continued: "I grew up in an environment where I heard that wars and rumors of wars were things that should not be taken lightly. That economic and religious freedoms, if not protected, would be lost."

"Do you still feel that way?"

"Yes, but I'm more isolationist than I was."

"So you went into the Marine Corps. Where did they send you for training?"

"The day after I graduated from high school I was sent to Parris Island. I stayed there for three months, after which I was sent to North Carolina for training in field telephone and radio communications. Then I went to my parent unit, Eighth Communications Battalion, for three months, and at that time, in December, 1965, I volunteered to go to Vietnam. In January, 1966 I had one-and-one-half weeks free leave, then I reported to Camp

Pendleton, California for advanced infantry and jungle warfare training, after which I was shipped out."

"When did you arrive in Vietnam?"

"In May of 1966. I landed at Chu Lai Airbase—which was taking mortars. It was a quick step from a commercial airline to a large quonset hut for processing. I was assigned to the First Battalion, Eleventh Marines—it was a 105mm artillery battery—as a wireman. I was part of a team that kept the land-lines functioning in the field.

"To get me used to the climate, for the first three weeks, I filled sand bags. After that I was assigned to a four-man wire team. We had a three-quarter ton truck. Three of the men worked on wires and the fourth stood guard—as shotgun. The shotgun man carried an automatic weapon. It was a week on duty and a week off; there were three teams."

"How long were you on that duty?"

"I was there for two months. Then they shipped me out on an operation to guard an ammo dump with twelve other men. The ammo dump was about the size of a football field, or a little larger. We only had grenades and our personal weapons to guard it, and we were in 'Indian territory.' It was one-hundred percent alert every night, and work all day. When the trucks came, we were the labor to load them."

"How long were you there?"

"It was three weeks. Then I was shipped back to my parent unit and to a wire team. We were sent to the First Marine Division near DaNang, which was on combat operations off and on. I was assigned as a radioman to an infantry unit where I didn't know anyone."

"Were you a replacement?"

"Yes, the life expectancy in the field for officers, machine gunners, and radio operators was very short. The reason was that the NVA was trying to destroy the command structure of our units."

"How long were you in Vietnam before you got hit?"

"It was September 7, 1966. I had been shipped back to my regular wire team and we were repairing communications. We were standing in a group, four of us—something that we had, up to that time, never done. The NVA had downed miles of communication lines. We had started at 5:30 in the morning to repair them and we were getting tired.

"At the particular place where we had stopped to repair the lines, we were standing in a group about three feet apart. The NVA command detonated a booby trap which blew up right in the middle of us. There were three hand-grenades which went off all at once.

"Two men were killed instantly, including the team leader. One man had multiple shrapnel wounds and was unconscious. I was the only one standing at the edge of the hole where the explosion took place. Everybody else was blown all over the place. I had shrapnel in my legs, and the explosion had ruptured both of my ear drums—I couldn't hear anything."

"Did you return to the States for recuperation?"

"I was sent to Okinawa to recoup, and I finished my thirteen months overseas there. I had put in papers to go back to Vietnam but the Commanding Officer told me, 'no way'; I was going back to the States. I spent thirty days free leave and then was assigned to various units in the States."

Second Tour in Vietnam

"I volunteered to go back again. I had to waive my rights for a one-year tour of duty in the States. I arrived back in Vietnam in February, 1968, just in time for the Tet offensive."

"That was good timing."

"I thought so too when I got off the plane. I landed in DaNang and wound up in Hue assigned to the First Battalion, First Marines."

"What was your duty?"

"I was just a grunt."

"You were a replacement, I presume."

"Yes, the units were suffering anywhere from fifty to sixty percent casualties at the time, and they just needed warm bodies that knew how to shoot to kill."

"What was your rank, then?"

"I was a Corporal, E-4."

"Why don't you tell me the circumstances leading up to your out-of-body experience?"

"In the last week of June, 1968, I was up in the hills, Hill 881-North, near Khe Sanh. While we were on the hill we were running daily search and destroy missions in the bush. I was holding three jobs at the time: a wireman, a radio operator, and a grunt. We were suffering a lot of casualties so we had to do extra duty.

"We went up on the hill as a fully manned infantry company, over 250 men with 81 mortars, and within thirty days we had lost between 20 and 30 percent. The last half of June we got word that we were going to evacuate the hill, just turn it over to the NVA—we were just going to pull out and leave it to them.

"We were told that because of the lack of helicopters 82nd Airborne was going to evacuate us off the hill. This was supposed to happen in the last day of June and the first day of July. To prepare for the evacuation we tore down all our bunkers and all our trench lines. Airborne never showed up."

"Good night, you were sort of exposed weren't you?"

"That's right. When the NVA saw us blowing up our bunkers they started dropping mortars and rockets on us daily. With our bacon hanging out like that our Commanding Officer, a Captain, was really angry and he called in helicopters. Some Chinooks came and took us off Hill 881-North and put us on Hill 681, five miles away.

"The night we landed on Hill 681, on July 6th, we ran into heavy fire-fighting. It lasted from midnight to about five A.M. We had NVA coming into the wire—it was face-to-face fighting. I usually carried fifteen magazines that hold twenty rounds apiece, six grenades, and full bandoleers for extra ammo. In the morning, after the fire-fight, I had one magazine left, with, maybe eight rounds, no grenades—everybody was in that same situation. We were all running around looking for ammo.

"Around seven o'clock, after everybody had relaxed for a while, we decided it was time to stock up on food, more ammo, and other necessities. Everybody was tired, they didn't want to do anything, so I got angry and said: 'The hell with you, I'll do it.' I started humping ammo for the people that were near me and ammo for the 81mm mortars."

"How far did you have to go to get the ammo?"

"Approximately one hundred yards. About nine o'clock I was on my ninth or tenth trip, and we started getting some 122mm rockets, 82mm mortars and small arms fire. I was tired, I was angry, and I was put out by the whole situation. When everything started coming in I said to myself: *the hell with it, all they can do is kill me*. "On my last trip, I was told this later by one of the Corpsmen who attended me, when I came over the crest of the hill a 122mm rocket landed about twenty feet behind me. When it went off it picked me up and threw me twenty feet down the hill. I landed on both my knees with my head on the ground. My right arm was behind me. I was dazed—I wasn't unconscious, just dazed.

"When I looked down where my right arm was I didn't see anything. I swore, and thought: *They got me, they really got me this time*. I felt for my arm and pulled it out from behind me. It was all torn up. I didn't pay much attention to the rest of my body. I was looking for a Corpsman and I got up. One of the guys I knew told me to look at my legs. I did, and saw that they were in shreds and were bleeding profusely.

"I collapsed and lay there on the ground. They came over and took my flak jacket off, what was left of it, and attempted to stop the bleeding. While the Corpsman was working over me, I just . . . I had a feeling of: *I'm tired, I'm going to sleep, I've had enough of this*. I almost lost the will to live. I closed my eyes—the pain had just started catching up with me."

"Hadn't they given you any shots for the pain, yet?"

"While I had my eyes closed one of the men asked the Corpsman why he didn't give me a shot of morphine. He said that he couldn't, it would just leak back out. I had shrapnel wounds in both feet, both legs, both cheeks, both arms, both hands, the back of my neck and the small of my back.

"After hearing the Corpsmen talk about me, I felt that my time was up."

A Different World with People Dressed in White

"I first became aware that everything was black. Then I saw a light coming towards me, and I remember wondering why there was no pain. It felt so good. The light, at first, was like a candle. But it kept getting closer and brighter until it was a blinding light."

"Could you look straight at it?"

"No I couldn't. I tried everything not to look at the light."

"Why was that?"

"I don't know. I wasn't afraid of it. It was extremely bright. The light finally caught up to me, and I opened my eyes, not literally, but I looked at it. And I saw a river.

"Across this river there were a lot of people waving at me. They were gesturing me to come across. They were people that I hadn't seen before, and they seemed really happy. I was getting a feeling of warmth, of happiness, of great tranquility.

"As I began to walk towards the river and the people on the other side, I felt a hand on my shoulder. I tried to turn around to see who was putting a hand on me and I . . . I couldn't move. A voice that I heard said: 'No, it's not your time, go back.' Then I was back. I opened my eyes, and this Corpsman was pounding my chest. He was screaming at me: 'Don't you dare die on me.' An hour later I was choppered off the hill."

"When you saw the river, what was the terrain like on both sides of the river?"

"On my side it was fairly white, like a brand new coat of white paint. Closer to the river there were shades of green. The water was a shimmering blue, and I could tell it was moving. On the other side of the river it was white, but it had color also."

"Did you see shrubs and things of this sort?"

"I saw trees, bushes, flowers—vividly colored flowers."

"Were the bushes, shrubs and flowers similar to what you had seen on earth, or were they different?"

"Similar, in that their growth patterns were similar, but their sizes were more robust, their colors were more vivid, and everything was very warm."

"Did you have a feeling that you knew any of the people on the other side?"

"I've often asked myself that. At the time I thought: *I know those guys*. But I couldn't see their faces. All I could see was their bodies. I knew they were gesturing to me but I just couldn't see their faces. I could see their hands fine, and I could see their physical makeup all right, but not their faces."

"But you had a feeling that you knew them?"

"Right. It seemed like there were people there that I knew. Maybe my team leader who was killed earlier, and maybe some of my other Vietnam buddies. But I couldn't swear to it. I knew a lot of men in Vietnam who had died, but I had no relatives who had died."

"Could you tell how they were dressed?"

"Everybody was in white. Some had robes, and some had shirts and trousers, but they were all white."

"Did it appear that there was light coming from them, or could you tell?"

"It was light behind them, but I couldn't see way beyond them. I knew that they were overjoyed to see me."

"Did you see a bridge?"

"No I didn't. As I walked towards the river and the people, someone stopped me. I couldn't move; my eyes were locked straight ahead looking at these people. And the voice simply said: 'Don't be afraid about not going over there. It's not your time yet."

"Did you have the feeling that you could walk over the water if you had wanted?"

"I never had the feeling that I was walking. It was more like . . . I was just moving. And when the hand came on my shoulder I had such an overwhelming sense of love and tranquility; everything that we here are looking for and have such a hard time finding, I had completely, in abundance, and I didn't want to come back to the earth."

"Why didn't you want to come back?"

"Because it felt so good there."

"Did you have any feeling of what it was you were supposed to come back for?"

"No I didn't. After I was told that it was not my time, I would have to go back, I had things to do, that was the end."

"Was it quick when you came back into your body?"

"The blink of an eye."

No Pain, Just Knowledge and Love

"When I came back I had pain in abundance, and it was instantaneous. There was no pain on the other side. I knew . . . everything worked good while I was over there. My body worked good, my hands worked good, my legs worked good. I had the feeling that I knew why things are as they are—why all the problems on the earth were as they were. It was an overwhelming feeling of knowing, but I couldn't tell you now what I knew."

"Did that feeling come over you when you felt the hand, or was it before that?"

"It was when I was going towards the people and felt really good."

"When the hand touched your shoulder, you didn't get a chance to turn around and see who it was did you?"

"No. All I can tell you is that, as I see it, it was God's hand."

"That's what you felt?"

"Right."

"And it was just a single contact where the hand touched your shoulder?"

"Actually, after it touched my shoulder, I felt an embrace—as if I were being embraced from the back by someone. And I could see a bright light from the side."

"How did that feel?"

"When I was embraced, I felt a warmth all through me. And there was the feeling of . . . of love. As if it were all the love there is."

"Do you mean you felt that all the love in the world was there?"

"No, it was like that was all the love there was, everywhere. It was like . . . I can't explain the feeling. It's beyond words."

Life After the Experience

"After the experience, when I thought about it, it scared me. When I was, quote, back here, it scared me to death—and it still does. What really scares me is death."

"Why do you feel that way?"

"I've been pondering that for years. I don't know if it's because of the thought of the loss of going through the routine humdrum of life, or the thought of not being around to physically touch my children. I have this feeling that I want to live forever."

"Well, David, you probably will in one form or another. Let me ask you, as you came back into this life, or subsequent to coming back, did you get a feeling for why you came back?"

"In a way—over the years people have sought me out with their problems. I've advised them to be more patient, and I've given them other advice. In ninety percent of the cases they've done what I suggested, and it has worked out well for them."

"One of your feelings, then, is that you've been able to help other people?"

"Yes, and unfortunately I've not always been able to help myself."

"What about children, have you had any feelings about a necessity to come back for them?"

"Yes, I love children to death. They give me a sense of immortality. I have three children, ages thirteen, eight and six."

"Have you told others of this experience?"

"Only Peggy, I think."

"Have your religious feelings changed as a result of this experience?"

"I was never a person for organized religion. I'm a Catholic. I'd like to clarify; all religions in some way or other feel they are the true religion. One is no better than the other, in my opinion. We all believe in one very important thing—no matter what we call him it still comes out, God. I don't care what peoples' religions are. It doesn't really matter. What I try to impart is that we are all here on this little planet, so let's try to cooperate. Why do we have to beat our heads against a wall and kill each other?"

"Do you feel, then, that there is a God?"

"Oh yes, I believe in God, I believe in an afterlife, and I believe in old man Satan."

"When you had your experience did it seem real or not?"

"It was vividly real. The other thing that gets me is that about four days before I was hit I knew I was going to be hit. And I knew I was going to die."

"That's interesting. Others I have talked to have had similar premonitions about death."

"Yes, you know, out there in the bush we didn't talk about death very often. Death was an accepted thing. On my second tour in Vietnam I kept myself quite friendless. I became a loner because I didn't want to associate death with people I knew."

"How long did it take you to recover from your wounds?"

"A little over a year. It took six months to learn how to walk again, and I had to learn to write left-handed instead of right-handed."

"Did they have difficulty saving your right arm?"

"When I was in Japan, where they first brought me, they were going to take my right arm and left leg off; the arm at the elbow and the leg at the knee. I became quite animated. I told those doctors that I was born with those suckers, and I was going to die with them. They said there was no way I would ever have the use of them again. I told them not to bet on it.

"When I was in Chelsea Naval Hospital in Boston I went through a lot of physical therapy and many operations on my arm—and physical therapy to learn how to walk again. I still have problems with my hand and my knee, and the pain in my arm is constant, but I do get function from them. It gets harder each year to remember when I wasn't in pain, or when I was physically whole.

"Do you have any messages you would like to leave?"

"The most important message I would like people to understand is that we are not who we think we are. We have that side of us that is extremely good, but we keep pushing it aside and concentrating on self. We keep thinking: 'I want money, I want things, I want fame.' It doesn't work that way. We have to take more time thinking of and helping others."

Chapter Nine

Young People

Chris Walker

A College Student

Carol and I met Chris Walker in his apartment near the Salt Lake Community College, which he was attending. He was a typical college student with books, athletic equipment, clothes, and other paraphernalia scattered about the room. He was 19, or as he put it, one month from 20, and a vibrant young man with dark hair and an enthusiasm for many subjects.

Chris explained that he was born in Torrance, California; he grew up in the Walnut Creek area of Northern California and about five years ago his parents moved to Utah. From the equipment in the room it was apparent that Chris enjoyed outdoor activities. He said that he liked to mountain-bike, ski, rock-climb, and bungee-dive. He was working full-time, as well as attending school studying aviation mechanics. He was a busy young man.

A Bicycle Crash

Chris started telling of his experiences: "The first one I remember was when we lived in Walnut Creek, about seven to ten years ago, and I had this bike that resembled a motorcycle. They were trying to resurface the road so it was really gritty. Our street going to our house had this big hill going to two manholes. My dad was jogging, and he said to me and my brother that the first one in the house would get a candy bar.

"I put my bike in third gear and started down the hill as fast as I could. They had pulled up one of the manholes, and when I got near it my front tire came off, or something, and I crashed. I was out for a few seconds. During that time I can remember being out of my body, and I didn't know what to think. It was just a few seconds."

"How do you know you were out of your body?" I asked.

"It just seemed like I was. I don't remember seeing me, but I remember seeing the bottom of the hill—and there were these green bushes, and I was, like, standing there right near the bushes. I remember my brother looking at me with really big eyes. My face was in the ground—and I couldn't see, the way I was facing—so I had to be out of my body."

"Did you have a helmet on?"

"No."

"Did you go to the doctor?"

"Yes, and he scrubbed me up. It hurt where the dirt was ground into my face."

"Did you tell your folks about your out-of-body experience?"

"No. They probably wouldn't have had any interest, so I never told them."

"Did you tell anyone?"

"Yes, I told my brother, and I told my friend."

"What was their reaction?"

"Not much, they just said, 'Oh really.' I've only been asked about it once since then. Someone wanted to know what it was like."

A Second Out-of-Body Experience

"My second experience was about five years ago when I was fourteen. We were still living in Walnut Creek, and I was using my uncle's bike—a total blue beast. There was this new development area, and we could take a short-cut through it to the shopping area. It was all downhill with new paved roads and everything was really fun. There was one turn at the very bottom where you could ride out from the hill. In the past there had been no center divider where you took the turn. But they put one in, and I didn't know about it.

"There were no houses in the development, yet, so there weren't any cars; if there was one you could see it from a distance. I had the route memorized and it was fun to go really fast. I went down it this one day and started coming around the last turn, when I saw the center divider. I thought: *Oh, oh, I'm in trouble.*

"I was banking as hard as I could, but I kept getting closer and closer to the divider. I'd been in enough crashes that I could tell I wasn't going to make it. I could see myself getting closer, and then . . . and then I saw myself sliding."

"You did crash then?"

"Yes, but the only thing I remembered, after seeing the divider get closer, was to see myself sliding . . ."

"You saw your body slide . . .?"

"Yes, and the bike slide. During that time I didn't feel any pain either. I thought to myself: *Now I've crashed, I'm all bloody, and I'm going to have all this gravel stuck in my shoulder. It's going to be painful, and as soon as I get back in I'm going to have to rub out all the gravel.*

"You knew you were going to get back in your body?"

"Yes."

"How did you know that?"

"It just . . . it seemed like I willfully stepped out—to avoid the pain temporarily. I seemed really calm. Some crashes, you know, you're nervous. In this one, for that split second, or however long I was out, I was calm and logical, even to thinking of how I would scrub out the wounds."

"When you saw your body and the bike skidding, did it seem as though time was passing fast, or slow, or was it . . .?"

"I don't remember that well . . . let's see. It just seemed like time was going normal. When I went back in, I don't think there was any time distortion."

"When you went back into your body, what was the sensation then?"

"Pain."

"Was it immediate, or were you unconscious for awhile?"

"No, I was conscious. All I did was slide, kind of on my shoulder. What happened was I slid ahead of the bike, and the bike slid into me, and . . . . Okay, that gives me a hint on time. When I slid and stopped, that's when I went back into me—and the bike was still sliding. In that period of time I thought of all this, so I must have been thinking fairly fast.

"I remember I stopped sliding, and I went back in; I looked at my hands as soon as I went back in. The bike was still sliding, and it hit me in the face. That hurt the most, and I had to get stitches in my mouth where it hit."

"When you were out of your body, what did it feel like?"

"Very peaceful. Like you don't have to worry . . . it takes a lot off your mind it seems like—normal everyday things, you know, like keeping your balance when you walk, or trying to stay a little warmer, or stay a little colder, or whatever. It was just total peace. I don't know what it was, my spirit or my brain; I didn't have to worry about balance, or about getting something tightened up to crash; I was just there."

"Could you tell what your spirit body looked like?"

"No."

"Did you have to go to the hospital?"

"Yes, they treated me for abrasions and for the damage in my mouth."

A River Accident

"One time when we were white-water rafting in the Tahoe area, we had life vests on. The guide said, if we wanted, we could jump into the water at this point because there were no rocks. Both my brother and I jumped in. The water was so cold it was hard to breathe, and my brother got back in the raft. I decided to stay calm and stay in the water.

"I started going down the rapids, and I struggled to stay above the surface. My muscles got tight, and I had a hard time breathing. The raft was behind me about fifty feet; I was going to yell to them for help but I couldn't, because my lungs weren't working. I was freaking out really bad, and there was one last part of the rapids; I went underneath the water. I was panicky—then I just let go and, relaxed. It seemed as if it got really warm.

"I didn't leave my body during this experience. After the total panic stage it seemed as though I became completely relaxed. I wouldn't have cared if I had hit a rock or had gone to the bottom of the river. I just lay there, until the next thing I knew I was floating. My life vest brought me to the surface. The next few hours I wondered why I had felt as I did."

Thoughts About Death and Life

"You asked me about death. I'm not really afraid of it . . . I might be if someone told me I was going to die."

"You're not anxious to do it?"

"No."

"Why not?"

"I guess I'm young. There are still a lot of ski days in my life."

"Is your religious affiliation the same as it has always been?"

"I guess I'm just young, because that changes frequently."

"What were you raised, and what's your current belief?"

"I was raised Roman Catholic for the first seven or eight years, in a private school. Currently, I believe in God, but I have an open view about the nature of God."

"Do you believe in life after death?"

"Yes."

"When you had these experiences, did you feel that they were an evidence of what might happen when you die, or not?"

"Yes, I've thought about it, but not in detail."

"Have you read any books on the subject of near-death experiences?"

"No, but I've heard about some cases."

"Do you have any last messages you would like to leave?"

"Not really."

We shook hands with Chris and wished him a good life. He grinned and wished us the same.

Kim

A High School Student

Kim was a tall, long-legged, attractive young lady who looked to be about eighteen; but, as she informed Carol and me, she was only fifteen. She came to our home with her mother in January, 1991. She told us that she had been raised in the LDS church. She was enthusiastic about telling us of her experience. She began:

"I had to go in the hospital for an operation on my leg last July, and it was for tibia torsion. Tibia torsion is twisting of the bones. I went to Primary Children's Hospital here in Salt Lake City.

"The operation itself took two hours, and it went okay, but afterwards I had problems. I was in the recovery room, and when I came to, the pain medicine did not work. I woke up to full pain, and I went immediately into shock.

"I was in pain for about an hour-and-a-half, and two doctors gave me different pain medicine. Only one of the medicines worked. They took me to my room, and the next day, despite the medicine, the pain came back. My leg was hurting so bad that I wanted to scream.

"My Mom was sitting next to the bed, and I opened my eyes. I wanted to say something, but the pain was so bad I couldn't talk. My mouth wouldn't open up, and my vocal chords wouldn't work. Then I just sort of blacked out."

A Lady in White

"When I came to there was blackness all around. There was a ball of light, like in a tunnel, and . . . I still don't know how to explain it. It was just blackness all around, kind of like being in a tunnel. It wasn't really a tunnel, but that's the best way I can describe it.

"I was standing there, and I saw this brilliant light—not like heat-warmth, more peace-warmth. I got curious, and I started going toward it. I heard somebody call my name; I turned to look, and there was this lady.

"She was dressed all in white. Her hair was white, and it was flowing down her back—it came to about her knees. She was really pretty, she was glowing, not just from the light in the distance but from herself. She called me by name and said: 'It's not your time.' I didn't quite understand, and she repeated the message; that it wasn't my time, and that I had to go back.

"When she told me, the second time, that I had to go back I remembered the pain, and everything, and I didn't want to go. I wanted to go toward the light; I felt so good, I felt so happy. She repeated the message again, telling me that it wasn't my time, and I must go back. She said everything would be okay. Finally, I agreed and turned around to return.

"Then I woke and it was a haze. I told my Mom, and there were nurses and doctors poking at me. The pain came again, and it was hazy for awhile. The angel said it would be okay, though, and it was.

"What did it feel like, Kim?"

"It wasn't like a dream, but I was confused. I didn't see my body or anything, and yet . . . . When I came back I just woke up and took a deep, deep breath."

Kim's mother interjected: "She had stopped breathing altogether. Her heart stopped and the monitors went flat. The doctors and nurses ran in, and suddenly Kim took a gasp. They pumped oxygen into her, gave her extra medicine, and put her to sleep. They got rid of the pain."

"Kim, have you told this experience to anyone besides your mother?"

"No. They would probably think I was crazy."

"How do you feel about your experience now?"

"When I think about it, the feeling of peace which I had is still with me."

"Do you have any last thoughts?"

"Yes, if anyone has an experience like this they should know that they aren't crazy."

James Niitsuma

An Artist

I visited James Niitsuma at his home in Salt Lake City. He greeted me with a smile and showed me how he had decorated his house. He told me that he was involved in art, and his house reflected that interest. From the decor, and from his conversation, it was apparent that James was also interested in the meditative techniques of eastern religions. He indicated that his heritage was Spanish and Japanese.

James began: "I was born in Salt Lake City in 1965, and I grew up here. I grew up in an environment where, in my family, we didn't have boundaries. As a consequence, I lived an abusive life style—physically, mentally, and emotionally. But I learned from these experiences."

"Okay, why don't you tell me of the circumstances leading up to your accident?"

"On June 6, 1986, I was dating a lady, and I decided I didn't want to see her anymore. She was angry, and she told me that it would be easy to kill me. I had never had anyone tell me that before, so I didn't believe her. We went for a trip together in her rented car, and I fell asleep. She took the car up to ninety-miles-an-hour, and rolled it. She had her seat-belt on, but I didn't because I was asleep.

"Just before the car rolled, as it turned, my spirit left my body, and I didn't feel anything. The car rolled three times and landed on top of me. When the helicopter got there I was pronounced dead. It took an hour-and-a-half for the helicopter to get there so I lost a lot of blood. We were about an-hour-and-a-half from Reno, in the desert."

Viewing His Body—A Life's Review

"There was a little dog with us, and while my spirit was out of my body I could see the dog licking my face. When the helicopter got there, they took the car off me and my heart stopped, then started again. The nurse said it was a miracle. It stopped again, and they had to revive me.

"While they worked on me, the nurse was cutting off my sweater. It was a $350 sweater, and I asked her if she understood that it was a $350 sweater. She told me that she wasn't worried about my sweater, she was worried about trying to save my life. As soon as she said that, I went into a coma, and my spirit went into a bright light. I was in the coma for three days."

"Let's see, James, it sounds as if your spirit left your body twice."

"No, I didn't go back into my body. I could see them working on me from outside my body, while it was under the car."

"How did you talk to the nurse, then?"

"That's the strange thing. I could see them working on me, and I could see my lips moving. I could hear the nurse, yet I was outside looking at her."

"Okay, what happened next?"

"Then there was this bright light, I was surrounded by it. I felt very warm, content, and happy—I had never felt like that before. It was just a beautiful feeling."

"Did you see anything besides the light?"

"I sort of saw a figure, but not like a human figure of human flesh. I had a warm spiritual feeling. I could see a form but it was . . . it was a spiritual form. There was a great, bright light coming from it."

"Did you communicate with this form?"

"Yes, I talked to it, and I saw my life flash before me. I saw twenty years go by. It wasn't all about material things. I saw my friends, and my family, and some experiences that I had had with some very close people."

Return to Life and a Poem

"I was asked by the Great Spirit if I wanted to come back, and I said, yes, I did. Then there was a flash of light, and my spirit gradually entered my body. As it went in I felt pain, lots of pain. It was extreme pain, not like when I was in the bright-white light. When I was in the light I felt beautiful, I felt wonderful, there was no pain."

"What damage had been done to your body by the accident?"

"Later I found that I had cracked my collar bones, broken my pelvis, torn the urethra from my bladder, broken cartilage in both my knees and my elbows, and I had fractured my skull."

"Do you feel that you did die during this experience?"

"I know that I died."

"It wasn't just a dream or a hallucination?"

"No, I know it wasn't. Even my family has said that I've changed as a result of the experience."

"How have you changed?"

"I pursue my art, and I have become more sensitive to people. I express myself more."

"Do you have any last messages?"

"Yes, I don't believe in religion, but one night after the car accident as I was in meditation I received this poem. It just came to me. I believe it expresses my feelings as well as anything does. So, this poem is my message:

the eye of God is my destiny,
he creates a living symphony,
a place where humans are to be,
a place of truth and dignity,
a place of mixed culture activity,

a place with peace and harmony,
a place of love for you and me,
in time the eye showed sincerity,
which touched my heart momentarily
but lasted until eternity,
in the end it was all about soul tranquility.

Nyk Fry

A Musician

Nyk Fry was working in his recording studio when I called on him in late February, 1991. He was a young man with dark curly hair, even features, and a slender build. He had a decided British accent accompanied by a ready smile. His studio was filled with numerous musical instruments, including a grand piano, and with complicated-looking electronic recording equipment.

He offered me a stool to sit on, he took the adjacent stool, and we got acquainted between his phone calls. He told me that he was born in Boston, Massachusetts, in 1965, and his parents moved to England when he was three, where he grew up. His father had a PhD in chemistry and was attracted to scientific disciplines, not religion. His mother, also, was not attracted to any formal religion. He explained that, currently, he was a single young man, was much involved in his music work, and was attending a University Ward of the LDS Church.

Nyk began his story: "My father had been around the world before he got married, and during his travels he obtained a Book of Mormon. When I was quite young I found it and asked Dad what it was. Because of my parents' orientation I was wary of religion, but he explained that the book had something to do with The Church of Jesus Christ of Latter-day Saints—that name stuck in my mind.

"Somewhat later I was at school, and I developed a friendship with a fellow on the Rugby team. He didn't drink alcohol, and neither did I, and we began to talk about it. He told me he was LDS. The way he saw it, he had an excuse for not drinking, and I was just crazy. There were three LDS members in a school of eight hundred students.

"I was much involved in music and I had a band. My friend asked the band to play for a Church Roadshow; one thing led to another, and I joined the Church."

"When was that?"

"It was eight or nine years ago."

"Is that what brought you to the United States?"

"Well, you see, this is what ties up with the experience I mentioned on the telephone. To start with, when I first got baptized I was really zealous. I wanted to change the world. I was fortunate in that when I walked to work, about five miles, it took an hour-and-a-half, and I had an opportunity to think, and to read. That helped me spiritually.

"I began to think about a mission, but I got conflicting signals from my prayers. In a way I wanted to go, but in another I didn't feel right about it. I talked to my Bishop, but I still wasn't sure. It didn't seem right for me.

"In the meantime I became a professional musician. Some friends had moved to Bountiful, Utah, and I decided to take a holiday and visit them. It was a pleasant experience, I liked Utah. On the plane back to England I began thinking how I had enjoyed it."

A Decision and a Strange Experience

"It was the summer of 1988, and during the return flight we hit substantial turbulence. I had let the seats down and was lying across four of them, with my seat strap across my body. I was trying to sleep when we hit some particularly bad turbulence. I was jolted awake, and immediately the thought hit me: *I've got to go back to Utah.*

"I tried to dismiss the thought, believing it was just from the euphoria of the holiday, but the thought kept returning. I struggled with it for several weeks and then decided to take action, to go to Utah. And, it was just like a movie. I managed to sell everything, and things seemed to break my way. My parents accepted the idea also."

"Where were you living then?"

"In Tadworth, England, and it was about three weeks before I was to come over, in November, 1988. I was lying on the sofa watching TV and at one point I felt I had fallen asleep. I had this dream in which I was walking from our Stake Center to the car park. The car park was incredibly dark, I couldn't see the ground. It kept getting darker, and at that point . . . I realized I wasn't dreaming any more. Everything was really black and I felt myself . . . I felt like I was going down. I was sinking—I struggled—it was total unpleasantness.

"I knew I had to stop this, whatever it was, and the only words . . . it was hard to speak or do anything. I didn't know what to do, but the only words I could summon in my mind were: *Heavenly Father.* At that very moment

I heard this sound of . . . the only way I can describe it was a mixture between a wolf and a horse. It was a horrible sound. And then I 'woke up.'

"My heart was beating rapidly and my parents were looking at me. I asked them what they heard or saw. They said I must have had a nightmare. But I'd never had anything like that happen to me before. It seemed too real to be a nightmare. It was something outside of me that was controlling, not me."

"Did you ever have a feeling of what, or why, this happened?"

"My summing up was that some force was trying to stop me from going to Utah, but it was right for me to go. I knew I should go, I wasn't sure why, but I suspected it was related to music. My patriarchal blessing said that my mission was going to be music."

A Motorcycle Accident

"About a week later I was traveling on my cycle at about twenty-five miles an hour, . . ."

"Was the weather clear?"

"It was eight o'clock at night, or so, and it was a nice, clear evening. A woman was in a parked mini-car with no lights on. When I got next to her she appeared to be confused, and she turned into me. She hit the crash bar on my Honda, and I struggled to control the bike. She knocked the bike sideways into the mud, and I went down into the mud and hit my head."

"Were you wearing a helmet?"

"Yes, that's a law in England. The next thing I remember was people lifting the bike off me. Witnesses said I was very lively and didn't want to sit down. My next recollection was that of waking in the hospital and wondering where I was, and who I was. I wasn't that badly hurt, no broken bones, but I was confused. When I saw my parents I gained some orientation. I figured out who I was.

"I tried to talk, and I could tell there was something wrong with my brain. My lip was twisted and numb when I tried to talk. Otherwise I felt fine. Part of me wanted to jump up and say everything's okay. The other part was thinking that I'd better not move. The head nurse took my blood pressure and looked concerned. Other people were pricking my feet to see my reactions. I was interested in what they were doing.

"I lay there drifting in and out of sleep for some hours. It got harder and harder for me to speak to people. My vision was strange, also. I could see all right, but everyone seemed to be in a tunnel. My impression of those I saw was that they were farther and farther away. It seemed a great effort for me to talk to people.

"Then I began to get the same feeling of darkness I had previously experienced. The darkness seemed to be under the bed. It was as if bomb doors had opened and I was there in the bomb-bay, waiting to drop into the darkness. My perception was that on top of me was light, and below me was darkness. It felt as though someone were pulling on my back.

"It seemed at the time that I could walk out of the room, or . . . or I could fall backwards out of a door. It seemed very easy. It seemed obvious. I felt I had a choice to do that—like relaxing very slowly into a big pillow. It seemed that I was relaxing away out of my body.

"I remember thinking how easy it would be to relax, but I didn't want to die. My passion . . . my feeling was, NO! As soon as I decided that I didn't want to die I was instantly awake. The feeling of light and darkness also disappeared. I was back to reality, my head hurt, there were nurses around, and I was fully conscious of my surroundings."

Thoughts on Freedom of Choice

"I later did a lot of thinking about the experiences. My summing up was that I was prey to these sorts of things because I was doing something with my life that the Lord wanted me to do and Satan didn't want me to do. I also decided, as a result of these experiences, that you really do have a lot of choice—as to what you do, where you go in your life, and when you die. Not that you have control over accidents, and such, but under the circumstances I was in I felt that I could easily have chosen to die."

"After this experience on the motorcycle did you come to Utah?"

"Yes, about two weeks later I made the trip."

"Has it been a good experience?"

"After selling everything I had in England I came over with three-hundred dollars. I stayed with friends for awhile. Within two months, after Christmas, I went through the Yellow Pages and called the first studio I found. I called them and they told me they had an opening, and I was hired. Within a month I was working with the Osmonds. Since then, among other projects, I've run a laser show at the planetarium, and most recently I produced the soundtrack for the musical *A Day a Night and a Day.*"

Chapter Ten

Two Young Women

Elizabeth Vorwaller

A Car Crash

Carol and I visited Elizabeth Vorwaller in her condominium in Salt Lake City in mid-March, 1991. She was immaculately dressed and wore an attractively short hair style. She was gracious in her mannerisms as she invited us in.

Elizabeth told us that she was born in Salt Lake City in 1961, and she grew up in Chicago where her father had a teaching position at the University of Chicago. About four years ago she came to Salt Lake to be near her parents who had moved here for business reasons. Elizabeth had worked in the broadcasting industry and was currently seeking a position in that field.

She began telling us of her experience: "The experience happened about five years ago while I was living in Chicago. It was a car accident. I was driving down the street, and I can't remember how the accident happened at all—I have no recollection. I was alone in the car, around twelve-thirty A.M., on a dark fall evening. There weren't many cars on the street, even though it was a main thoroughfare.

"I crashed into something. When the car was examined, later, the engine was slanted in the frame of the car, and there was other damage. But I don't remember the crash. When I woke up no one was there. There was no other vehicle, and there were no people around me."

A Personage in White Clothing

"I was alone in the car, and there was blood all over my face. My head had hit the windshield and the glass was cracked. I was unconscious for, maybe, 30 to 45 minutes. During that period I can remember something like a dark atmosphere around me. I had a floating sensation.

"I couldn't see myself; I was viewing in front of myself. I was talking to someone, it was a male person. From what I can remember he was wearing white clothing and had dark long hair—almost Christ-like in appearance. We were having a conversation, and I remember being asked if I wanted to go with him or to stay. I was frantic at the thought; I told him that I wanted to stay on earth, because I felt that I had something more to prove. I felt that my life wasn't finished yet."

"When you saw the individual, did you know who it was?" I asked.

"Yes, I felt oddly familiar with this person, and I talked to him as if I knew him."

"Do you remember who it was now?"

"No."

"What happened after you finished talking to him?"

"I woke up, and I drove home. I don't know how I did it, but I did. I was in shock and I didn't feel any pain. When my roommate saw me she brought me to the hospital."

"What did they say at the hospital?"

"They said I was lucky to come out of it, because any injury to the neck or head can be fatal. They told me that I had a concussion. I was in the hospital for three days, of which one-and-a-half days were spent in traction."

"When you first went out of your body and saw the individual, do you remember a bright light or anything of that sort?"

"There were no bright lights at all. There was no one else there. There was no form of . . . no land or anything. It was like we were almost floating."

"Can you describe a little more about the individual?"

"He had shoulder-length brown hair and a white robe—from what I could tell his robe was long, it covered his whole body except for his face and neck."

"Did the individual glow or appear bright?"

"Do you mean where an actual light surrounded his body?"

"Or . . ."

"He was bright in appearance, his face, but there was no, like halo, to speak of."

"How bright was his face?"

"Not any brighter than that light over there." Elizabeth pointed to a lamp glowing on a table stand.

"When the individual communicated with you, was it vocal communication, or mind-talk, or what?"

"He was speaking with his mouth, and I did the same. I couldn't hear everything, though. All I know is he did ask me if I wanted to go with him, or if I wanted to go back to the car."

"Why did you feel so strongly that you wanted to come back?"

"I've always had a strong need to help other people. At that point in my life I was helping others, but I was going about it in the wrong way. I still wanted to help, though, but in the right way."

"What do you feel the right way is?"

"I made the mistake of bringing some people into my home and trying to change them. I now feel that you can't force change on people. They have to want to change."

"When you were out of your body how did you feel?"

Weightless, there was no weight and no pain."

"Did you feel that you had arms and legs?"

"I felt as if I had the same form as the person standing next to me, on my right side. But I didn't feel as though I were standing on the ground, with weight. I was just floating."

"Do you have any last messages?"

"The main thing is to do unto others as you would have them do unto you, that's what comes to mind."

Stephanie LaRue

Early Memories

Stephanie LaRue, was waiting for Carol and me as we drove up to her home in West Valley City, Utah, in late March, 1991. She was a svelte, self-assured young woman with auburn hair worn in a short stylish cut. Her blue eyes were striking as they smiled at us. She informed us that she was 40 years of age, but she could have passed for 30.

Stephanie was born in Sacramento, California, but her folks moved to Utah when she was two years old. She grew up in Utah, went to school at a Catholic parochial school, and later attended the University of Utah where she become a Registered Nurse. During the Vietnam war she served on Oahu as a nurse, then in Arizona for a period. She moved back to Utah, updated her studies in cardiology, moved to Montana for eleven years, and then returned to Utah. Stephanie said she was married to a good man, and they were seeking to adopt children.

I asked Stephanie to tell us of the background leading up to her experience. She began: "Let me start by saying the first thing I remember in my life, this life, was looking in a mirror when I was about five or six years old. As I looked at myself I remember saying out loud to myself, 'You are not the person in the mirror who you appear to be,' or words to that effect.

"I recall that as I looked at the little girl in the mirror with short, curly red hair and missing teeth, I didn't look that pretty. Yet, inside, I felt this marvelous spirituality. My parents weren't that religious so they didn't teach me to feel that way, but at the time I felt that the reflection in the mirror was not the real me.

"As I grew older I would sometimes get flashes of thoughts, scenes, or events that would later come to pass. On one occasion, for instance, I called up my mother and asked her if she felt it. She asked, 'Felt what?' 'Why the earthquake, of course, I responded.' She told me that she hadn't felt any earthquake—an hour later we had an earthquake. Also, if there is going to be a death in the family I usually know it is going to happen.

"As a consequence of these intuitive feelings, I have found that as they come to me, in my everyday life, if I respond to them I feel good. Things work out well when I do what my gut feelings tell me; when I don't, I get in trouble."

Illness and an Operation

"I had female problems for several years; they called it endometriosis. It's non-fatal; little tumors spread throughout the female tract. I was trying to have children, and they cauterized the tumors, but, in time, the tumors spread badly and the physicians had to perform major surgery. So on July 26, 1980, they performed a complete hysterectomy.

"The operation took place at the University of Utah Medical Center, and after the operation I was in severe pain. I knew that pain was normal but, for some reason, the pain seemed more than I could handle. They gave me morphine, but I found out that my body did not use morphine, it didn't block pain for me.

"While they were trying to find a solution for the pain, I began to hemorrhage internally, and I developed a temperature of 106 degrees. I also eviscerated, the stitches ruptured and everything came back out from the first operation. Needless to say I was in great distress. I felt awful.

"I knew that if I shut my eyes and went to sleep I would die. I was fighting to live, it was just a feeling that I had. They took me back into surgery, but, because of my deteriorating condition, they didn't give me a general anesthetic.

They gave me demerol and, I think, valium in the arm, and they performed the surgery as quickly as they could.

"I didn't know it at the time, but the doctors told my husband that I probably would not live longer than 45 minutes. He called my parents and they rushed back to the hospital.

"When I came out of surgery the second time I had lost massive amounts of blood, and my chemistry profile was terrible. Fighting pain was, for me, like running a marathon. I knew that if I stopped I would die. Finally, after I felt that I had gone beyond the end of the race, a sense of calmness came over me, and the pain went away. My husband was holding me in his arms in my hospital bed, and I felt contented because the pain had gone."

Out-of-Body—Complete Knowledge

"All of a sudden, within the blink of an eye, I left my body. It was so fast and so natural. I wasn't afraid—of course I didn't know that this was death."

"How did you know that you had left your body?" I asked.

"I turned around and saw myself in the bed."

"What did you look like?"

"I remember saying: 'That's not the real me,' and I pointed at the hospital bed. 'This is the real me; that's only a shell,' and I pointed back, again, at the hospital bed."

"Could you see your husband?"

"I could see my husband, and I could see myself. And I remember, while I was out of my body, going through the hospital drapes and thinking: *After all these years why do they have to have these green drapes?* And I didn't have to part them, I just walked through them.

"About this time I had an experience that I'll never forget. It was an experience of complete tranquility, peacefulness, wholeness—whatever the word wholeness means; like mind, body, and soul. Also a feeling of total, total knowledge without asking.

"It's like you and me sitting here, now, and wondering how far the universe expands, or . . . just questions we have on earth about the geography of the earth, craters, or anything. This feeling I had of total knowledge was just that, I knew everything without asking. It was an incredible feeling.

"I turned around and looked at my body again, and I knew why I was there; I didn't have to ask. The only way I can relate to it is to observe that I was more alive in that realm than I am talking to you, here, now. Another way to relate to it is . . . like you and I are more awake now than when we are asleep at night. That's how much more aware I was in the other realm."

In and Out of Body

"I turned around and looked at my body. I guess it wasn't time for me to go, because I got back in. As soon as I got back in my body there was a fear in me. I wasn't exactly sure what was going on. I jumped up as weak as I was with all the tubes hanging from me, and with my husband wondering what I was doing, I went around the corner to look in the mirror. I used my fingers to touch my face, my arms, and my legs, to verify that I was really back in my body.

"This happened off and on for the next few days."

"What happened?"

"I would leave my body and come back—the pain was so bad, or I was so sick, that I was going in and out of death. So, each time I woke up I looked around to make sure where I was. During those times, I didn't have the knowledge or experience that I did the first time. After that first time, though, whenever it happened, maybe three or four times, I welcomed it. The pain became less intense, and I didn't fight it anymore."

"The first time when you went out, Stephanie, did you see any light or dark spaces?"

"No, I didn't see black or white, nor did I see a tunnel. But everything was complete, in perfect harmony."

"When you say that you walked through the hospital drapes, did you walk through a wall, or what?"

"I remember that I was coming back from somewhere. I know that I left the hospital, but I don't remember where I went. I remember going down the hallway to visit a sick friend that I had met before surgery."

"When you traveled to these various places, did you walk, or was it by some other mode of locomotion?"

"I felt as though I traveled more by thought than by anything else. It wasn't like I had a body."

Feelings of Love, Wholeness, and Power

"When I left my body I was encompassed with a higher power. It felt like complete wholeness, tranquility, peacefulness, . . ."

"Love?"

"Oh definitely love, definitely. It . . . there are no words in the English language to describe it. It's more than love; the word love is just the tip of the iceberg, so to speak."

"When you had that feeling, did you have any understanding about where the feeling was coming from, or what was driving it?"

"It was everything. It was an accumulation of everything that ever lived—like the trees, the flowers, every human being, animals, anything that lives or breathes, a blade of grass. It was a totality of everything. Also, when I came back into my body I knew that everything had its place, its purpose, and there was a reason for everything. Even poor children that die of cancer at a young age, somebody's life that is taken; everything has a reason. But you don't *know* that until you are on the other side."

Coming Back—Subsequent Experiences

"I came back because I felt that there were things that I still had to do on this earth."

"Like what?"

"I could be wrong, but I had the feeling that I'm supposed to have two children. I felt that there would be a special spiritual person coming into my life. And I knew that I had to be there for that person or persons."

"When you came back into your body, did you feel that it was hard to come back, and did you have any say in it?"

"I just knew I had to come back, and there was a lot of pain when I got back."

"Was it hard to get back into your body?"

"No."

"Do you know how you got back?"

"No, I wish I did."

"Do you feel that the experience was truly out-of-body, and that it was a real experience and not a dream or a hallucination?"

"I'd bet my life on it."

"Did you want to come back?"

"Now I wish I hadn't."

"Why is that?"

"It's just that . . . once you've had something so good, and so perfect, why settle for less?"

"You apparently felt, though, that you had to come back for a purpose. And I presume that became an overriding issue with you?"

"Yes, it did."

"Has your experience changed your feeling about religion?"

"In terms of formal religion, not particularly, but it has made me more spiritual. I consider myself deeply spiritual, but not necessarily religious."

"Do you have any evidence of this increased spirituality?"

"Yes, sometimes I have experiences where I will see a light, like an aura around somebody, and I know, somehow, that the person is important to me. One example is my present husband. I was walking in a bowling alley, and out of the corner of my eye I saw this bright light around a man, but his back was facing me. I thought to myself: *I wish I could meet him. I know he is a good person*. Shortly thereafter, in the bowling alley, somebody called my name. This person introduced me to the man I had seen with the aura, and now we are married."

Chapter Eleven

Family Ties

Joy Melvin

Joy Melvin seemed to be a happy, self-aware person as Carol and I visited her home in Sandy, Utah. She retained a permanent, gentle smile throughout our interview, except when she was moved to tears, and she appeared to radiate love. She showed us the exotic fish which her husband raised in three large salt-water tanks. One tank had a friendly octopus which kept changing color as he scooted to the various areas in the tank.

Joy informed us that she was born in 1960 in Salt Lake City and was raised in Holladay, Utah. She was close to her parents and siblings, although her parents divorced when she was about 16. She had two brothers and a sister; they were all raised in the LDS religion, although Joy hadn't been active in the church for many years.

She married her high school sweetheart when she was 18, and he was killed in an automobile accident when they were 21. In 1984 she married Jeff, her present husband, and they had two children, a boy and a girl aged six and three at the time of our visit.

Visit by a Deceased Grandmother

Joy began her story:"When I was about five or six years old, on a fishing trip with my family to Flaming Gorge, it was really late at night, and my mom told me to run over to the bathrooms they have at the campground. I was running with my shoe laces untied, and I tripped on my shoe. I got down to fix my shoe, and . . . and there was this really, really bright light.

"The light was very bright and I looked up. It was my grandma. I knew it was her—from her pictures—and, I just knew it was her."

"Had she died previously?" I asked.

"She had committed suicide when I was about two."

"Was that on your father's or mother's side?"

"My mother. . . . I remember her brown curly hair, she had naturally curly hair. I kept looking at her feet because they weren't touching the ground, and I asked her what she was standing on. She talked to me—I think—it's just like I felt her words inside me. She told me that she loved me so much and to tell my mother that she was okay.

"She said that she was fine, she would be waiting for my mother, and everything was okay. I think the whole thing was more for my mother. I don't know why she didn't go to her, but she kept emphasizing that I should tell my mom that she was really happy where she was."

"How was your grandmother dressed?"

"She was wearing a white robe, and there was a glow behind her. Her feet were bare, and she wasn't standing on the ground."

"Did you tell your mother?"

"Oh yes, I ran back. I was bawling, I wasn't sure why, and I was a little scared."

"What did your mother say?"

"My mother just hugged me and cried and cried and cried. My brothers were sitting in their sleeping bags, and I remember them making fun of me. My Mom just kept hugging me and saying: 'It's true, it's true.'"

Agony Over Deaths of Husband, Brother, and Father

"I mentioned that my first husband died when I was twenty-one, in 1981. Nine months later my oldest brother was killed in a car accident. Then a year-and-a-half after that my dad died following minor surgery from a blood clot. All three of them died suddenly, and it was really bad on my family. It devastated us all.

"I had been with my husband since I was twelve years old. We were good friends and pals. And then my brother and my father—when I was so young. It bothered me continuously, even after I later met and married another good man, Jeff, and had a child.

"I especially had this bad thing about my brother, because I went to see him in the mortuary the night of his accident. I picked up his bloodied clothes at the hospital, and I was so upset that I went to the mortuary, very late. The mortician let me see him, but his legs, you couldn't . . ." Joy began to cry. "You couldn't see his legs. I wanted to look under the blanket but the mortician wouldn't let me."

Out-of-Body in a Colorful World

"In 1987 we were living in our home in Riverton, Utah, and I lay down on our couch. I wasn't feeling well. I had the flu, or something, and I lay down to rest. I put Andrew down for a nap; I didn't have Natalie yet.

"As I lay there, my face felt warm, and I felt as though I were moving my head from side to side, like I was saying no, and yet my head didn't feel like it was moving on the couch. The next thing I knew, it felt really weird, I just came out here." Joy pointed in the general direction of her head.

"Where is here?" I asked.

"At the top of my head, in my head area. It happened so fast. I felt myself come out, and then I saw a fog—lots and lots of fog. And there was a pulling in my abdomen, like something was pulling me.

"I got through the fog and there was . . . it was kind of like mountains, but they weren't mountains. See, I have to describe things that you can picture, but it's not how it was. They were sort of, like mountains, but you could see through them, and they had colors in them. Colors like pastels. Colors that . . . there's just no colors that I've ever seen. Pinks and . . . kind of like pinks, I don't know how to describe it, oranges and . . ."

"What about shrubbery and flowers, were there . . . ?"

"No, no, no."

"Just bare mountains?"

"They were almost . . . they almost looked like glass. You know, I just don't know how . . . they were shiny."

"Was there light coming from them?"

"There was light behind them, like before the sun comes up in the morning, and you can see the mountains with light behind them. That's how it was. It was sort of a pinkish-yellowish color.

"I was walking, and . . . and when I was walking I felt really warm. It wasn't temperature warm, it just was warm. And there was sound, it was . . . it was like music, but it wasn't music. I don't know how to describe it any other way, but it was like music."

A Reunion with Deceased Relatives

"I rounded a corner and there stood my dad, my brother, and my first husband. I remember running to them. I ran up to my brother, I ran my hands down his body and . . . and down his legs where the mortician wouldn't let me look. He lifted me up and he said: 'I'm whole here, Joy, I'm whole here.'

"Then, I remember . . ." Joy had difficulty continuing. "I grabbed my dad and I could feel him, and I could smell him . . . smell his smell. My dad used to call me 'Sis.' He didn't say a lot to me, there wasn't a lot said, only he said that he was okay, it was wonderful, and it was beyond his dreams.

"It's almost like I saved my husband for last. He had long blonde hair, and I remember I buried my face in it—I could smell it, and it felt like it did before. And there was this love between all three of us. There was this love.

"All of a sudden the pulling started again in my stomach. I started going back. It was slow at first, and I didn't want to go. I wanted to stay, it felt good there. I *really* wanted to stay, but the pulling kept going. The next thing I knew my body had a big jolt, and I sat up.

"I know it wasn't a dream—it was real. I had been down for less than a minute. I just lay down, and that's what happened."

Further Thoughts About the Experience

"For three days after that I felt groggy. But after that experience I could go on . . . I could go on and live my life again. Because, before the experience, I married Jeff, a wonderful man, and I couldn't . . ." Joy was overcome with emotion. "I couldn't love him as I should, because I was so hurt. After this experience, though, I was able to, you know, get it together with my husband, and my son, and make a happy life. And that's why, I think, they allowed me to see them."

"That's a wonderful experience, Joy. Let me ask you a few questions. When you first came out of your body did you see yourself lying there?"

"No. I just knew I was moving my head, and yet it wasn't moving on the couch. I wondered what was going on, and then, bam, I saw the fog."

"How do you know your head wasn't moving?"

"Because I could feel my head lying on the couch. Yet, I could see from side to side that my head was moving. Another thing, my body eyes were closed; I was going to take a nap, but I could see. I don't know how else to describe it."

"Did you see a bright light or anything like that?"

"No, not until I walked through the fog. Then there were all those pastel colors."

"Now you say you walked. . . ."

"I moved forward. I assume my legs were moving—I don't know. I could feel a pulling at my stomach. And then when I was going back I was being pulled, and . . . and when I went back I was moving fast, so I guess I wasn't walking. At first when I was going back it was slow. Then it got faster and faster, and there was resistance on my part. It felt almost as if my body was in a V where I was being pulled.

"There's another thing. I was aware of the sounds in my living room through this whole thing. My phone rang during all this, and I ignored it. You know, it didn't seem relevant."

"That's an understatement. Okay, now you saw this beautiful mountain that was shiny and had the pastel colors, but you didn't see any shrubs, is that right?"

"I don't remember any shrubs. There's another thing too. When I saw my family, there were other people there also. I noticed them, but I didn't acknowledge them, and they didn't acknowledge me. When I first saw my family and the other people, I remember thinking that this was like a way station. It wasn't heaven, or whatever, it was just a place where I could come—because it wasn't my turn."

"Do you remember how your relatives were dressed?"

"They were wearing clothes that were familiar to me. My brother was in his jeans and a flannel shirt, my dad was in a sweater and dress pants that my mom had bought him, and my husband . . . I don't remember what he was wearing."

"You say the place where you saw them was a way station. What do you think . . .?"

"After it all happened and I processed it in my mind I remember . . . I remember being there and thinking that it wasn't heaven. It was like common ground where we could meet; they were not in the physical but I was. I'm pretty sure of that, and I'm not sure how I'm sure, I just am."

"When you communicated with your relatives, did you do it by talking?"

"No. I could hear them, but it was like in my head. But I think I was talking—I think, I don't know. Or maybe there were no words exchanged, we just knew how we felt. You know, you'd think if you saw someone who was dead you would have a million questions. Well that's how it was for me before this experience. But when I finally got to see them there was nothing that needed to be said. Except for the tremendous love we felt for each other."

"Why didn't you need to say more?"

"I don't know. It was just that love feeling. My dad said: 'Hi Sis,' and a few other words and hugged me. The only other one who said something was my brother, as I ran my hands down his body, when he said that he was whole."

"And you could feel your brother?"

"Yes, I could feel him and the others too."

"And you had a body that went to this way station but felt as if it were a real body?"

"Yes, it felt real."

"And when you moved, you didn't necessarily walk?"

"That's right, but I felt like me. I remember seeing my hands run down my brother's leg."

"Did you feel it was a real experience or a dream?"

"I knew it was real."

"How did it feel?"

"I was under tremendous pain and anxiety before the experience because of all the deaths. When I was there I didn't take the pain with me. I didn't take my nerves with me. It was just . . . I never felt so accepted, so loved, and so calm. When I came back I had all the normal physical things again, and this thing, this body to lug around. I felt . . . it was like all the beautiful things in my life intensified a trillion times. It was nothing I had ever seen or felt before. Love doesn't even began to describe what I felt, but it's the only word I know to explain the sensation."

Marcia Anderson

A Young Mother

Marcia Anderson bounced into our home on a beautiful spring day, 1991. She was a petite, strawberry blonde, with a touch of freckles, and an effervescent personality. She spoke enthusiastically with both voice and hands.

Marcia told Carol and me that she had been born in Boise, Idaho, on Easter Sunday, April 17, 1949. She was raised in an active LDS home and stated that she had a testimony of the truthfulness of her religion, which she had obtained on her own. She was the oldest child of seven children.

She obtained a bachelor's degree in education from Brigham Young University, and she did her student teaching work in Salt Lake City. There, she met her future husband, Dan, who had returned from a mission for the LDS church. He was attending the University of Utah where he was studying accounting. They married in 1970 in the Logan Temple. At the time of our interview she and Dan had five children, four boys and a girl.

Carbon-Monoxide in the House

Marcia began her story: "We had a habit of going to Boise, Idaho, each year for a couple of weeks in February. We stayed with my folks, and Dan did income tax work for some clients in that area. On the last day of February, 1978, we returned to our home in Cache Valley, Utah. It was a typical, cold winter evening in Providence—two miles south of Logan. During our absence, for two weeks, we had closed the house up tight so it would stay warm.

"It was late when we got in, near midnight, so we got the four boys into bed and dumped the suitcases on the floor. As we got the boys into bed I sensed some uneasiness in the home, and I told Dan about it. He was tired from the long drive, and he told me it would be okay. He said: 'Let's just go to bed.'

"We went to bed, and I lay there not sleeping. I still felt uneasy about something, and I got up two or three times and looked around. There was just something wrong, it didn't feel right. I remember asking, in prayer, if there was something wrong in the house, for our Heavenly Father to please help us.

"The children and Dan were all asleep, and ultimately I drifted off. I woke up about two-thirty or three A.M. with a really bad headache. It was terrible. I couldn't remember ever having had a worse one. I woke Dan, and he got me some aspirin, which I took.

"We went back to sleep until about six-fifteen in the morning, when I awoke, again, with the same terrible headache. I had never had such an awful headache. I didn't want to wake Dan again, so I got up and went into the kitchen where we kept the aspirin. I was reaching up above the stove to get it when I lost consciousness. I slumped into the corner in the kitchen."

Out-of-Body-A Decision

"In that instant, with my physical body slumped on the floor, *I* was standing above the floor looking down at my body. All the pain was gone, and I felt wonderful. I was really calm, and I felt completely at peace. Everything was fine.

"I did not leave the kitchen. I wasn't standing on the floor, I was standing above the floor. It didn't seem frightening, it didn't seem . . . it wasn't strange, it just seemed absolutely the normal tide of events. Nothing was out of order.

"I was looking at this slumped over thing on the floor—but it wasn't really me. I was here, above the floor. As I stood there . . . at that moment I knew exactly what was wrong in the house. It just came, it filled my mind. I knew it was carbon-monoxide, I knew how to fix it, I knew that fresh air had to come into the house. It just all seemed to follow with the progressive orderliness of things.

"Also, at that moment I thought of my children, and as the awareness of motherhood, my stewardship, and my place with them filled my mind, I made a conscious choice. I had a choice to stay there, with them, or to proceed to some other place—away from the kitchen and away from the house. As the thoughts of the children filled my mind, I knew I needed to stay with them; I wanted to more than anything. I needed to . . . I needed to complete the stewardship that was mine. Their total well-being, at that point, just filled me."

Recovery

"I had been standing above that body during this period, I don't know for how long; it seemed as if it were just a normal event. As I thought of my children, I knew that I had to check on them. I reentered that slumped over body that was on the floor, and in an instant, it just . . . I helped it get up—it couldn't get up. I leaned on the counter top for strength and helped it pull itself up. The pain came back, the terrible pain, it was vicious. I knew that I had to get a door open, so I staggered over to the sliding door and opened it.

"As I got the door open I looked and saw my husband stumbling down the hallway. He seemed to be in shock, and he kept fainting, falling, getting up and then falling again. I yelled to him that he had to get to the front door.

"As soon as the fresh air came in I began to feel better. My six year old son came staggering down the hall, and I told him to get his two brothers out of the bedroom and take them out the front door. Dan, my husband, was in shock. He was outside in the dead of winter, walking in circles in his bare feet, saying that this couldn't have happened to us.

"I went to the other bedroom for my four-and-one-half month old son. I'll never forget the feeling of complete joy that filled me as I entered the room and saw his little eyes peering at me. We collected all the children, got in the car and went to our neighbor's house. She was the Primary President. We laid down on our neighbor's bed, and she took care of our children.

"For about the next six hours we lapsed in and out of consciousness, and we all were throwing up, almost continuously. I don't remember how many times she changed my baby, but she showed loving care to all of us. Her husband, and other men from our ward, including our bishop, whose last name was Bishop and who also happened to be a doctor, came and checked us and the house. Doctor Bishop made sure that we did what we were supposed to during that period. After he checked the house, he later told us that the level of carbon-monoxide was so great that none of us should have awakened.

"It turned out that the furnace was improperly adjusted, and that, coupled with the house having been so tightly sealed for two weeks, led to the excess of carbon-monoxide. It was a simple matter to fix once the problem was identified.

"When we felt well enough, later in the day, the doctor told us to go for a walk. We did, in lovely Providence, and we had this tremendous feeling of closeness to each other. We literally cherished each other. We felt a Presence in the home as we shared the precious moments together that evening. My husband's blessing informs him that he has a guardian angel assigned to him."

Visitors—Beings of Light

"That evening we went to bed about eleven o'clock. I had been asleep for about an hour, in a very peaceful sleep, and for some reason I woke up. From my bed, through the sliding glass door, I could see the Logan Temple, just beautifully. I awoke for no reason and was enjoying the sight of the temple, and . . . ," Marcia cried as she remembered, "and I saw two people. They were above the floor in front of the sliding glass door.

"They were rather translucent; I could see the outline of their bodies. I could kind of see through them, in a way. I couldn't tell you what their faces looked like. I knew that they had a body, and I knew that they had a face. They were smiling with a peaceful kind of aura that was there. There was a brightness about them, a white light. I was totally awake and I wasn't frightened.

"I smiled at them and nodded my head up and down. They told me they were going. They didn't speak audibly—I didn't hear them through my ears. I heard them through my mind. I said, 'thank you,' and they left. The tears started to come, and I said a prayer of thanksgiving to my Father in Heaven at that point. They had been with us all day, I knew they had, they had been there. We felt them."

"When you saw the two individuals, could you tell how they were dressed and whether they were male or female?"

"I don't know whether they were male or female. They were in white robes, translucent long robes."

"When you communicated with them did you do it vocally?"

"I whispered a thank-you to them, but they did not speak to me audibly. They just smiled and . . . and it was their presence that brought such peace."

"When you were out of your body, did it feel as if you had a body?"

"Yes. I felt just like I was me. That's probably what I learned most from the experience—death is nothing. It's no big deal! We worry needlessly about death. Death is normal. It's this flesh that you leave behind. The real you continues. Life is eternal, it never ends, there is no stopping place.

"Did your spirit body feel as if it had arms and legs?"

"Yes. I knew I was standing, but not on the floor. I felt just like me with this wonderful feeling of calmness; no pressure, no frustration, and no worries."

"Did these experiences change your feeling about religion?"

"They didn't change it. The Church has been such a part of me forever . . . all it did was make sense. It wasn't strange, what happened. I knew that's what it would be. I don't think my faith is faith, it's beyond that point, it's my knowledge."

Chapter Twelve

Diverse Experiences

Joanne Jones

A Bleeding Ulcer

Robert and Joanne Jones were waiting for me in their home in Salt Lake City when I drove up. They welcomed me and we traded news of our early life. It turned out that Robert and I had both spent part of our youth in a small town, Dunsmuir, in Northern California.

Joanne explained that she had been born in 1930 in Cleveland, Ohio. When she was six years old, her parents moved to California where she grew up. She and Robert were married in 1954, and they joined The Church of Jesus Christ of Latter-day Saints in 1957, although they were not fully active members until 1986 when they went through the Salt Lake Temple. They had three girls, two of whom were still living.

Joanne began telling of her experience: "About 25 years ago I started with an ulcer. Like a lot of people I kept on smoking. About seven years ago we decided to go to Jackson Hole, Wyoming for the weekend. I hadn't been feeling good—the ulcers were kicking up, but I just thought they'd do their thing and I'd be okay again. Well, when we got there the ulcers had other ideas. They perforated, and I ended up in the hospital."

"Where was the hospital?"

"It was in Jackson. They kept me there overnight, enough to stabilize me so they could bring me in the air-lift ambulance to Salt Lake. I ended up in the LDS Hospital for eighteen days. After I got in the LDS Hospital . . . Robert knows more about what happened there than I do—you tell him, Robert."

Robert continued: "In Jackson, they put eight pints of blood in Joanne, and on the way down they put three more in her. The blood was pouring out through the ulcers as fast as they were putting it in. At LDS, they operated and took out the lower half of her stomach—they found three ulcers near the duodenum. They put a butterfly, a temporary bypass, in her intestine. They pumped a bunch of blood into her, and she was getting ready to go home, and the next day her spleen ruptured."

"She must have been near death," I remarked. "How much blood did she get throughout the ordeal?"

"She got seventy-six pints. People from our Stake donated much of the blood. Anyway, they went in again and removed her spleen, the rest of her stomach, and eight inches of her intestine. Okay, you tell what happened next, Joanne."

Out-of-Body in a Beautiful Place

"After the last surgery, I think it was in the morning, the weirdest thing happened. I was lying in the bed; my body, anyway. But I'm not there. And this is the strangest thing, I look at my . . . that is, my spirit, soul, call it anything you want, the part of me that's spiritually connected, it's out of my body. My body is there—I look down and I see me. Just a tired, sick old woman lying there.

"And then, I was in this most beautiful place I've ever seen in my life. It was outside, with mountains, and animals, and children. There was a country road, and I was aware of myself being there, not my body, but me, Joanne Jones. And I was kind of walking—floating, if you will—down this country road."

A Wonderful Face

"There was an entity coming toward me. At first I didn't know whether it was a man or woman. The person was dressed as we've been led to believe men were dressed at the time of Jesus Christ, in a white robe. Anyway, soon we were face to face, and I've . . . I've never seen a more wonderful face in my life.

"What did he look like?"

"He was fairly young; I'd say around 35 or 40 years of age. He reached for me, embraced me, and said: 'I love you. Not yet, my daughter.' That's all there was to it. I found myself back again in my bed in the hospital."

Other Impressions About the Experience

"When you were first out of your body, Joanne, and could see yourself, did you see any darkness, or lightness, or were you just suddenly in this other world?"

"No, it's like I was transported from where I was to this other world. There was no tunnel, no light; it was just my spirit, or my soul going from here to this other place. It all happened in a hurry—the whole thing—maybe sixty seconds."

"What did the surroundings look like in the other place?"

"Well, okay, there were mountains, beautiful mountains, trees."

"Were there flowers?"

"It was mostly foliage, more beautiful, all kinds of beautiful stuff. Not necessarily from any one region, just gorgeous . . . it was beautiful. That's all I can say. The water was . . ."

"There was water there, too?"

"It seems to me, I can't remember exactly, there was either a river, or a fall. . . ."

"What were the colors like?"

"They were vivid. Not like here; if you imagine the most beautiful place you can think of here."

"Yosemite?"

"It's . . . it's a hundred times more vivid, more wonderful than that. You can't believe it, the colors were magnificent—you can't describe it."

"When you saw the Savior, you say he was good-looking?"

"Yes, I found him to be an extremely attractive person . . . beautiful, with a strong, gentle face. A man who . . . he *was* a man, you could feel it, yet he was something else. And the embrace . . . I could feel the strength, and the love, and the gentleness."

"Was there light; did you notice any brightness about him?"

"You mean around him, like a halo or something. No, I don't remember anything like that. He was dressed in a long robe. And he was this very gentle, beautiful, loving, male entity."

"Did you speak to him?"

"I don't remember saying anything. Only what he said, and then I was back in the hospital with my doctors, John Bowers and Mark Muir. They were standing on either side of my bed holding my hands. There were tears in their eyes, and John said, 'You are one tough lady. I don't know what happened, but you've come back from someplace.'"

Jackie

A Stopped Heart

Jackie greeted Carol and me at the door of her apartment on a windy spring day in 1991. She was busy preparing for a barbecue later in the day. She interrupted her preparations to visit with us.

Jackie was born in Colorado in 1959 and was raised in various parts of the country. They traveled extensively because her mother was a successful entertainer. Jackie proudly displayed a recent record release by her mother.

Two areas where she spent considerable time were New York and California. She went to school at St. Michael's Academy in Manhattan. Ultimately the family moved to Utah. Jackie married the first time at fifteen, just after graduating from high school, and she was divorced at nineteen. She had a daughter from the first marriage. She married again, three years ago, to a good man from Brooklyn whom she characterized as a service brat.

She began her story: "I was 22 years old in 1979, and I was living here in Salt Lake. I had just returned from Japan, and I was having a terrible problem with jet lag, and with insomnia. To help me through the problem I went to this doctor. He didn't do a physical on me but he prescribed 900 mg Placidyl tablets, one of the strongest sleeping medicines they make.

"Normally my heart rate is very slow, but the doctor didn't know that since he didn't check me. On the evening that I got the medicine I went to a party at Len's, my best friend's house, and I had a glass of brandy. At bed time I couldn't sleep, so I took a sleeping pill; the combination of the brandy and the sleeping pill made my heart stop.

"Later Len found me; I had already turned blue. He couldn't feel a pulse, and he took me in his car to St. Mark's Hospital. He was very upset—he thought I had taken the whole bottle of sleeping pills.

"At the hospital they rushed me into the cardiac unit and did everything they could to try and revive me. By this time Len was frantic. The hospital people told him that he couldn't sign the papers, or anything, since he wasn't related. He got my sister to come to the hospital.

"My heart had been stopped at least ten minutes, and the doctors told my friend there wasn't much they could do for me. They had shocked me, twice, with electrical paddles, and they had given me a shot of adrenalin with no success. When they told Len he began crying, sobbing."

Watching the Doctor Explain Her Death

"Okay, my body was in the emergency room, but I was out in the waiting room with Len and my sister. I really didn't walk out there. I was just standing next to Len when the doctor was talking to him. Len was crying. I remember talking to him and asking him why he was crying, but he couldn't hear me. It was as if I weren't there, to Len, to my sister, and to the doctor.

"Then, it seemed as if I were somewhere else. But I could still hear the conversation they were having. Len was screaming that I couldn't leave him now. He had been having problems, and I had helped him. He kept screaming that I couldn't leave, I couldn't die. He was pulling on my sister and crying.

"I was in a place where I didn't feel . . . it wasn't like I was physical. I could still hear them, though. It wasn't like I was floating around, like in ghost stories. It's that I was still there, like a presence, and I was feeling relieved. There was no pain, but no . . . just not physical.

"I remember light, everything was very light. And very, very . . . like relief. But I kept hearing Len's voice, and he was crying for me to come back.

"Then I remember going and getting into my body, and I don't remember anything after that. I was in a coma for seven days. After they revived me I was unable to remember any of the period that I was in the coma. The doctors were extremely shocked when I came out of the coma and there was no brain damage. So that's what happened."

Further Examination of the Experience

"Okay Jackie, let me ask you a few questions. When you were out of your body, how did it feel?"

"It felt like I had no weight."

"Did it feel good or bad?"

"It felt good—I felt free."

"Can you describe the light?"

"It was everywhere. It was just light, it was . . ."

"What color was it?"

"Like a pale blue."

"Were you in it or was it off in the distance?"

"No, I was in it. It was all around me."

"Did the experience feel real, while you were there, or did it feel like a dream?"

"No, it was real. I remember feeling that Len and my sister were pulling me back. Like I couldn't leave. I had an opportunity to leave . . ."

"Oh, you felt as if you could leave?"

"Yes I did. I think I could have, I think I could have left. I think they pulled me back."

"Did you want to come back?"

"No. . . . I guess I did." Jackie laughed as she considered the question. "I guess I did. You know, I was really, really close to him, and I felt like I was abandoning him. So I felt like, . . . I guess I'd better come back. I was at a point, though, where I could have left. I felt that I had to make a decision."

"Did you have any feeling about where you might have gone if you had made the decision to go?"

"To a higher plane. I felt like . . . I didn't feel in danger at all, there was no peril. I felt that I was headed toward happiness—beyond happiness, euphoria.

"Did you ever tell anyone about your experience?"

"Yes, I told Len after it happened. At first he didn't believe me, he just said, 'oh, sure.' Then I told him of the detailed conversation he had with the hospital people about signing papers and the later conversation with the doctor and my sister. That convinced him. He said there was no way that I could have known what he said unless I had been there. He was the only person who ever believed me."

A Friend Commits Suicide

"Another strange thing happened recently. My friend, Len, died; he committed suicide. And I truly believe he came here right after he died. We were inseparable for years and years. He was my best friend from grade school. We had come from similar backgrounds, broken homes and things like that, and he had other problems. He never had a supportive family, and it was too much—he drank.

"It happened last Labor Day, in September, and the coroner later told me the estimated time of death. At that time I was working on my computer here at home, and . . . all of a sudden, at the exact time of his death, a door slammed in another room. None of the windows were open, or anything, and I had this really funny feeling that he was right here with me.

"I don't think that he could leave this . . . I think he was really troubled and couldn't leave. I've never been troubled by things. I've had a hard life, but I've had a happy life. I've never hated anybody, and I've always felt that

I would have a good place to go after this life. But my friend hated everybody. I think his grief kept him here."

"It's too bad that he felt that way, Jackie. I'm sure you helped him all you could. On a separate issue, have you ever read anything on near-death experiences, such as what you experienced?"

"No. Most books are in text form and I don't like to read text."

"Has the experience changed your religious beliefs at all?"

"A little. But I've always been spiritual; I descended from the Irish. I've always been Christian."

"Do you belong to any formal religion?"

"Not now, but I was raised Unitarian Universalist. They teach theology from all perspectives and tell you to look inside yourself and make your choices."

"Has your feeling about death changed?"

"Before the experience I wasn't sure if there was something beyond death. Now I know that there is something beyond this life. This is not the end."

Ray Berg

A Life's Review

I met Ray Berg and two of his boys at their apartment in West Valley City, Utah in early spring, 1991. Ray told me he was on disability because of some health problems. He was born in Omaha, Nebraska in 1940. His mother was from Switzerland where she joined the LDS church. His father was born in Logan, Utah; he worked for the railroad and moved the family to Omaha as a result of his job. When Ray was seven years old, the family moved back to Utah where Ray was raised.

Ray began his story: "In 1967, when I was nearly 27 years old, I was with a lady friend and four or five other couples. We went on an outing near Saratoga, by Lehi, to go on rides, eat, go swimming, and just have fun. I wasn't a swimmer, I never learned to swim, I never cared for it that much.

"To join the rest of them I went in the outside pool; I was on the edge at the deep end talking to some friends. There was a ledge that we were sitting on, and there was another ledge where we put our feet.

"After talking for a while I decided to walk out into the pool. I forgot that we were at the deep end. As I pushed out from the edge, I ended up near the middle of the pool. I went under the water and went down at least three times.

"The lady I was with knew I couldn't swim, and she pushed me back to the edge. Another friend saw us and thought we were just fooling around. He pushed me back into the deep part.

"During those periods when I was going up and down in the water, probably only a minute or two, I saw a review, like a movie, of my whole life. The entire twenty-six-and-a-half years flashed before me. It was just the highlights—not every little event in my life. It was, sort of, like fast forwarding a video recorder. It was my whole life in a matter of seconds.

"I don't remember, now, any specific scenes. Other than just, boom, the whole highlights of my life being shown. That was about it."

"How did you feel when this was happening?" I asked.

"Well, I was so upset when I was bouncing around in the water I really didn't put much thought into the film-like scenes. Later, I got thinking about it, and I heard of the same thing happening to others. I've told several people about it—one close friend thinks it's nonsense."

"Was it in color or black and white, or do you remember?"

"Umm, let's see. I assume it was in color, but I don't remember for sure. I assume it was color, because at the time I remember it being just as I lived it.

"I do remember thinking at the time: *I'm only twenty-six. Do I have to go now?* I didn't want to leave this life then, I wanted to continue to live. I felt it was a bad time to leave."

Ray wanted to be sure that his boys understood that his experience was real. I thanked him for telling of his experience and left.

Doris

Problems in the Navy

Carol and I visited Doris and her brother at their mobile home in West Jordan, Utah in the spring of 1991. Doris explained that she was born in Utah in 1921, but her parents moved to Iowa shortly after she was born. She was raised in Iowa until she was fifteen, during the Great Depression, when she had to leave home. She didn't particularly like Iowa because there weren't many Mormons there, and she had been raised in the LDS church.

When she was twenty years old, during World War II, Doris joined the Navy. She was stationed in Washington D.C.

Doris began telling of her experience: "During my early life I had been told by my Dad that I was stupid. When I got in the Navy and I took some tests I found out that wasn't true. The Navy tests showed that I had an IQ at the college level. That made me feel great.

"I got stationed in Washington D.C., in 1943, in Communications. I was running a decoding machine, and it was boring—I wanted to be an aviation mechanic. I put in for the necessary military school but, it turned out, my tested mechanical aptitude was too low, so they didn't accept me.

"They had taken me out of the secret decoding work, and the only place they had available was the mess hall. After finding out that I really had a brain, to be put in the mess hall just did me in. I was so furious that I decided I was getting out of the service.

"Back in those days you didn't get out easily. I tried to think of ways to get out, and I finally came up with the idea of not eating. My not-eating campaign started on Christmas day. I went through the line and didn't pick up any food. Someone noticed, and they sent me to the Captain's office.

"He asked me what I was doing. I told him I was mad at the Navy and I wanted out. I informed him that I wouldn't eat. He sent me to the doctor, and she gave me a bottle of pink medicine—I later threw it out and continued my non-eating campaign."

Looking Down on Body Which Continues to Walk

"I didn't eat for fourteen days. On the eleventh day, after I finished my duty with the spuds, I was walking back to my bunk and as I passed a cinder-block wall, all of a sudden, within the snap of a finger, I found myself high above my body. My body continued to walk below me.

"Naturally, I went into shock. I never had expected anything like that. I had never even heard of it. It took me at least a minute to get hold of myself. In the meantime my body kept right on walking below me.

"When I got hold of myself I figured I had to do something about it. I thought: *I just can't stay up here in the air with my body below me.* I came down to my body, which was walking, and I hovered in front of it.

"As I hovered there, with my body walking toward me, I studied the head and shoulders to try and figure out a way to return to my body. I almost despaired because I couldn't see any way to get back in. Suddenly, like the snap of a finger, I was back. That's all there was to it."

"How did you feel when you were out?" I asked.

"Light, very light. I didn't look around or anything when I was out; I was in shock. I was stunned—I just couldn't believe that that was where I was. I wanted out of the Navy, not out of my body."

"Did you hear any voices, or anything of that sort?"

"No. Nobody was around. I could see the cinder-block wall below me, the sidewalk, and the landscape."

"Did you have a feeling of peace?"

"If I did I didn't notice."

"How long were you out?"

"Two minutes at the most, maybe three."

"And your body was walking along during this period?"

"I could see it, it didn't miss a step. I apparently had control of it, but I don't know how."

"When you got back in, did you have any ill effects?"

"No. Within three days I stopped my diet, when the Navy agreed to let me out with an honorable discharge."

"You got out of the Navy then?"

"No, I decided to stay in. I guess all I wanted was my own way. I stayed in and served my one-and-a-half years."

"Has that out-of-body experience affected your thinking?"

"Well, I know that it's no big deal to get out of your body. And I've read a lot of books on the subject since the experience happened. I also know that the person that is *you* is the spirit inside of your body."

"So you believe it was your spirit that was out?"

"Oh, yes."

"And you think your experience was real, not a dream or anything like that?"

"It was no dream. You don't dream while you're walking down the street."

"Do you think there is a life after death?"

"You bet I do. I don't even think—I know. And there is a God."

"Do you have any messages to leave for others?"

"I'm not one to advise other people, but I think what we do here is pretty important."

Chapter Thirteen

A Suicide Attempt

Katrina

A Terrible Childhood Experience

Katrina was a lovely dark-haired lady, somewhat overweight, who came to our home in the early spring of 1991. Carol and I tried to make her feel comfortable before we began taping her experience. She was obviously nervous and under considerable emotional strain. The things she was about to divulge were difficult for her to talk about; she was reluctant to share a very private experience and expose it to public scrutiny. She told us she had not slept the previous night in anticipation of the visit, which she almost cancelled.

Katrina was born in 1955 in Colorado where her father worked in the oil fields. She went to high school in a small community near Provo, Utah after moving there to be near relatives of her mother. She was raised in the LDS church.

She graduated from LDS Business College when she was eighteen. She obtained excellent grades and was trained as a secretary and received later training as a paralegal.

Katrina told her story to Carol and me with great difficulty. I will not repeat the details of some of her conversation because no good purpose would be served in so doing. The reader must understand the rudiments of what happened to her in her early life, however, in order to comprehend why she later took some of the actions that she did, and why the outcome during her out-of-body experience was as it was. This chapter, although extremely distasteful in terms of what Katrina suffered, is presented to show that the Lord understands whatever happens to us, no matter how dreadful in our minds, and extends his infinite love.

During Katrina's early youth, her father was a contractor, as well as a supervisor for Standard Oil, and he built the Mormon chapel in the small community that they lived in. When Katrina was six years old, and a beautiful child, she often accompanied her father to the church which he worked on.

Katrina enjoyed being with her father while he worked. It was a sort of fantasy world where she could play and be near her father. On one occasion, when Katrina was six years old, her father had to leave the church to go to the lumber yard for a short period. He asked Katrina if she wanted to go with him or if she preferred to stay and play with her doll until he returned. Katrina chose to stay. Her father left her in the care of a man whom he and Katrina trusted.

During the period when her father was gone the man performed horrible physical and sexual acts upon Katrina. He also threatened that terrible things would happen to her if she ever told anyone. The acts and subsequent threats were so terrifying that Katrina was marred for life. She never told anyone about the incident until years later, and then only when she was forced, in therapy, to face what had been hidden in her mind as a horrible experience too awful to admit, even to herself.

As a Young Adult

Katrina began her story: "That experience affected my life in many ways. I was terrified of men, for example. When I became dating age, I was scared to death when guys started calling me up for dates. I couldn't bring myself to date before my twenties. I involved myself in my studies, instead, and became a straight-A student.

"There was a young man who was the President of the Young Adults, a returned missionary, who was very nice to me. He never made improper advances, or anything, and I eventually married him in the Salt Lake Temple. It later turned out that he was sterile and couldn't have children—I wanted them. He had other physical and emotional problems which were related to his sterility. He hadn't told me of these problems before our marriage, and he was kind enough to let me get an annulment. We were married for a-year-and-a-half.

"I started dating again after a period and guys acted like, I guess normal men do, wanting to be affectionate, and it scared me. I wanted to be something like a Nun where I didn't have to face these problems and the feelings within me. The closest thing the LDS church had to being a Nun was a mission, so I put in for a mission.

"I wanted to go badly. I went to several temple sessions—I had already received my endowments when I was married. In the temple I kept getting the feeling that I shouldn't go. I really wanted to go, though, so I pressed the Lord, in prayer, and told him that I wanted to serve. I reminded the Lord that in the Doctrine and Covenants it says if you desire to serve you are called. I got a response which was, in effect: *Okay daughter, go. Your desire will be granted.*

"I got my mission call in 1979 and was one of the original districts to go through the Missionary Training Center. When I got to the MTC I immediately realized why He had told me, in the temple, that a mission wasn't for me. I was in a sea of men; everywhere I looked were men. There were two thousand men and a hundred-and-twenty-seven sisters.

"I had a breakdown being around that many men. I did the best I could, but I couldn't function. I talked to my Mission President, and he felt that I should go home and get some counseling. So that's what I did.

"I went into counseling at that point with LDS Social Services. They had experts that worked with me, but I still couldn't tell them what really was bothering me. I dropped out of therapy.

"I moved back to Colorado and lived with my mom. I got a job and tried to stay away from the guys. I found it increasingly difficult to stay away from men, because, unfortunately for me, I was good looking; at the time I weighed about a hundred-and-thirty pounds.

"I met a man who had been divorced and then joined the LDS church. He was on his mission when I met him. After he was released from his mission he came back and we were married. I didn't know him well, but I felt comfortable with him."

Fear for Children

"I became pregnant—and I totally freaked out. At the time I didn't know what was bothering me, but later, after therapy, I understood that I didn't feel that this world was safe for children. The thought that I had to bring a child into this world terrified me.

"Shortly after my pregnancy I made my first suicide attempt. I was really, really, afraid it would be a girl. I tried to drive my car into the river. In the back of my mind was the thought that I had to protect my child.

"When the baby came it was a boy. I felt I had done a grave injustice to this small, helpless child by bringing him into an unsafe world. I couldn't bring myself to take him to church—because of what had happened to me. Churches were not safe places for children, in my mind, so we had him blessed at home."

"Did you tell your husband why?" I asked.

"No, I couldn't. I hadn't told anyone. I went from being totally active in the church to being totally inactive after I had my baby, and no one could understand why. I didn't know myself why I stopped being active.

"We ended up moving back to Salt Lake City, and I became extremely overprotective of my son. I actually became house-bound for four years. I wouldn't answer the door, and I wouldn't answer the phone. I couldn't understand why I was acting like this, except I felt that I was safe and he was safe. Additionally, I wouldn't let anyone baby-sit him.

"When my son was still a baby he got the idea that he shouldn't be put down, because I carried him all the time. I put him in a kangaroo type pouch and carried him wherever I went.

"When it came time to put him in kindergarten I couldn't do it, I just couldn't. I remember the first time I took him out of the house to a grocery store and he saw another child. His face took on a look of amazement and delight. He laughed and carried on, because he had seen another child that was like him.

"He wanted so badly to go to kindergarten, to play and to be with other children. I knew I needed counseling, really badly. I begged my husband to get someone that would come into the home and help me to get over my phobias. But he wouldn't do it—he dealt with things by staying away. He wasn't supportive at all. All I could do was pray for help.

"I was desperate and I forced myself to take my son, get in a car and drive to Colorado where my mom was. When I got there she was down at the church, so I drove to where she was. At first I couldn't force myself to go in. I drove around the church several times. Finally, I started to go up the stairs, when . . . I don't know what happened. I still, to this day, don't know how I could have tripped and fallen. It felt like I was pushed, and I fell down and broke my arm.

"It was a severe break and I had to have surgery. The doctor who treated me recognized that I was severely depressed. He put me on an anti-depressant and got me in touch with a therapist; she diagnosed my emotional illness as an extreme separation problem."

Help from Therapy—Then Disaster

"We started what turned out to be three years of therapy. I felt better than I had in my whole life when they put me on the anti-depressant. We gradually got to the point where I could put my son in school. It was hard for both my son and me. I could hardly wait to pick him up at three o'clock, but I did it.

"Over a period of three years I was gradually able to function again. I still hadn't told the therapist what had happened to me as a child, though—I had never talked about it. I had maintained 27 years of silence.

"My therapist mentioned the problem several times, because I had difficulty with bulimia, an eating disorder where you eat compulsively to put on weight. I wanted to look nice, but I couldn't handle the attention from the men, so I would eat and put on weight. Then I would feel bad, because I didn't want to look that way, and I would throw up what I had eaten.

"She began to delve into what was causing the bulimia. She kept suggesting that it was a sexual abuse issue that I hadn't dealt with."

"Did you remember it, Katrina, or was it something that you had put out of your mind?" I asked.

"I had really forced it back. It was something that was incidental, way over in the corner. There was no emotion to it, I buried it pretty deep. I explained it to myself as a bad childhood nightmare, which I hadn't forgotten as I had other childhood dreams.

"Also, at this point something happened in my husband's life to change him—his whole attitude changed. He went from a very giving person to one where . . . he had the idea that females were second class people and were subservient to males. He started hitting me, physically abusing me and my boy.

"Being depressed and unable to cope I stayed in the arrangement longer than I should have. I began to feel suicidal. My self esteem got even lower. I wondered: *How could God let this happen? Why didn't God love me? Didn't I matter to him.*

"To make matters worse I was pregnant again, and I flipped out thinking that it might be a girl.

"My husband beat me pretty severely one night, and I went to the hospital. I lost the baby. I lost my faith in everything.

"In the back of my mind I had always wanted a girl—even through all of this—and I got pregnant again, on purpose, to replace the child I lost. The beatings became even more severe, and . . . and out of desperation I made a really bad decision. I went and got an abortion.

"I had made the abortion decision consciously, and when I did I thought: *I am going to go to hell*. But as a mother I wanted to protect my child from this earth and from things that would hurt girls. I felt as if I would rather send that child back to God and go to hell myself than to bring the child into an unsafe world. I prayed that God would understand and give me another chance with those same spirits at a later date. I felt awful."

Attempted Suicide

"Last August, after a divorce from my husband, I made a decision to end it all. I got a medical journal and figured out what pills, coupled with my anti-depressant, would be fatal. I took them. I felt like I was human garbage.

"I told my ex-husband, who was there at the time, to take my son to work with him. He didn't know I had taken the pills. I told him I wanted to be cremated and flushed down the toilet if I should die. I felt that was where I belonged. I laid down on the bed to die.

"I first became aware of a blackness, a void. It felt very peaceful. No earthly problem or care followed me there. I was aware I existed, but I felt no pain. For the first time since being a child I felt free from emotional pain. I knew what was meant when the Lord said that the earth would be cursed for our sakes. This felt so natural in comparison to earth life. I came to the conclusion that our earth experience was the unnatural state and this one, the spiritual state, was the correct state of being.

"I had the feeling of fighting with someone or something. I felt I was being pulled away from the blackness, and I desperately wanted to stay.

"As it turned out, my ex-husband had decided not to take our boy to work with him. He left him at home with me. My child later told me I had been screaming, throwing myself around on the bed fighting something, and it had scared him so badly that he called my step-mother. She came over and spent an-hour-and-a-half trying to revive me."

A Marvelous Experience and a Message

"I remember leaving the void and entering a garden. The garden was similar to a wooded or forest area, but it had plants that were tropical in nature, sort of like you would find in Florida.

"There was the most beautiful music. It was not something I heard with my ears. Rather, it was something I felt with my soul.

"There were animals; birds, butterflies and small furry creatures, one resembling a fawn. I could communicate with these animals. It wasn't a verbal exchange or a question and answer scenario. It was, instead, as if I were a part of them. They seemed to receive their life force from the same source I did. We were part of a collective consciousness, part of a universal whole.

"It was like I had increased awareness. On earth our body has five senses, but over there I had more than the five senses. Part of the expanded awareness was the ability to perceive thoughts, to peer into the souls of all living things, and to communicate with them.

"In this manner it was communicated to me by a person whom I understood to be my 'guardian angel,' the person who was assigned to work with and help me, that I was not supposed to be there. I was going to be sent back, because I had not yet learned what I was supposed to learn on earth.

"And it's like I asked: 'What is that?'

"Trust in God, came the reply. *Allow yourself to receive the beautiful body he intended to bestow on you—and to glorify God with. Stop abusing and defiling your body. Let your body be worthy of the spirit which inhabits it, and trust in God to protect you. Let go of the fat which you were using to keep men away; trust in God.*

"Additionally, I was told I had been trying to get my self-worth, my satisfaction, my reward from the wrong place. I had been trying to get them from flesh, from my husband, from my family, and from my friends. I was told that I was looking in the wrong direction. I should have been connecting with Christ and with God, not with man, for my identity.

"Something told me to look, and I turned and looked. I saw a beautiful girl, a young child of about eight or nine years with long brown hair. There was a small boy standing next to her who resembled my brother. I understood that these were the two children I had lost. The girl was the one I had lost from the beating, and the boy was lost from the abortion. They were beautiful children and I . . . I had a feeling of remorse and a great sense of loss.

"Then another message was communicated to my soul. I understood this person to be Christ speaking to me. The message was: *Oh precious child of God, I will restore that which the locust has eaten*. I knew it meant that those children would be mine.

"I was amazed at the mercy, understanding and love given to me while in the Savior's presence. There was such total acceptance and love—no condemnation whatsoever.

"Standing in His presence I received a new perception of myself and of my worth. I had left the earth thinking of myself as human garbage. In a few moments in His presence, and feeling for myself what he felt for me, I totally reevaluated my worth. I *did* matter; He *did* care. Even more than that—he loved me, he forgave me.

"I was so overwhelmed by the utter love and peace and mercy that I did not want to leave. I wanted to dance to that beautiful music. Even though

I knew that someday I would hear the music and feel the love again, I begged not to be sent back."

Return—A New Understanding of Life

"Then I was back. The nurse was saying to me: 'You're in Holy Cross Hospital. You are in critical condition, and we don't know if we can save you. Even if we do you'll have heart problems the rest of your life.'

"Since that experience I haven't felt suicidal at all. Everything has changed. I'm not interested in money anymore. I wanted money to buy security, to be safe, in a nice house, with an education. I used to think if I could be a lawyer I could bring people who hurt women and children into court, and . . . and those things don't matter now.

"The only thing that is important to me now is doing right by the people I love. All I want is to do the best I can for those that I love. I now feel that God loves me. I had never felt such an overwhelming sense of peace, and acceptance, and total love, total . . . there was no judgment. Just mercy and acceptance.

"I certainly don't feel suicidal anymore. Yes, I would like to be back in His presence, but I wouldn't want to kill myself to get there. I want to do what I'm supposed to do, to do right by my son, and to have those two children that were promised to be sent back.

"I thought for sure I was going to hell. You know, I had an abortion, and I tried to kill myself. But I know when my time comes I will go to that beautiful place, and it will be just as peaceful and lovely as it was when I was there." Katrina paused and wiped the tears from her face. She had cried throughout most of the interview. I waited for a period while she regained her composure.

"How is your health now, Katrina? Have you developed heart problems?"

"Interestingly enough, my tests show normal."

"How is your boy doing?"

"He's doing really well. My former husband has improved, also. He has gone back to the Church, and he spends time with our boy; something he never did before."

"Have you gotten over your phobias?"

"Yes, I finally told my therapist what had happened when I was young. And I've been able to go back into churches and feel safe."

"Did they ever catch the man who abused you?"

"I think so. In any event he is dead now and it doesn't matter. I hold no anger toward him.

"Another thing occurred, though. I found out later that the church where it happened burned down. They built something else in its place, and it burned down too. So, you see, the Lord cleansed his church."

A Final Review of Katrina's Experience

"Going back to your out-of-body experience, when you went out of your body, do you remember seeing your body?"

"No, the first thing I remember was the blackness."

"And the blackness felt peaceful?"

"Peaceful in that I didn't have any earthly problems to worry about, but in the back of . . . these words do not describe it. They are so inadequate. I was aware of fighting something, desperately fighting it. I didn't want to come back; I wanted to stay in the blackness. I don't know whether I was fighting against coming back—or what I was fighting."

"When you were in the other world what was your body like?"

"When I went into the garden I was in a different body than the one I had left. I was not overweight, I was maybe even a little on the thin side. I seemed to be a young woman; not adolescent, but not the 35 years old that I was at the time. I had long black hair and my body was perfect. Just as beautiful as it could be. And I had more senses than the five senses we have on this earth. I had more perception. My body wasn't heavy, it wasn't cumbersome, it wasn't burdensome. It was beautiful and I didn't want to leave it."

"What do you mean by more perception?"

"Well, we perceive things here in three dimensions. It seemed like on the other side there was more than the three. You have . . . you can do more things. It's really hard to describe."

"What about knowledge?"

"Oh, anything I wanted to know I understood before I could even formulate the question."

"So what sort of things did you feel you wanted to know?"

"Well, I wanted to know why I had been through the things that I had been through. I wondered about others, people I loved who had hurt me, and . . . and I felt like those things didn't matter. That was their problem. All those things were old and would fall away, and they would be as dust in the dirt.

"I understood that I was looking in the wrong place, I was looking down, I was looking in the dirt. I should, instead, look up. I should look up to Christ. Those things that bothered me so much didn't matter anymore. All the pain I had experienced in life became insignificant standing in the presence of such love. All doubt was removed about whether or not I mattered. I was overwhelmed by the mercy and non-judgment.

"Another thing came to me while I was getting this knowledge. It was that when I fell down and broke my arm on the steps of the church . . . that happened because my guardian angel pushed me. It was so I would get the help I needed."

"When you saw the other world with the tropical environment, do you remember what the colors were like?"

"I remember green and brown. That's about it."

"Did you see a light?"

"Yes."

"What was it associated with?"

"Coming into the garden. I've read other people's experiences, and the light itself was not the overwhelming thing that I've heard other people describe it as. What overwhelmed me more than the light was the feeling of peace and love. That seemed more important than just the light."

"When you communicated with the persons did you see them?"

"No."

"So it was just a feeling of a presence?"

"Yes."

"And you felt the beautiful music?"

"Yes, and I've listened to hundreds of hours of music trying to find it. I've found something that sort of captures it, but it still is too harsh."

"Do you know the name of the piece?"

"Yes. It is Daniel Kobialka's version of 'Pachelbel's Kanon.' It's classical and it's pretty soft, but it's still too harsh."

Chapter Fourteen

Chased By An Evil Spirit

Dee

A Bad Marriage

Dee was waiting for Carol and me as we parked in front of her house in Salt Lake City. Her living room was light and cheery, and Dee matched it with her cheery disposition. One beautiful but shy cat sat on a small rocking chair; another, a ragged-looking waif of a cat, poked its head around the corner and looked timidly at us. Dee told us that she had rescued both cats from the animal shelter where she worked.

Dee said that she was born in Indianapolis, Indiana in 1949. She was raised in the Catholic church by an Irish-Catholic mother and by a father who was a convert to that church. She had a happy youth and went to high school in Indianapolis. She went to nursing school for two years but did not graduate. She began to tell her story.

"In 1969, when my first husband was stationed in Virginia, and we were living there, I had become close friends with another girl, Janey, whose husband was a Corporal. My husband was a Sergeant. Both of our marriages were bad, and we tried to help each other; we spent every waking minute together.

"Janey got pregnant and she was very unhappy about it. She said: 'Look what I've done now. I've got a really rotten marriage, and now this. What am I going to do?'

"Janey was about seven-and-one-half months pregnant when we left Virginia. My husband got an early-out discharge. We came back to Indiana and we stayed with my mom and dad.

"My parents could tell that I was unhappy, but I'm not the type of person who tells my problems to everybody. I just wanted, somehow, to get out of the marriage before I got pregnant. The possibility of getting pregnant was the scariest thing, because I did not want to bring a child into the marriage.

"It was summer time and it was hot. My mother and dad lived in an old farm house. I can remember thinking: *Gee, some months have past—Janey is going to have that baby. I'm not going to be there.*

"We had planned so much for me to be there. As I thought about it, I was tired, and my mom told me to go upstairs and lie down for awhile so I would feel better.

"I went upstairs and lay on the bed. I looked at the ceiling and was thinking: *Look what I've got myself into. I'm 21 years old and I'm miserable. Janey will have that baby and I won't be there to help. What will she do?*

An Out-of-Body Trip to a Friend

"As I thought about Janey, the very next second, I was floating . . . like I was walking down a staircase, and I came right down onto the base in Virginia. While I looked at the base from above I thought: *Oh my gosh, look at this! This is great. There's the house I used to live in.*

"I walked down the street, going south, toward Jane's house. I was going fast, it was like a floating walk. I walked right up to Janey's house, and I walked through the closed screen door.

"I could see Janey sitting there with a cigarette, drinking coffee, and rubbing her temple. When she rubbed her head I always knew she was depressed. I knew, looking at her, that she had had the baby. She had shorts on, and she never wore shorts. I gave her a pair but she would never wear them, no matter how hot it got, because her husband made fun of her legs.

"She seemed super-depressed and I decided I didn't want to bother her. I wanted to see the baby, though. That was the most important thing in my mind. So I went upstairs, floating up the stairs, right into the baby's room. I looked around and it seemed so sweet. When I looked at the baby I knew it was a boy. I just knew. I remember thinking that it looked more like her husband than her.

"The next thing I knew I was back in Indiana. Smack—boom! I was back in Indiana. I was upstairs on the bed and I could feel the fan blowing on me. I ran downstairs and told my mom what had happened. She told me to get on the phone and call Janey.

"I called Janey and told her I had just been at her house. She started laughing. I told her that she had on a pair of blue shorts that I gave her. She agreed that she did, and she asked me how I knew. I told her, again, that I was just at her house.

"Janey said I was just dreaming. I explained that it was no dream, and that I saw her fat little baby boy. I remember when I first saw her, when I was out of my body, that she had a piece of paper, and she was writing. She told me that she had just been writing me a letter to tell me that they had the baby, and that they had named him John. We talked a little longer and she promised to send a picture."

"Did she believe you?" I asked.

"No. Janey's a real skeptical person. I couldn't talk religion to her, she just laughed it off. She said something about the power of the mind, and she mentioned that I knew she had blue shorts because I gave them to her, and she said I was just guessing she would have them on.

"My mom believed me though. I thought the whole experience was great, and I tried to repeat it for weeks. But it never happened again until later. I thought: *What a great way to travel*." Dee laughed as she thought about it.

"We moved out of my parents' house, but the marriage continued to deteriorate. I finally left him and got a divorce."

A Second Bad Marriage

"The next incident took place in the winter of 1983. I had married again, and this marriage was worse than the first one, but I didn't want to end it. My husband used to tell me that if I ended it I would be a two-time loser. That preyed on my mind, because I had a little girl and she loved her daddy. I didn't want to break it up.

"It was a bad marriage early on, but I kept thinking I could change him. At first he was gentle and nice—then that changed. After the birth of our daughter we moved to Salt Lake City. Both my husband and I had good jobs. He worked for the Union Pacific, and I worked at the airport in the control center.

"One day, out of the blue, he said let's move back to Indiana. I was sick about it, because I loved Utah. We both had good jobs and I liked the climate."

"Why did he want to go back?" I asked.

"He was homesick; he was the oldest of ten kids. He missed his brothers and sisters. He was a country boy and I was a city girl.

"The minute we got to Indiana we went from living a good life to being desperately poor. I hated it, because I kept thinking that there was no reason we had to be so poor. All he had to do was get himself together and get a job, but he wouldn't do it.

"Things got worse and worse. Finally, we were living on unemployment, and we saw an ad in the paper where there was a house for rent for one-hundred dollars a month, with fifty-two acres of land. He said that we could farm it.

"I hated the house from the very beginning. It sat way out in the woods; the nearest neighbor was three-and-a-half miles away. I didn't like that much solitude; it scared me. The climate was sticky; we were in an old farm house, and the only noises we heard were the crickets and locusts and other bugs. To a country person those are great sounds, but to a city person it was disgusting. The noise, to me, was deafening.

"We had started chopping wood to get ready for the winter. My husband was gone most of the time; I was alone with our little daughter, and as it began to get cold I had a terrible time with the stove. My mother-in-law kept calling me and telling me how to stoke it, remove the ashes, and so forth. I knew diddly about wood stoves.

"I felt abandoned, in a house that I hated, miles from the nearest neighbor, and in a miserable environment. We didn't even have running water—I had to haul it.

"Finally, it reached the point that when my husband was home, which was seldom, he would sleep near the wood stove on the far side of the bed. It was a big, old-fashioned bedroom. I slept, separately, on a couch in the bedroom; my little girl slept in the bed with her dad. We all bundled up with covers in an attempt to stay warm."

Emotional Trauma—Then Out-of-Body

"One night, just before dawn, I was lying on the couch and shivering because of the cold. I had on a pair of blue-jeans, heavy socks, a wool sweater, a bathrobe, my coat, and blankets—and I was freezing. I could hear my husband snoring, and I was miserable. I remember thinking: *Come spring I'm getting out of here. I don't know where I'll go, but I'm taking Sara and I'm getting out. I won't spend another winter in this lousy house. I hate it here. I hate winter here, and I hate summer here. I'm going to get out.*

"The next thing I knew I was out of my body; I was over the bed looking down and I was thinking: *Here we go again*. It seemed like the first incident had happened only yesterday.

"I remember floating above the bed looking down at my husband, looking at Sara, and looking at myself on the couch. I thought the scene was peculiar, because I saw this . . . it was like a spider's thread coming from my chest on my body up to me—where I was floating. It seemed to be fastened to me. I remember wondering how far the thread would let me go."

"Could you feel this thread fastened to you?" I asked.

"I couldn't feel it, actually, but I could sense it, and I could see it. And I wondered how far I could go."

"What did it look like?"

"It was like a string off a spider's web, like it had dew on it, or something. As I wondered how far I could go, the next thing I knew I was floating right up through the roof, and I was outside. It was just starting to get dawn, way out in the country, and I thought how wonderful it was. I started moving above the treetops and down the road to the bridge.

"I wondered if I could make it to the bridge, which was way down at the end of the road, and I saw, off to my left, cows in a field. The cows were lying down, and I could see the steam coming from their noses where it hit the cold air.

"I kept thinking how great and how wonderful it was as I continued to head for the bridge. I looked up and saw the stars twinkle—it's like there were a zillion stars."

An Evil Spirit

"The next thing I knew was . . . there was something behind me, and I was afraid. I felt this awful presence—and I knew that it was after me. I looked back and I saw that my string, which I was hooked to, was getting tight. I was afraid, and I was thinking: *What is this thing behind me?* I started to circle, because I knew I had to get back to the house.

"The thing was coming after me fast, and I had the feeling it could kill me. I was moving through the tops of the trees, and I was thinking that I couldn't break my string, and I had to get back quick. Then . . ." Dee's hands were visibly shaking as she tried to continue with the story.

"This . . . this thing, this awful, this terrifying thing—I could feel it on me. It was pushing me away from the house, and I could see the string getting tighter. I was sure I was going to die. I was frantic for Sara, frantic over the idea that if I died she would be stuck with my husband. I felt I had to get back, but the thing kept trying to push me away from the house.

"Every time I would circle and try to get back to the house the thing would come up behind and push me. I knew I was going to die. I could feel the tug at my string. I was being chased by something that was evil. And it wanted *me*. It wanted to destroy me. I was terrified and I was crying, and I remember thinking: *Oh God, help me, help me God.* I got all my strength to go as fast as I could—I could actually feel this thing on the back of my neck."

Return to Her Body

"The next thing I can remember was: SLAM! I was in my body and I was screaming. My husband and my daughter woke up, and I was screaming and shaking. My husband said: 'What's the matter with you? You were only having a dream.' I told him: 'That was no dream. Something was trying to kill me.'

"My husband just . . . we were total opposites. I couldn't explain this to him. My little girl was terribly frightened because she had never seen her mother scream. She was only four years old.

"I got up, paced the floor, and put fire in the stove. My husband kept insisting it was a dream, and I kept telling him it wasn't. I told him I hated the house and that we had to get out of it. I also said that if he didn't get me out of the house I would leave.

"The next day I drove in the Van to my mother's house, fifty miles away, and told her about it. She said that I had to get away from my husband. She told me to look at myself, how distraught I was.

"After that, things got progressively worse in our marriage. We moved out of the farm house, bought a house closer to town, but it only lasted a year. He physically abused me, and I couldn't stay. I came to Utah with my daughter."

Other Thoughts About Experiences

"The evil spirit experience was horribly real. Look, I'm shaking just thinking about it. I know that if that thing had been able to push me away so that my string broke it would have killed me. I believe that these two incidents happened, maybe as a warning, a signal, or something, so that I would get out. I stayed in the second marriage because of my daughter.

"Before I left Indiana I was very suicidal. I wouldn't have committed suicide, there is no way, but I felt like it. I was depressed and I was filled with hate. I was ripe for the experience I had with . . . with that thing.

"I've had to repair my life since then. Little by little I've gotten things back together. That incident pretty well scared the hell out of me."

"Let me ask you a few questions, Dee. On the first incident, do you remember a string being attached to you?"

"No, not on the first one."

"In both experiences, how did your body feel when you were out?"

"I don't know what you call the other thing, my soul, my spirit, or what, but there was no feeling. The first time, when I glided down from the air, there was no feeling. Just a lot of thought."

"Did you feel as though you had a body?"

"I didn't think about it. I knew where I was—in Virginia."

"You felt like you were walking?"

"Yes. It felt like walking. My body didn't feel heavy. You know how your body feels . . . I remember when I walked through the closed screen door, and I thought that this was great. Then I walk-glided up to the bedroom and thought how terrific it was.

"As soon as I got my wish I was back. The important thing was to see the baby. I loved Jane dearly, and I wanted to see the baby."

"So that was a good experience?"

"That was a wonderful experience. And I remember—I don't know how to express it, how I was zapped back into my body, or what made me go back . . . . I believe when I started thinking about Indiana and wondering where my body was, as soon as I started thinking about my body, zap, I was back. And I knew I wasn't asleep. I knew that for sure."

"So it wasn't a dream?"

"It was no dream. As soon as I was back I could feel the heat again—it was so hot."

"And you didn't feel the heat when you were out?"

"No, there was no heat. It was a nothing sensation, a floating feeling."

"You didn't see any lights or anything of that sort?"

"No. No flashing lights; should I have?"

"We can talk about what others have seen in a minute."

"It was bright, if that's what you mean. It wasn't a fog. It was, like, brilliant-bright. There wasn't a distinct light. It was just very bright."

"Around you, or where?"

"It was everywhere, everything was bright. Brighter than it normally would have been."

"Was that true in both experiences?"

"No, because the second experience was at night. It was just before dawn and I could see the frost on the ground and the steam from the cow's nose. I could see a mist on my string. My string had a glimmer to it."

Feelings of Terror in Second Experience

"When I first became aware of the presence of the thing, in the second experience, it was the most terrible feeling that I've ever had in my life. It was like I was going to die, or worse."

"What did you feel that the presence was?"

"I thought that it was the Devil, or a spirit that was trying to get my body. That's what I thought. I've always had a healthy fear of evil spirits. As soon as I felt this presence behind me I knew that this was ugly, this was terror, this was the worst . . . it was the most ugly, the most horrible thing that I had ever encountered. It was going to get me—it was going to destroy me—it was after my body.

"I knew that if it broke my string I would be dead. It kept pushing me away from the house; it was trying to get me as far as it could from my body. It wanted my string to break. The most important thing in my mind was to get back to my body, so I wouldn't leave my daughter.

"The terror was awful. I could feel myself wanting to scream. I was flailing my arms, grasping for something to pull me back, but there was nothing to hold onto. I was fighting to go back, and I flailed my arms to try and get the thing away from me. It was the most horrible experience I had ever had. Even today, when I think about it I am terror-striken. Look at my hands!" Dee's hands continued to shake as she remembered the experience.

"When I got back into my body I was screaming, because I couldn't . . . maybe that's it. I guess I couldn't make vocal noise out of my body. Maybe I was screaming, and as soon as I got back to my body I could vocalize it. It was a blood curdling scream—because that was the most terrifying thing that had ever happened to me."

Chapter Fifteen

People Meeting People

Tracie

Diabetic Coma

Tracie was a typical blue-eyed, sandy-haired teenager who came to our house with her father in early spring, 1991. She was full of the enthusiasm of youth but she seemed more mature in her demeanor than most teenagers. She told Carol and me that she was born in 1975 in Salt Lake City, Utah. She was raised as an active member of The Church of Jesus Christ of Latter-day Saints. She began her story:

"Last October my friends and I were spending the night together for a social get together. The previous night I had some trouble breathing, and stuff like that, so I went to the doctor—but he couldn't figure out what it was.

"When I went to sleep on this particular night, the next morning they couldn't wake me up. For six hours, somebody told me, they couldn't wake me."

"Did they ever determine why they couldn't wake you?" I asked.

"In November the doctors said, probably, but not for sure, it was a diabetic coma."

"So you couldn't wake up. What happened?"

"I was just lying there, and it was like I couldn't wake up, but I could hear things going on around me. I could hear people talking, and they were trying to wake me up, and stuff."

Blackness, Light, and People

"Then it was like I went through this blackness—sort of like empty space. It's hard to explain what it was really like. Then I went through the same kind of thing, except it was bright red. And I came into this, sort of like a room, which was bright-white. Everything was white.

"It was a really bright light. It was brighter than anything I had ever seen, but it didn't hurt my eyes. I could look at the light. I just stood there for a moment because everything was so peaceful. It was just like there was love and warmth in the air. It was really nice.

"It was like there was a corridor. I looked up the corridor and there was a group of about five people standing there. Some were female and some were male, and they were turned away from me at first. They were walking really slowly.

"The people turned around, and it was like they were expecting somebody. You know, it's like they were waiting for me to be there. They just stood there and waited. No words were spoken, but I just felt like I was to go to them. Sort of like mind waves, or whatever you want to call them.

"I went up to them, and they just really welcomed me. It was very nice. I felt as if they were waiting for me, and they wanted me to be with them. So I walked up this corridor with them for awhile. And all of a sudden there was, sort of like, a window. I looked out of it, and I saw my body lying there on the couch. People were still trying to wake me up.

"I didn't feel like I wanted to go back. It was so nice where I was. So much nicer than it was, you know, on earth.

"We continued walking some more. And . . . I can't remember anything for awhile. It just doesn't come to mind. But I know something else happened.

"The next thing that I do remember is that we came to another small room. It's like there were windows on two sides of it. I felt that I should go to the window on the left, so I did.

"When I looked through the window, I could see that my parents were there, this time, with my body. Someone had called my parents. And I felt as though I were getting farther and farther from earth life and more into the new life. I could see that someone had called the paramedics, because they couldn't wake me.

"The paramedics put ammonia up my nose. I felt this burning when they did and it hurt. I tried to get away from it—I was really scared—I didn't want to go back. I liked it where I was. The paramedics said something like: 'Don't fight it,' and they used that stuff again.

"Then . . . it's hard to explain . . . it was sort of like a high-powered vacuum that was pulling me back. I was trying to get farther along the corridor, but I couldn't. They were pulling me back.

"All of a sudden, they, the people who were with me in the corridor, were gone. They disappeared somehow. I didn't feel like they deserted me, or anything, I just felt that they were trying to tell me they loved me, but I had to come back. There was something I had to do.

"I was still fighting, even though I felt they were trying to tell me to return. So I went back through the redness and the blackness again. Then I was back in my body again. I wanted to close my eyes and go back where I had been, but the paramedics made me keep my eyes open. They wouldn't let me go back to sleep. That was it."

Further Review of Tracie's Experience

"Okay, let me ask you a few questions, Tracie. When you first went into the darkness, did you see your body then?"

"No. It was just the blackness, then the redness, then the bright room."

"How did the brightness feel?"

"It was just very peaceful, and it felt safe."

"How were the people that you met dressed?"

"They were wearing long white robes—silky material."

"Did you feel that you knew the people?"

"No, I . . . I didn't recognize them, let's put it that way."

"But you didn't feel that you knew them?"

"I felt like I had been with them before. But I just didn't recognize them. I knew them somehow, but I couldn't realize it then."

"Did you hear any voices?"

"Not verbal voices, but, like I said, through mind waves. But it couldn't be translated straight into English. It was just sort of—they gave you . . . I don't know. It's hard to explain."

"As best you can translate, what feelings did you get from the voices?"

"Like I said, they loved me, and they wanted to be with me, but I needed to go back because there was something that I needed to do."

"Oh, so you needed to do something?"

"Yes. I haven't figured out what yet, but . . ."

"When you looked through the windows, what was it like?"

"The first time I looked, I just saw my body lying there with my friends trying to wake me. I didn't really know why these things were happening. But it wasn't like I was worrying about it. It was like I was really peaceful, and I knew that I would find out why this was happening to me."

"Before you went to the second window something else happened to you."

"Yes."

"And you don't remember what it was."

"No I don't. I don't recall what it was."

"That's too bad."

"No, it's . . . it's sort of like I'm not supposed to remember it. I just get the feeling that I'm not supposed to recall what went on there. It was sort of withheld from my memory."

"When you saw your body the second time, what were your parents doing?"

"My mom was really upset, and my dad was standing around like he didn't know what was going on."

"Where was your spirit body when you felt the paramedics putting the ammonia up your nose?"

"I was looking out the window, and I could see them putting it up my nose. It didn't register with me right away, I didn't feel it then, and I turned away. I just knew they were trying to get me back. I was looking for the people and they weren't there anymore. That's when I began to get the feeling that they loved me, but I had to go back. Then I started to feel the stuff in my nose."

"How did your spirit body feel?"

"It was still very peaceful, but I was sort of scared. Because I didn't really . . . it's hard to think of going from someplace which is so peaceful to . . ."

"Did your spirit body feel as though it were a body?"

"Yes it did."

"And did it feel as if you had arms and legs?"

"Yes, but it was way lighter. It felt so much lighter."

"When you traveled did you walk?"

"Uh, . . . it's sort of like floating, right above . . ."

"Were the people standing on the ground when you saw them?"

"When I first saw them they were."

"Later, were they?"

"When they were standing still they were. But it's like I said, when they moved it's like they were floating."

"When you were in this new world, did you see anything about the new world?"

"Not about anything I can consciously remember. I only just saw the whiteness, and the corridors, and . . . I don't think I was supposed to know about it. That's the way I feel."

"But you saw a building, because you went into it. What did the building look like?"

"I don't know what the outside looked like because when I . . . the brightness was when I was going into the building. I didn't see the outside. I only saw the inside."

"What did the inside look like?"

"Of what I saw, it was just the main room, then the corridor, then the other room."

"You didn't see any drapes, or pictures, or anything of that sort?"

"Only the whiteness. And the people in the brightness—the people seemed to glow with brightness."

"When you got back in your body did you hurt?"

"Yes I did. I started crying because I hurt so bad."

"When you were in your spirit body, did you hurt?"

"No, I didn't feel anything. Anything physical, that is."

"What's your feeling about death?"

"I think that it is really peaceful. But I think that there is a certain time that people are supposed to die."

"Has the experience changed your feeling about religion?"

"If anything it has reinforced it."

"So you believe that there is a God and there is a life after death?"

"Yes."

"Did your experience seem like a dream?"

"At first it did. I didn't really believe that it happened. I had heard people talk about such things before, but I didn't believe them."

"So you thought it was a dream at first?"

"Yes."

"Did it continue to feel like a dream?"

"It became more life-like, you know, as . . . that this was really happening."

"What do you feel about it now—was it real or a dream?"

"It was, definitely, real."

"Do you have any messages for other people?"

"I'd just like to say to other people who haven't had this kind of experience that they should believe those who tell them about an out-of-body experience. It would be really hard to make up something like this."

Maureen Daniels

Paroxysmal Hemicrania

Maureen Daniels and her husband Todd were waiting for Carol and me in their apartment in Murray, Utah, on a lovely spring evening in 1991. They were a young couple, obviously very much in love, with enthusiasm for life and for each other. They had been married since the previous September, and they were expecting a baby in the next September. Maureen was a trim blonde with freckles.

Maureen indicated that she was born in 1960, in a suburb of Boston, to an Irish-Catholic family with six children. She was raised in a large, close-knit family in a small town—she had 36 first cousins living near her. She moved to San Francisco when she was 21, by putting her finger on a map, to become more independent.

She began telling of her experience: "It was August, 1983, in Arlington, Massachusetts, and I was in a situation where I was running after a car that had hit my cousin's car, along Massachusetts Avenue. All of a sudden I got a piercing pain in my head. It was so severe it pretty much put me out, and they got an ambulance."

"You hadn't been hit, or anything, had you?" I asked.

"No. At first they thought it was an aneurism, but it turned out to be chronic paroxysmal hemicrania. It's a nerve disorder of the brain which is in the pain center of the brain. It sends false pain signals. There actually is no pain, but the pain center tells you there is. The only methods they have for treating it are surgery, which I declined because of the risks, or morphine.

"While I was in the hospital, for two weeks, I got regular morphine injections. The nurses felt bad for me, with the pain which I had, and I think they got off schedule with the injections. I was being transferred to Mount Auburn Hospital in Cambridge, and they must have given me tons of morphine to make the drive. My parents and brother and sister were with me during the transfer.

"While I was in the elevator of Mount Auburn to go to my room, they code ninety-nined me. I could hear them announce the code ninety-nine, and I could feel them running with me. After that I don't remember what they did with me. My parents who were with me in the elevator, told me later."

Feelings of Love—A Visit by Deceased Grandparents

"The voices faded from my consciousness. Then there was . . . I wouldn't say there was music, but there was a knowing of . . . of a calm sound. Not unlike waves, or a seashore, which I frequently went to. It was as if there were a beach kind of sound. And there was a feeling of brightness, not necessarily a bright light, but a feeling of being surrounded by love.

"Approaching me from the front, and I recognized them immediately, were my grandparents. My grandfather had died in 1968, and my grandmother had died three months before the incident in May, 1983. We grew up in a duplex with them, and I was very close to them. It really hurt when my grandmother died.

"They approached me. I knew that it was them, but they weren't old as my grandparents had been. They walked very upright, with no arthritis, and with no wrinkles—but I could tell that they were my grandparents. They came, and they didn't physically embrace me, but I felt embraced by them.

"They greeted me, and loved me, and then they started talking between themselves. They weren't arguing, but they were having a conversation. My grandfather was telling my grandmother, Mary, that I couldn't stay. She was very excited that I was there. She couldn't wait to have me with them, and to be with me again.

"My grandfather kept saying: 'No, Mary, she can't stay now. It's not her time to stay.'

"It felt like a long time that they talked back and forth with each other. Grandmother finally said: 'He's right. It's not your time, but we will see you again.'

"The next thing I remember was getting mouth-to-mouth resuscitation. That's about all I remember."

Final Thoughts About Maureen's Experience

"Well, Maureen, that was a choice experience. Let me ask you some questions about it. What did you feel like when you left your body?"

"A knowing. A calmness—it wasn't a fear at all."

"You used the word, music. Why did you use that word?"

"I guess because I like music and it calms me. I felt calm."

"You also used the word love, even before you saw your grandparents. Was that what you felt?"

"Yes, I felt it in the brightness. I didn't actually see a light source, but it was a brightness."

"What did your body feel like when you were out?"

"It felt very light. I don't really remember walking, I remember *being*. I don't remember floating. When I first saw them they were walking, and I saw them on a surface. I was on the same plane with them."

"What kind of clothes were your grandparents wearing?"

"They had on clothes that I remember them wearing in life. My grandmother was in a housecoat type of dress, and my grandfather was in his straight-legged pants with cuffs."

"Did you want to come back?"

"I felt very calm and happy there. I went along with what they said. I was happy to see my grandmother and, I think, I would have been happy to stay with her. I felt that happiness."

"Did you have a feeling for why it was you should come back?"

"Only that they told me it wasn't meant to be at that time. They told me it was all right to come back, and that they would see me later when this happened again."

"So was it their decision, or your decision to come back?"

"They told me, and then I agreed."

"You said there was a feeling of knowing. What did you mean by that?"

"I don't want to say all knowing, but . . . but it was a feeling of knowing what was going on. I really didn't question what was going on. I had a feeling that it was right, that this was a very normal happening."

"Were you glad to get back?"

"Yes, I felt this joy. I couldn't wait to talk to my mother, her sisters, and her brother."

"Did you feel pain when you got back?"

"Not immediately. But then later the pain came back to my head."

"Did you tell the story, immediately, to your parents and your family, and did they believe you?"

"Yes."

"Did it feel like a real experience, or was it more like a dream or a hallucination?"

"I questioned it, but it felt too real to be a dream or a hallucination. It was very real. It was more real than this life. I would say that it was something which there was no question about—there was no question that this took place and happened."

"Has the experience affected your religious, or other feelings?"

"There is no fear . . . I can't really say that I was ever fearful of death, and I won't say that I'm looking forward to it. I have a lot to do here. But when it does come, I know that my grandparents are there waiting for me."

"What is it that you think you have to do?"

"Have my baby. I would have thirteen of them if I could." Maureen laughed as she thought of the prospects for future children. Then she commented: "I feel I have a lot to accomplish here—with a family—and to leave behind."

"Do you believe in a life after death and in a God?"

"Both. I believe in God and that there is a life after death."

"Do you have any messages to leave for others?"

"That there is a lot of beauty out there. I think each of us have our own beauty, and I believe that we each experience our own beauty after death."

"You say there is a lot of beauty out there and after death. Did you see anything, in your experience, to lead you to believe that that was true?"

"I didn't see anything, but I felt it. I think it's that all knowing feeling that I had."

"When you saw your grandparents, did you see anything of the environment they were in?"

"It was just this bright . . . but I felt as though they had come from an environment . . . I wouldn't say that this was a way station, or whatever, but I felt it was something so that I wasn't put into a situation immediately. It seemed that we were in a place which was somewhat of a way station."

Shirley James

A Helping Person

Shirley James came to our house in late April, 1991, and Carol and I greeted her. Shirley was a petite lady who smiled anxiously as she took her place next to me on the couch. She later said that she was emotionally moved as she recounted her story—she had never told anyone about her experience before.

Shirley was born in Salt Lake City in 1934 and was raised here. She had six of her own children which she had raised, largely by herself, and then she helped raise other children. Her parents were LDS, and she was brought up in that church, but she had not been active for a number of years.

Shirley began her story: "My first husband died when we had only been married for two years. He drowned in Utah Lake in 1952, when my first child was eight months old. Then I remarried and had five more children.

"At one period of my life I was living in Idaho. My sister-in-law became ill with cancer, and at the same time my other sister-in-law, my brother's wife, became ill with a heart problem. They both struggled for about five years with their illnesses.

"About the last nine months of my husband's sister's life I took care of her. She said she didn't want anyone else to take care of her. Even during her last days in the hospital she wouldn't let the nurses touch her. They had to get me to come, because she said I didn't hurt her. She said God had blessed my hands so that I wouldn't hurt her.

"She passed away and we brought her to Salt Lake for the funeral. She asked that I dress her and fix her hair, so I did. The day that we buried her, when we got home from the funeral, the telephone rang. It was my brother's wife's mother looking for my brother. She said that his wife had just passed on.

"I felt terrible and got hysterical. We stayed in Salt Lake, because I was asked to dress and take care of my brother's wife. I had been under a lot of stress during the previous months taking care of my husband's sister, as well as taking care of my six children. During that period I found out that my husband had been stepping out with another woman.

"When I got back to Idaho I went into a real deep depression; I began to think about suicide. I didn't know how I could keep living, and how I could keep care of my children. I knew my husband was going to leave me."

Emotional Trauma and a Visit by Deceased Relatives

"I lay down on the couch—I was just lying there thinking about dying. I felt that I couldn't go on. Then a light, and I can't say it was a bright light, it was an indescribable light, appeared in the room. It just lit up.

"I was watching the light when . . . I can't say they floated, they appeared—my husband who had died, my two sisters-in-law, and my grandfather and grandmother who had passed on."

"Did you know your grandfather and grandmother?" I asked.

"Oh, I knew everybody. My grandfather and grandmother didn't pass away until I was in my twenties, and I was close to them. I lived with them as a child for awhile.

"Each of these people came toward me and then passed me. As this was happening, I felt overwhelmed by love. I was not frightened. I felt warm.

They didn't speak to me; it was like telepathy. It came from their heads to my head. And they each said: 'It'll be okay.'

"Then they just disappeared. But I was still overwhelmed with love—for days. It didn't go away, the feeling that I had no worries. Every worry had been lifted from me. I didn't care what my husband was doing. I didn't feel sorry for myself anymore, and I felt a great, great, great love for my children. I always loved my children, but this was some kind of a . . . I can't explain it.

"Each spirit that appeared before me during this episode was absolutely glowing with health. Their skin—they looked happy, and there were no differences in age. Although my husband was only twenty years old when he died, and my grandparents were in their seventies, there didn't seem to be an age difference between them.

"My grandparents were dressed in their temple clothes, in white. My sister-in-law, who was my brother's wife, was in her temple clothes. And I guess it was temple clothes my husband was wearing. Their clothes were all very white robes.

Additional Analysis of Shirley's Experience

Shirley paused and looked emotionally drained. She rested for a moment, and then I asked her a few questions:

"Now when you lay down on the couch and first saw these people, were . . . ?"

"I was not asleep. I was not asleep. I was crying and I felt miserable."

"And when you saw the people you felt good?"

"I felt warmth and love. I was totally engulfed in love."

"Did you see the brightness first or . . . ?"

"I saw the light first, then each one. The ones in back were kind of faded, then as they appeared they became more distinct. Then each one just went away."

"Did they seem happy to see you?"

"Very much so. Their love told me that."

"And their communication was not vocal?"

"No. Their mouths didn't move. Thoughts came from their mind to my mind just as if they had said it. I knew exactly what they had communicated."

"What sort of things did they say?"

"They only said one thing: 'Everything will be all right.' There was no conversation. That's all they said."

"Did the incident take very long?"

"I don't think so, but it was hard to judge time."

"When they were through did the light go away?"

"Yes. I guess it went with them."

"And when they disappeared you still felt good?"

"I had no worries. I did not think of suicide. All I could feel was the love and the astonishment of the whole experience. I had a hard time believing what had happened to me. The feeling of love and warmth lasted for days, even weeks."

"Have you told others of this experience?"

"No."

"Have you read other materials, such as Raymond Moody's books on near-death experiences?"

"I've read parts of some of the books; that's all."

Chapter Sixteen

On Trial For Their Lives

Kathleen Pratt Martinez

A Birth Emergency

Kathleen Pratt Martinez met Carol and me at our home in late April, 1991. She seemed to have a deep understanding of her ancestral roots. Parley P. Pratt, an early Apostle in The Church of Jesus Christ of Latter-day Saints, was her maternal great-great-grandfather.

Kathleen said that she was born in Provo, Utah, in 1946, and she grew up primarily in Salt Lake City. She was raised as a member of the LDS Church, and she had two older brothers. At the time of our interview she was divorced and had three children, two girls and a boy. She was currently attending Phillips Junior College to become a paralegal.

She began her story: "My oldest daughter, whom I had when I was twenty-one, was born out of wedlock. When I was pregnant with her, my grandmother, Mary Stark Pratt, argued that I should have the baby and not have the fetus aborted, nor should I give the baby up for adoption. I loved my grandmother deeply, and I listened to her. At the time that we talked she had cancer; she died three months before my baby was born.

"During the birth of my daughter, when I was in labor, I didn't dilate properly, and they took me into x-ray to see what the problem was. In x-ray they found that they would have to perform surgery, because the baby was improperly placed for delivery. So they put me under anesthesia to do the surgical procedure; that's when I had the experience."

Deceased Relatives Conduct a Trial

"I first became aware of an immense dark area. Lining the left and right sides of the dark area were personages in white clothing. I couldn't distinguish any particular faces, but I realized, from a sense that I had, that they were members of my family who had died.

"At the end of this dark area, in the distance, was a throne-type, high-backed chair, with a personage in it. Again, I couldn't distinguish a face, but I felt that this personage had some higher power in the spiritual realm. The people seemed to be the judge and the jury for my situation.

"At the left side of me stood my grandfather, Rey L. Pratt, whom I never knew in this life, and my grandmother, Mary Stark Pratt, his wife, who had passed away three months previously. I could also see my spirit, and I looked somewhat different from what I did on earth. I had long hair and darker-complexioned skin than I normally did, and my stature was more petite than here.

"Through thought transference I knew that I was on trial for my life. The trial was to determine whether or not I would be allowed to continue in this life—based upon whether I would do the things I was supposed to do, and cease transgressing.

"My grandfather felt that I probably would not be able to continue. Evidently there was some mission I was supposed to perform. He felt that they might have to select someone else, because I wouldn't be able to carry it out. I apparently was not a strong enough character to follow through with whatever I was supposed to do.

"My grandmother took my defense and said that she thought that I would, and she said I should be given the chance to prove that I could do this. I, of course, didn't understand fully what they were talking about, except that I wanted to go on living. I told them that I had planned to continue with my schooling. I mentioned what I wanted to study, and I said that I would live my life uprightly from this point on. I asked them to give me another chance.

"So, it was decided—my grandfather looked at me, and at this other person in the chair, and they kind of viewed each other—and it was unanimously decided among them, through thought transference, that I would be given this chance.

"I turned to my right, and I saw this spirit that was going to be my child. The spirit, a male, appeared to be a very old person; in chronological terms he looked to be about ninety, with piercing eyes. He seemed to be very knowledgeable, very intelligent. He said nothing, he looked at me, and we both turned—and I saw this shaft of light. I went down the shaft of light, almost instantaneously, and my spirit seemed to enter my body through the forehead.

"The next thing I remember was hearing the doctors say: 'She's coming around. I didn't think she was going to make it. Let's have her deliver this baby, now.' When the baby came it was a girl.

"At the time it was confusing to me because, based upon my experience, I thought I was going to have a boy. It wasn't until some years later that I got my boy. That was the end of the experience."

Questions and Responses

"Let me ask you a few questions, Kathy. You say that the first thing you became conscious of was the darkness, and of people on either side?"

"Yes, it was not like a room, or anything, it was like a void. There wasn't anything around that I could distinguish, it was like space, dark space. The only things distinguishable were the people on either side of me—away from me though, not close to me, kind of forward from me—and then beyond that, the throne-type chair with the personage in it."

"When you first went out you say that you recognized your spirit body. How did you recognize it?"

"I just knew. It was as if I were watching a picture, except that it was me in the picture. It was almost like I could see everything, yet I was a part of it at the same time."

"Did your spirit body appear in human form?"

"Yes—female."

"How were you dressed?"

"I remember looking at myself from behind and seeing my bare shoulders and long hair. I had on a light-weight skirt, and I was bare footed. It seemed that my grandparents had on street apparel. Their clothing was similar to what we wear now rather than the white that the others had on."

"You mentioned the 'others.' Who were they?"

"They seemed to be the spirits of my family. I perceived that my Aunt Gladys was there, she was S. Dilworth Young's first wife, and she had died a few years before this incident. I perceived that she was there, yet I didn't see her; I sensed her presence. And I sensed that the other personages were family members, but I couldn't distinguish exactly who they were."

"Did you notice any light, or something of that sort?"

"There was light, because I could see the people. Things were illuminated, but they weren't brilliant. It was as if I had come into a dark room and someone had turned on a light, enough to illuminate it."

"How did your spirit body feel when you were there?"

"I didn't feel anything except a fear of not being able to come back. A fear of dying."

"Did you feel any pain?"

"No, there was no pain. I was just intensely involved in the actions that were going on."

"The individual who sat in the throne-type chair—did you have a sense of who that was?"

"No. I couldn't see his face. I just knew that it was someone of great importance, and it was someone who had the power to say yes or no when it came to my living or dying."

"What kinds of issues were raised in the discussion which ensued in their minds?"

"The primary issue, I think, was the concern as to my moral character. It was a concern about whether or not I was going to be able to put my life back together. As I mentioned before, my daughter was born out of wedlock.

"The mission that I was to have, evidently, required that I have a sufficiently good moral character to be able to carry it out. I was supposed to refrain from making these kinds of mistakes, to stay close to the doctrine of the church, and to try and live an exemplary life."

"Did you have a feeling for what your mission was?"

"I didn't. I was completely lost. It wasn't until I had my son that it became clear to me."

"When you came back, you felt that the tribunal had made the decision for you to come back, and it wasn't your decision?"

"Yes."

"But you wanted to come back?"

"Yes, definitely. I was literally fighting for my life. I wanted to prove that I could do what I was expected to do—without really knowing what it was. I wanted to live a better life and to do better by myself and by my child. I promised that I would do what was right. I was told if I did not that I and my child would die."

"Did you feel that the place you were in was a nice place, or a bad place?"

"It was indifferent. It didn't have a spiritual feeling either way."

"Do you remember anything about traveling to and from this place, or were you just all of a sudden there?"

"I was all of a sudden there, but in coming back I remember coming down the light. It was a shaft of light, straight like a laser beam, but wider. It almost looked like a cloud, except it was very white and brilliant."

Purpose of Her Return—A Vision

"You mentioned that, later, you understood what your mission was to be. Can you explain that?"

"When my youngest child, my son, was six weeks old, I had what I consider a personal revelation about him. Just before I woke up from a night's sleep, in a vision, or whatever, I found myself entering an old fashioned temple, or tabernacle, similar to what might have existed in biblical times. There were cloth drapes, supported by poles, which formed the walls.

"In the vision, my husband and I, and I was carrying my son, walked through a doorway. We were in modern-day clothes, and we were greeted by a man. The drapes covering the walls were of a muslin-type cloth, but in the corner there was some striped, Hebrew-type of material. It had a different weaving and was colored deep crimson and yellow with defined stripes. The floor had Persian, not elaborate, but functional, types of rugs.

"The man who approached us was a very old man with a long white beard. He had a muslin-type covering on his head, with a band around it, similar to pictures of biblical shepherds. He had on a white robe, but over that white robe he had on another robe with the striped material.

"From the main room, the old man led us to another room which had an . . . not an altar, but more a high mantle type thing. More like a table—it was wide. It was draped with a plain, light-colored cloth.

"The room itself was illuminated with a light that I had never seen before. It was a goldish sort of color. But it was so bright that it was . . . it was awe inspiring. It was like something from another world. It was soft, yet it was so illuminating. I have a hard time describing it, because I have never seen anything like it in this world. The closest thing I can come to it is something like a sunset—but that wasn't it either.

"The old man took the baby from me, laid him down on the table, and he undressed my boy. He started checking him like a physician would.

"I questioned what he was doing with my baby. He said: 'I need to make sure that the baby is perfect, because the mission for which he has been selected will require that he be perfect.'

"I asked what mission that was, and he responded: 'All I can tell you is that he is to take the place of a very wise old man.'

"While I was talking to him, my son, even though he was just a baby, had crawled off the table. He had climbed up into a font. The font was made of some type of stone with a thick, wide rim around it, and it was on a pedestal.

It was fairly deep, but not real deep. It had liquid in it which wasn't water. The liquid appeared to be some type of oil.

"My son started swimming in the font, and the man looked at him. Then he said: 'Look how unafraid he is. For his mission he needs to have no fear.' Then the vision ended.

"I never knew who the old man was until . . . you're going to think I am crazy. I was visiting at Temple Square and, . . . and it came to me that this man was Father Abraham. It also came to me that my trial was about whether or not I could properly raise the boy for his spiritual mission."

"How old is your boy now, and is he spiritually inclined?"

"He's nine years old, and he's very spiritual. When he was only two or two-and-one-half years old, I would read the scriptures to him, and he would sit and listen. He is quite artistic, and he is very loving."

"When you had this vision, did it seem like a dream?"

"No, it seemed like it was real. It was just before I woke up."

Final Thoughts About Kathleen's Experience

"Are you still puzzled about the incident where you returned from your spiritual trial with the old male spirit?"

"Yes. I don't understand why I had a girl baby when the spirit was a man. I had the impression that this male spirit was to be my child. I also got the impression that he didn't have to come if he didn't choose to."

"You said the girl was born out of wedlock?"

"Yes."

"And you were given a new chance to demonstrate that you would live a more circumspect life?"

"Yes, that's true. I was supposed to prove myself."

"Could it be that the old male spirit was to be your son—only later—after you had married and lived closer to the teachings of the church?"

"But it seemed that he was coming down with me then, when I went to the shaft of light. Why was that?"

"Perhaps he was allowed to view the birth of your daughter. He may have accompanied you to earth in order to watch you for awhile."

"I had never thought of that before. It makes sense; it would sure explain much of what has baffled me about the incident."

"Are there any messages you would like to leave to people who might read this?"

"My message would be to Latter-day Saints, since that's my religious persuasion. No matter how much hypocrisy may seem to exist with individuals, or what we think they do wrong, *never* fall away from the doctrine. If you deviate it will take you years to recover—to put your life where it should be. It took me years to get back to where I should be, even after the experience with my daughter. The problem was that I was jeopardizing my whole future, my eternal future."

"So you believe in a life after death?"

"Oh, definitely. My feeling is not that death starts a new life, but rather that it is a continuation of this life—but in a different order. And in a more perfected state than we are living now."

Jean

Illness; Then a World of Knowledge

Jean came to our home in June, 1991. She was a cheerful, dark-haired lady and she seemed anxious to tell us her story. She explained that, after being born in Utah in 1946, she had been raised as a Mormon. She began her story:

"In 1986, I was a student at Weber State College, and my daughter brought a little girl she had been baby-sitting home. The girl had hepatitis, and I caught it immediately. On top of that, I'm diabetic, and I became extremely ill. I couldn't even get out of bed.

"One day I was lying in bed, terribly sick, and . . . and I know this wasn't a dream—it wasn't like other dreams. It was more than a dream. It's hard to explain exactly what it was, but I suddenly found myself in this beautiful patio garden area. There were a group of buildings around, and the buildings were—I just knew they were libraries. They were educational buildings.

"The garden areas were so gorgeous. I had never seen such a well kept-garden. And the colors of the flowers were so vivid. I can remember exactly, and even the cement was pure white. The sidewalks, and the benches, and the patios were beautiful. There were people all over the place, and I just stood there in the middle of the garden looking around.

"As I looked, groups of children came running across the lawn with a teacher. There were other people walking around, and sitting on the benches, and leaning against the trees; they were all reading books and studying.

"I got so excited, because I recognized the buildings as 'The Libraries.' That's what I called them: 'The Libraries.' I knew that every single building was a different subject. All the knowledge in the universe was stored in those libraries. I was excited because I wanted to go and study and read everything. Since I had just been in college it made it all the more exciting; to be where all that knowledge was available.

"I was really surprised to see groups of children there. Another thing that surprised me was that everybody I saw was dressed in a different time period. They were dressed, I guess, in the time period that they had lived on earth.

"While I was standing there looking around, a group of men in dark suits, white shirts, and ties—they looked like Mormon Priesthood holders—came up to me and told me to follow them. I followed them into one of the buildings. It was beautiful inside, with mahogany, and cherry wood, and . . . just a beautiful interior."

A Courtroom and a Trial

"We walked up a winding staircase which was crowded with people. At the top of the staircase we entered a room that was similar to a courtroom, or a high-council room. In the center of the room there was a large elongated oval table with chairs all around it. In the corner there was a fenced off area with a beautifully engraved fence. There was a platform behind the fence in a sort of closed circle. I was asked to stand there.

"These men then went and sat around the table. As they sat there they began discussing whether or not I should be allowed to stay or to go back. Some of them were for me staying, and others were saying that I had to go back. The ones saying that I had to return were very determined. The ones who said I could stay, they just sort of said it was okay for me to stay; they weren't as adamant as the others.

"They started asking me questions. One of the questions was: 'Is there anyone to take care of your children if you stay?' I told them that there wasn't anyone else. They then agreed, unanimously, that I had to return, and they told me so.

"I didn't want to return. I wanted to stay and read those books in the library. I was so excited about the library, and I really wanted to stay and to study. They reiterated that I had to go back.

"They all gathered around me in a circle, put their hands on my head, and said a prayer . . . I guess. Anyway, I felt a downward pulling sensation. Then I was in my own bed.

"As soon as I woke up I knew I had to get to the doctor. I called him immediately and he put me in the hospital."

Questions and Responses

"Okay, Jean, let me ask you a few questions. When you first became aware that you were in a different place, did you have a feeling of where it was?"

"Yes. There wasn't any fear involved. It was peaceful, and I knew exactly what those buildings were. I knew I was in a garden area in the spirit world. I knew what it was and what the purposes of the buildings were—I recognized them.

"Everything was so calm and quiet. There were so many people around, yet there was no conflict. Everyone was happy and busy—everyone was so busy. And I felt at peace and excited."

"Those almost sound like contradictions, to be at peace, yet excited."

"I was excited because I wanted to read those books. I can't portray to you how excited I was thinking about all the knowledge that was stored in those libraries. I had this great desire to study and learn everything I could. In fact, I still have that desire."

"You mentioned the beautiful scenery. Was it similar to what we have here?"

"Yes, there were trees, beautiful trees, and flowers, and shrubs, but . . . but everything was enhanced. The colors were so much brighter. And everything was perfect. There wasn't a single weed in the place."

"You said that you didn't want to return to this earth. Why did you want to stay?"

"Because I was so excited about the libraries and about getting to study there."

"When it was decided that you were to come back, did you agree with that decision?"

"No. I went yelling!"

"Is that right?"

"Yes. When they had their hands on my heads and when there was the downward pulling—the whole time, I was yelling that I wanted to stay."

"So it was not your choice to come back?"

"No, it was not."

"Yet, you recognized that if you didn't come back there would be no one to care for your children?"

"That's right. There would be no one to take care of them nor to raise them as I knew they should be raised. Also, if I didn't return, they wouldn't have the love that I could give them."

"Under those circumstances, it appears that you at least partially agreed that you should come back."

"Yes. I guess so—but I left yelling."

Recognition of People—Other Experiences

"Is there anything else about the experience that you remember?"

"Well this sounds silly, so I wasn't going to say it. But walking up the staircase I recognized one person."

"Who was that?"

"Benjamin Franklin. I recognized him from his pictures. As I passed him I thought: *Wow! But where else would he be? What more natural place for such a man than the libraries where all the knowledge was.*"

"Did you recognize anyone else?"

"There was one General Authority."

"That's a General Authority from the LDS Church?"

"Yes. I don't remember his name. He was going down the stairs while I was going up."

"Did you have any feeling of who the people were who conducted the trial?"

"No. I knew they were Authorities, and I knew they were in charge of making the decision, but that's all."

"You didn't feel that they were your relatives?"

"No. But I had some other experiences in which relatives were involved."

"All right, why don't you tell me about them."

"My husband died when he was relatively young, and I was pregnant with my third child. I was three months along, and I was really sick with morning sickness and other problems. It was the night before the funeral, I was so sick, and I couldn't sleep. I was throwing up, non-stop, and I was sitting on the edge of my bed thinking that if I didn't get some sleep I wouldn't be able to make it to the funeral.

"At that moment, I was wide awake, and I became aware of two people standing in the corner of my room. One was my husband. The other was a personage, a male, wearing a long white robe. I couldn't see the face of this personage—I wasn't allowed to see his face. They were about two feet off the ground, and they were standing there looking at me.

"My husband turned to him and said: 'Does she have to suffer like that?' The personage in the robe raised his right arm to the square. Then they disappeared and I lay down. The next thing I knew it was morning and I felt wonderful."

"How did your husband look?"

"He was dressed in the dark suit that he was buried in. He looked like he always did, but healthy."

"Was there any light associated with either individual?"

"Yes, around the messenger there was light; that's why I couldn't see his face. It was a bright glow."

"That was an interesting experience. Is there anything else?"

"Well, there was another incident."

"What sort of incident?"

"It was a different kind of experience. I'm not sure you would be interested in it."

"Tell us about it."

"In the 1980s my youngest sister was called to go on a mission for the LDS Church to Bolivia, and she asked me to give the main talk at her farewell. I was excited about it; I'm a speech and drama teacher, and I was sure I could do a good job.

"Her farewell was at her ward in Salt Lake City, and I was sitting on the stand waiting for the Sacrament Meeting to start. As I sat there I became aware of a whole group of people standing in the back of the chapel. They were all dressed in temple clothes.

"As I looked at the people, all of whom had previously died, I saw my father, my grandparents, and my aunts and uncles. My husband was not there. While I watched them my father came forward. He told me that he was pleased with the talk I was going to give.

"Several months later I wrote my sister and told her what I had seen. She wrote back and thanked me for telling her. She said that for months prior to her mission she had prayed and invited each of these deceased relatives to be at her missionary farewell."

Chapter Seventeen

A Life's Review Midst the Stars

John Stirling

A Fascinating Man

I first met John Stirling on a beautiful spring day in 1991, up Emigration Canyon, northeast of Salt Lake City. Fresh greenery was evident throughout the canyon, and the sky was a cobalt blue with puffy white cumulus clouds drifting across the heavens. It was a good day to talk about eternity.

John's voice was cheerful and full of the joy of life over the telephone, but I wasn't prepared for the great bear of a man who greeted me that day. I had pulled into his place, which had many automobiles in various stages of disrepair in front, and I walked to a shop area with the sounds of car repair machinery emanating from within. I knocked timidly on the door, and a voice responded.

A burly man with long hair, a beard, and dirt spread over him from the work he had been doing, greeted me. His smiling eyes repudiated his gruff appearance. As John's interview proceeded, and as John's emotions became evident, I concluded that he wasn't the gruff individual that he appeared to be—he was a marshmallow with a great love for people.

John invited me to sit on a chair, and he sat adjacent to me; we began our conversation sitting in the great outdoors of the Wasatch Mountains. John told me he was born in 1953 in Salt Lake City, where he was raised in a family consisting of his father, his mother, and three older sisters. He went to high school in Salt Lake City, and he went to college for three terms to study art. He had traveled extensively.

A Personal Crisis and a Motorcycle Accident

John began: "In September, 1978 my wife left me and took my son. She wouldn't let me see him for quite a long time, many months, and I was pretty miserable. Through the whole thing I didn't want a divorce, I wanted to get back together with her, but she didn't want to get back with me. She was angry, inside, and couldn't pinpoint reasons for it. At the time my son was two years old.

"I was having a rough go of life in general. I was tired of it, pretty sick of living. I bought a motorcycle, a Yamaha 650, to have something to do at nights when I was bored or lonely; because I don't watch TV. I used to drive through the canyons for diversion, to think about things and to relax.

"One Friday, during the day, I had a really strange feeling. I called everyone I knew that was close to me. I couldn't explain my conversations with them, but during each conversation I told them I was going somewhere. I didn't know where, and they would ask me where I was going. I said I didn't know—I told them I might go to Denver. I also told them that I might not talk to them again for a long time.

"I was really agitated and nervous all day. I called my mother and told her that I didn't know where I was going, but I thought I would be leaving on a trip somewhere. I said I would talk to her when I knew where I was going. As the day went on I had mood swings, and I was filled with a lot of confusion. I tried to figure out where I was going.

"A friend came over to visit and we talked for awhile. I thought, with him there, I would be able to determine where I was going—so I could call the airport and book a flight—if I was flying. We ended up getting on my motorcycle and going for a ride up to the cafe in Emigration Canyon.

"We spent an hour-and-a-half or so at the cafe; we had some beer, and we left and began coming down the canyon. I used to race motorcycles, so I knew pretty well what they would do under different circumstances. As we came down the canyon, we hit a washout in the road, where the water had washed out under the road, and there was a bump.

"With the combined weight of my friend and myself, and at the speed we were traveling, the bump bounced the motorcycle off the road and into the gravel. It was about eleven-thirty at night, and as I fought for control in the dark I considered heading the motorcycle up the mountain instead of staying in the gravel. I opted to do that, to go up the mountain, so that gravity would slow us down.

"We headed up the mountain a short distance, then I saw that the mountain had been discontinued where road work had been performed. I yelled at my friend, that he had to get off. We were still going fast—about fifty-five, and he wouldn't get off. I leaned back and knocked him off.

"I then hit the rock, where it had been blown away, and I thought to myself: *Well this is it.* The right side of my body crashed into the rock where it had been, kind of, curved. The bike rolled over on top of me and stuck the rear view mirror on the top of my head—I didn't have a helmet on. Then the bike continued to tumble and ended up about two-hundred-and-fifty feet away."

Out-of-Body in the Stars

"I remember the crash and the bike tumbling, then I remember lying there, for just a split second, and thinking: *Well this is it, I'm leaving.* I turned around and looked, and I saw a body that seemed familiar. It looked like me, but I had no emotional involvement with the body laying there.

"I then felt great relief and joy—that I was leaving, and that I didn't have to endure, any more, the pain of the divorce, or the pain of missing my child. So I immediately, without any further thinking about it, took off, because it was what I had been wishing would happen.

"I could feel an ability in my spirit body to move at great speed, and I wanted to get where I was going as quickly as possible. I was going to a place that I *knew.* It was the place that I had *come* from. I wanted to get there as quickly as possible.

"I started traveling fairly slowly, in real time, when I first started. Then, as I got farther away from earth I traveled much faster. The stars started to look like the stars in 'Star Wars,' with a long trail, because of my speed.

"A voice came to me, as I was traveling at that high rate of speed, and . . . and I was so peaceful and comfortable. All the emotional pain that I had been feeling was gone. I looked at my hand, and I saw the shape of a hand, but . . . but it had an aura around it. It wasn't the same hand as an earthly hand. There was an energy field that defined it.

"And the voice . . . the voice asked me if I was done. And I knew the voice and it was . . ." John had difficulty continuing as he wiped away the tears. "It was a comfortable voice—a voice full of love.

"I said: 'Yes, I'm done. I don't want to go back there. I don't ever want to go back there.' The voice asked me a second time: 'Are you done?' And I said: 'Yes, I'm done. I don't want to go back.' The voice asked me a third time if I was done, and again I said that I was.

"Then the voice said: 'Well, let's look at your life.' And I saw . . . I saw my life flashed before my eyes. Everything from when I was a child up to the present time. And every emotion that I had during my life, when I saw the scene, I felt the same emotion. I could feel the reasons that I did things as I saw the scenes unfold.

"I felt very comfortable with my life as I looked at it. It was all in color and three dimensional, and it flashed in a circle as if it were a deck of cards. I felt very comfortable that I would not have to come back to earth.

"The review continued until it came to the previous Friday, when I had had my son over, on Friday night. And it . . . the review traveled all the way up to that time.

"The scene, you can call it a card that came up for me to see, or, the vision that came to my view, it . . . my eyes locked onto that night. And the life review stopped. When that Friday scene first flashed up it looked as if it were going to go by, but when my eyes locked on it, then I knew I had to come back.

"So I . . . I said yes I would come back. Because I knew I had to raise my son as best I could. There was no further contact with the voice after I said I would return. I came back to my body so much faster than when I left. It was almost instantaneous. I can remember reversing in space and then waking up in my body."

Return

"The first thought that came to me when I was back in my body was that I had to find Richard, my friend who was on the motorcycle with me. So I stood up and started screaming for him. He answered and came down. When he saw me his face showed fear. I asked him to show me where he was hurt. He had scraped his elbow and his shin a little bit.

"I told him I would go get some help from one of the houses in the canyon. He told me to stay put and he would go get the help. I told him that he should stay, since he was hurt, and I raised my hand to brush away what I thought was sweat from my eyes. I saw that the sweat was actually blood—then I looked closer at my arm. My hand was at a right angle to it.

"At that point I told him: 'Well, okay, I guess I'm hurt worse than you. You go get some help.' As he left, and I waited, I looked a little closer at myself. I saw that both of my feet were folded underneath at the ankles—I was walking on my ankles. I didn't feel any pain at all. I had the same peace with me, that everything would be okay, as I'd had when I first left my body.

"A girl came up, dressed in white, in a Volkswagen. She said that she had just gotten off from work, and she was a nurse. She told me to sit on her car. So that's what I did while I waited for Richard to come back with help.

"The girl and I talked together. I don't remember what she said, very much, but suddenly my friend was there. He said that he had called the ambulance, and they were on the way. And . . . and I don't know what happened to the girl in white who came in the Volkswagen. I looked for her for a long time after that, and I asked people in the canyon if they had ever known her. No one knew anything about her. She told me that she lived in the canyon.

"That's pretty much what happened."

Further Analysis of John's Experience

"That was a remarkable experience, John. Let me ask you a few questions. When you went out of your body, did you see any light or anything of that sort?"

"Not that I can recall. At that point my main concern was getting out of here as quickly as possible. I was familiar with where I was, and . . ."

"So you had a feeling that you had been there before?"

"Oh, I knew. Yes, I knew—there was no doubt in my mind. And I wanted to get out of here as quickly as possible."

"You say you knew where you were. Did you have a feeling of knowing anything else?"

"I had an internal knowledge of where I was going."

"Did you have knowledge of other things?"

"Yes. I had an expanded consciousness. It wasn't like an earthly booktype knowledge. It was a consciousness that was larger, more spiritual."

"When you heard the voice, did you see anybody; or was it just a feeling of a presence?"

"I didn't see anyone."

"You felt, though, that you knew the individual?"

"Oh, yes."

"Do you know who it was, now?"

"Well, I would say it was Jesus Christ."

"You didn't have a feeling, then, that that was the case—or did you feel, then, that it was Christ?"

"Yes, I did."

"When you communicated with him, was it vocal communication?"

"It was not a verbal type of communication. It was a communication within. There's something when you are there. . . . When you are on earth you may have all sorts of thoughts running through your mind, or all sorts of confusion in your mind, all at the same time. There, you don't feel that way. You are more at peace, and you are more sensory. Communication was within me and was given back the same way, without the spoken word."

The Life's Review

"The life's review came as a shock. When I heard the voice say: 'Well, let's see your life,' I didn't know how it would happen. It was totally unexpected, and it was right there in my view. It was as if both the voice and I were viewing it—and both of us could feel it as well as visually see it."

"Was there judgment in the voice?"

"Not at all. It was the same feeling you would get in a heart-to-heart conversation with a loving father about anything that concerned you. Not that judgment would be involved, but that you would both view the circumstances, see the way things were, and go on from there."

"So it was a teaching experience more than a judgmental experience?"

"It wasn't judgmental. I didn't know that I was coming back so I didn't realize, at the time, that it was a teaching experience."

"You mentioned that when you saw different events from your life you could also feel the emotions associated with those events. Did you understand that the voice also felt those emotions?"

"I felt, inside, that we both felt the emotions. As I recall, the life review started when I was two or three years old. The review, starting from that time, showed all the daily events, all the people involved, as I lived through the events. There were the funny times, the sad times, and my concerns at the time—for my age.

"So that when I was five, ten, or fifteen years old, for the wisdom I had at that age, I felt the same kind of emotions as I had when I was that age. I also knew where I was at, spiritually, for that given age. That's one of the reasons I felt comfortable with my life's review. Because I felt as if I really had tried as hard as I could, in accordance with what I knew at that age."

"Some people who have had this type of life's review indicated that they also felt, when they had done something good for someone, or when they had hurt someone, the emotions of that individual. Did you feel anything like that?"

"Yes. When I was younger I was a meek and timid kid, and I didn't do many things that would create a flash-back for me—adverse things that I would feel. My father died when I was a teenager, though, and I got kind of bitter and angry. Then I did do some things to hurt other people. I saw those events and felt the effect on the people. I also felt, at the time, my own bitterness."

"When you did something to help someone did you feel their response to that as well?"

"Yes. I could feel the joy and the happiness as well as the pain, depending upon the circumstances."

"When your father died, did you feel the pain again?"

"Yes. I felt the pain again, but it was a comfortable pain this time. It wasn't the hollow loss that it was the first time."

"Why was it more comfortable?"

"Because I was in eternity—and I knew it. And I knew that my father was there also."

"But you didn't see your father, did you?"

"No. After the experience, and I've thought much about it, I wondered why I was stopped midway to my destination. The conclusion that I came to is that if I had been allowed to go all the way, to be in the presence of the Savior, or to be greeted by my father, I would not have returned. I know that would have been true."

"As you saw the life's review unfold, did it seem as if it took a long time?"

"Not at all."

"But there were 25 years which you went through. That's a lot of years. How could you see that in such a short time?"

"Yes, it was a lot of years. But it just . . . it's hard to describe. It unfolded, it was large, it was three-dimensional, it was right in my view, I didn't have to turn my head or anything, and it just exploded right there. It was as if it were the ultimate movie—three dimensional, with feeling and color."

"All-in-all, though, you felt it was a comfortable experience?"

"Oh yes. I had worried much of my life about things that I did, that I might be doing things that would give me a failing grade in life. All the little things that I did wrong. In viewing my life, though, it was different than that viewpoint."

Other Thoughts

"You say that you saw an aura around your hand when you looked at it. Was that aura all over your body as far as you could tell?"

"Yes."

"How did your spirit body feel when you were out of your physical body?"

"Peaceful, calm, real, existing . . . ."

"Okay, so it didn't feel like a dream?"

"No."

"Did it feel as real as any experience in this life?"

"Yes, even more real."

"Has the experience changed your feelings about death?"

"It has changed my feelings about life more than it has about death."

"In what way?"

"It's the way I feel about people, now, and life in general—that we are all part of the same plan. We are all part of the same program; the greatest value, for any of us, is to try and help another person in their situation. We shouldn't interfere with others negatively, nor should we hurt another person. We should not, in any way, detract from a life. Rather we should add to other people's lives."

"When you were told that you had to come back, you really didn't want to, I take it?"

"I wasn't told to come back. I saw my son come up in the life's review and I knew, when my eyes locked on him, that I had to come back. And I said I would come back. I wasn't told to—I knew I had to."

"So it was your choice to come back, not somebody else's?"

"Oh yes. I saw him and knew I had to come back. I knew that I wasn't done with this life."

"As a result of the experience, have your religious feelings changed?"

"Yes."

"In what way?"

"I was raised as a Mormon. I was raised thinking, maybe, that God loved certain individuals more than others. Or that he cared about certain individuals more than others depending upon how they lived. I didn't find that to be true.

"I found that his love was extended to everyone, all the time. And that he understood why we are what we are, and why we are going through what we are going through. I found that we are all the same in the volume of his love. His love is not judgmental. He wouldn't think, for example, because we don't have the great amount of knowledge that he does, or the great strength that he does, that we are bad. His love is extended to everyone."

Physical Recovery

"Regarding your story, you left us with yourself sitting on the Volkswagen when your friend came back. What happened then?"

"I was taken to the emergency room of St. Mark's Hospital, and I was in great spirits. The doctor who received me was gruff and angry. He made it plainly clear that he didn't like motorcycles, and the accidents from them, and he wasn't going to put up with my accident very easily, either.

"The nurses who came in had to cut all my clothes off, with scissors, because I had road rash almost everywhere. I teased the nurses, as I saw their concerned faces, and I smiled and laughed at them. At that point my spirits were still elevated, and I could feel no pain.

"They put me under an anesthetic, after awhile, to reset the broken bones, and to try and get the rest of the gravel out of my skin. When I woke the next morning, it kind of settled on me, the situation that my physical body was really in. I hadn't noticed up to that time.

"I sat up in bed, and it was difficult because the bandages from the broken bones rubbed on the skin which I didn't have. I looked in the mirror. That was the first awareness I had of how bad the accident had really been. The skin had been ground off the whole right side of my face, from the center of the face outward, where I had hit the sandstone rocks. My face was all yellow, and red, and puffy, with no eyebrow, and I thought: *Boy, I've really done it this time*." John laughed as he thought about it.

"I still didn't really care, because the peace resided within me, and the comforting feeling that everything would be okay. It resided in my soul. For the amount of damage that my body had sustained the pain was very little. I was in intensive care for three-and-one-half weeks. One of my friends who came in to see me shortly after the accident nearly fainted. I tried to joke with him but he had to leave the room. A broken beer bottle had gouged a gash in my face from top to bottom, as well as the grinding from the rocks.

"After three-and-one-half weeks my skin had all grown back, and I looked normal. There were hardly any scars that could be seen. I had to use a wheelchair and a walker for awhile until my broken bones healed."

"How is your relationship with your son doing now?"

"Very good. I see him every other weekend. For years I saw him every weekend. He's fourteen now and a great kid. We have had good times together, and we are very close."

A Final Message

"After the experience I went through, I had to read everything I could find on Mormonism, and the Bible, and everything else, to find out if it was true or not. I found that the teachings were true, from the Bible through the Book of Mormon, and the Doctrine and Covenants; but too many times our priorities are mixed up. We forget the teachings of the New Testament—to love our neighbor, and to do all the other positive things written there.

"We get carried away with the temporal aspects of our own situations. We become involved in seeking money, or newer cars, or nicer clothes, or something, and we forget the things that, I believe, the Savior was trying to teach—concerning love and his way of love, his way of understanding. We should not judge our fellow beings, but we should love them, and serve them. Those were the teachings that He taught.

"There's another thing, too. Paul, in speaking to the Corinthians, and he was talking about our present place in eternity, and his comments were based on his extensive experiences, said: 'For now we see through a glass, darkly; but then face to face: now I know in part; but then shall I know even as also I am known.' It seems to me that this scripture sort of summarizes what happens in a near-death experience. I had expanded consciousness during the experience, I knew more than I did on earth, and I knew that I was known by the voice; by my Savior.

"But after the experience, when I came back, I still saw through a glass darkly—the experience itself was largely indescribable in terms of my earthly experience. How wonderful it will be when we can, as Paul says, see Him face to face, and know as we are known."

Chapter Eighteen

Personal Revelation

Gary Gillum

Studying for the Ministry

Gary was born in 1944 in Indianapolis, Indiana. His father was in the military, so as a child he traveled with his parents to various places in the world. Both of his parents were religiously inclined. Because his father was gone so much in his early life he was largely reared by his mother. She read Bible stories to him each evening when he was a child.

Because of a wonderful minister in his local Lutheran Church in Texas, Gary decided that he wanted to study for the ministry. He began those studies in Kansas while still in high school.

Gary began telling of his experience: "Initially my studies consisted of biblical interpretation classes; Latin, and German. Later I studied Greek and Hebrew. I had started on this course of action to become a Lutheran minister when I had my experience.

"It was the fall of 1962. I was 19 years old, and I had started my freshman year in college in Winfield, Kansas. It was St. John's College, a Lutheran institution, where most of us were studying for the ministry. I spent much of my time studying. On one occasion the Dean of Students called me to his office and expressed concern because I spent so much time studying. He suggested that I needed to socialize more and to be more relaxed.

"I tried to do that, but it was difficult, because I was so used to working most of the time. One method of relaxing was to walk through the tree-lined streets of Winfield, a beautiful community, and while walking, study my Greek vocabulary cards or my Shakespeare.

"Despite attempts to relax, often I would get discouraged because of the burden of study, and because of some of the things I was being taught. I would pray to my Heavenly Father for help. I prayed about life, and I prayed about some of the troubling teachings of the Lutheran Church. I couldn't believe, for example, that there was only heaven and hell, and if you weren't baptized you were confined to hell. I didn't think that was fair for people in Africa and other countries who didn't have a chance.

"About November, 1962, I was so discouraged because of personal problems, and because of other doctrinal problems I was having with the Lutheran Church, that I prayed and asked Heavenly Father to give me an experience that would wake me up and head me in a direction where I would find the truth."

"How long had you been in college by that time, Gary?" I asked.

"Three years. Anyway, after that prayer I resumed life as usual. One day, though, my roommate asked me how long I would be gone over Christmas vacation. (I had to go to California to see my parents, since my father was stationed at Edwards Air Force Base.) I told my roommate that I might not be back. He was puzzled and asked what I meant. I responded that I felt as though something were going to happen and I might not be back. He let it go at that and I never thought anything more about it."

"Did you know why you said what you did?"

"No. Not until after the experience. I went home on the train and saw my parents, but I didn't come back on the train. Our neighbor, who was also stationed at Edwards, had to go to Illinois for some type of Air Force class. He asked me if I would keep him company for that distance in his car—so I cashed in my train tickets."

An Automobile Trip and an Accident

"Jack, the neighbor who I was traveling with, had just gotten seat belts in his car. It was 1963 and that was still somewhat unusual. We wore the seat belts as we traveled along. We even discussed the seat belts and observed how important they would be to avoid serious injury when cars crashed.

"At five o'clock in the morning, on January 4, we were on Highway 54 heading toward Liberal, Kansas. We were on the Oklahoma panhandle, on a very straight stretch of road, and the sun was just coming up. The last thing I remember was a pair of headlights coming our way and then heading directly toward us. Jack swerved the car to the shoulder but the car hit us head on.

"It was a drunk driver. A policeman later said that we must have hit with a combined velocity of 110 miles per hour. We both had heavy Buicks, and that, combined with the fact that we had our seat belts on, probably saved our lives. But my injuries were massive. My spinal column had a compression fracture in the lumbar region, and my internal organs were severely damaged. Jack was in a similar desperate situation.

"I remember while they tried to extricate us from the car how wonderfully peaceful it was, and how great I felt. I'm sure I was in shock, but I was aware of what was going on. I also remember, when I first got in the emergency room, relieving myself of all the blood I had in me—all over the nurse. Sometime during that period they pronounced me clinically dead."

A Colorful Place of Light and a Choice

"During that time I had some unusual experiences, some of which pertained to my future life, which I didn't recognize until eight years later. The first thing I remember, though, was a personage, and I don't believe it was Jesus Christ, but . . . later I tried to remember—and I prayed about it—I got the impression that it was my paternal grandfather who had passed away six months earlier. He was very close to me.

"I saw a lot of light. The place was intense with color. It's like—everything we see in this life is three dimensional—it's like there was a fourth dimension there. That made everything more intense. And I felt a tremendous amount of love.

"Basically, I was given a choice to stay or to return to this life. Having prayed for some kind of experience, I sort of felt the question and the answer. It was: 'If I don't go back to earth and to my body, what am I going to miss out on?' And the answer was: 'If you go back, some day you will find the truth. Also, you have a lot of experiences still to have on the earth. If you stay here, you will have at least what you now see and feel, but if you go back to your body and come here later, and if you are faithful, then you will have much more than this.'

"While I was in this state, I learned—I probably learned much more than this—but I learned that the important things in life are service, love, and knowledge. I also had an inkling, because I now had an absolute knowledge that there was a life after death, that life would be more difficult for me than it otherwise would have been.

"That's about what I remember. I know there was more, but I can't remember it. Occasionally, at night, I have flashes of more of what happened, and I try to tell my wife, but I can't. It's really a strange feeling."

Interrogation About His Experience

"All right, Gary, let me ask you a few questions. First, why don't you explain a little more about the light you saw—what it looked like and how you felt?"

"It was very bright. It wasn't so much white, as it was kind of a yellowish-gold. It was around the individual that was there."

"Did the individual, himself, have light emanating from him?"

"Oh, yes."

"Describe, as much as you can, the individual."

"Just that it was a personage. Again, I can't be absolutely sure who it was."

"Do you remember the clothing of the individual?"

"No."

"And you felt love from the individual?"

"That's what made me want to stay."

"Did you have a feeling of knowledge about things?"

"That's one of the things that comes to me, now and then. Somehow, and I don't know how to explain this, but I'll do my best. Somehow I knew that I would recognize the Church when I found it. And that I would have a gift of discernment of things of the spirit."

"Did you feel as though you had left this earth and gone to some other place?"

"No, it was like I was almost in the same room. But, at the same time, it was outdoors—it was an outdoor scene."

"You were conscious, then, of there being some kind of scenery?"

"Right. There were flowers, trees and some kind of landscape."

"What did the landscape look like?"

"I don't remember what it looked like. All I remember was the intensity of the color and the distinct detail."

"Were you conscious of other people besides the one individual?"

"No."

A Vision of the Future

"That was the main experience. But I know, during the ten days that I was in the hospital, they had to keep reviving me. I was a mess physically. My kidneys stopped working and they had trouble finding a match-up for my AB blood type. I went out of my body several times during that period. On one occasion I had a different kind of experience."

"What was that?"

"It was even more strange than the first experience. I saw a building with tall spires, and I saw people in a room dressed in white clothing. The people were involved in a strange ceremony. I didn't understand any of it. It was totally foreign to my experience, and I didn't know what it symbolized, if anything."

"Did either, or both, of these experiences seem real, like a dream, or like a hallucination?"

"I know I had a lot of hallucinations, I guess from the medications for pain that I was receiving, but most of the hallucinations were frightening. They weren't peaceful and loving, they were frightening shapes, and they were evil-looking things and creatures. It was almost like it was an evil type of prelude to the good experiences that I had. It seemed that Satan was also trying to get hold of me through the chemicals and drugs that I was taking."

"Did the good experiences seem real?"

"Insofar as I knew that they existed, that they weren't just a figment of my imagination, that they actually happened—even though I couldn't explain them."

"You said that you were given a choice whether or not you were to come back. Did you have a feeling that there was a purpose in your return?"

"Just that I would find truth."

Finding the Gospel

"In 1969, six years after the accident, I was going with a girl who happened to be LDS. She was 'the angel' who was sent to help me find the truth. As a result of our mutual interest in each other, I listened to the missionaries as they explained the beliefs of the Mormon Church."

"Where was this?"

"In the last two years of my Bachelor's Degree I went to Concordia Senior College, in Fort Wayne, Indiana. I had graduated from Concordia and I was working at the Indianapolis Public Library where I met Lyn.

"When the missionaries started calling on me, my thought was that when I finally got around to finishing my schooling to become a Lutheran minister I would know something about the Mormons. I had no thought about becoming a member of that church.

"As the missionaries taught me, there was no contest when it came to reviewing the scriptures from the Bible. I could read them in the original Greek and Hebrew. But I was impressed by the individual testimonies of the missionaries. I had no similar experience from my Lutheran background. Lutherans are outwardly very unemotional about their religion. They would find it objectionable to view an emotional testimony meeting.

"The missionaries also told me about the promise in the Book of Mormon given by Moroni to know if the book was true—that I could know the truth by the power of the Holy Ghost. I took that promise seriously. I prayed about what I was reading in the Book of Mormon. As I did, I again experienced the light which I had previously seen during my accident. I didn't see any personage, but everything brightened up in the room. It was a personal testimony given to me to help me recognize the truth."

"Did you join the LDS Church, then?"

"Yes, I did."

"Did you marry Lyn?"

"Yes, but there was another experience that happened first. I had gotten hold of some anti-Mormon literature in the library where I was working. I wanted to find out some more about the Church. I read this material and became convinced that they were right. I also knew, after being baptized, that I was disappointing my parents because I had joined the Mormon Church. In their eyes, I felt, they believed I was going to become a non-Christian.

"So I walked into my fiancee's house, with my baptismal certificate, and I tore it up—into 47 pieces. I know that because I have it pasted together in my Book of Remembrance.

"All Lyn did was call her home teachers. Brother Williams and his wife came over right away. He didn't argue with me. He asked me to fast and pray. (I really hadn't learned how to fast yet.) I decided to give it a real try. So, for the next 24 hours I spent considerable time doing just that. And I got a firmer testimony of the truthfulness of the Gospel."

Visit to a Mormon Temple

"After our civil marriage, we wanted to be sealed in one of the Mormon temples. We were living in Provo as a result of a scholarship I got from BYU to get my graduate degree. We waited for a couple of years, and then we went to Manti to be married in the temple.

"That morning, when we were 17 miles from Manti, I recognized the spires of the temple which I had seen, years earlier, in my experience after the accident. I looked at Lyn, and I said: 'I've seen those spires before.' (I had never been to Manti in my life.) And when I got inside and saw the people dressed in white—bingo! I recognized the whole scene from my previous experience. In fact, after going through the temple I later wrote a short story, never published, entitled: 'With Him We Walk in White.'

Sustained by Personal Revelation

"As I previously told you, I had some difficult times. Lyn later got cancer and died. I married again and my second wife got cancer and died. I married a third time and it ended in divorce. Now I am married a fourth time to a wonderful woman—and we have seventeen children between us. It is quite a challenge.

"One thing that has sustained me is the ability to get revelation about my position in life. I think that somehow that experience that I had in 1963 has helped me to recognize that."

With that, I shook hands and left Gary in his office at Brigham Young University. He is employed there as Religion and Ancient Studies Librarian of the Harold B. Lee Library.

Joe Swick

Hit by a Car

Joe Swick met me on the BYU Campus shortly after my meeting with Gary. He was a student in Japanese language. Joe told me that he had served a mission to Japan for the LDS Church, that he had married a Japanese girl, and that they had three children, with a fourth on the way.

Joe was born in Seattle, Washington, in 1961. When he was about 12 years old they moved to Gig Harbor, about twenty minutes outside of Tacoma, Washington. His family wasn't too religious, but his mother was raised as a Lutheran, and as a boy he attended the Lutheran Church. Later he attended the Evangelical Free Church, and then, later still, he went to the Assembly of God Church.

Joe began telling of his experience: "I was about nine years old, I was with several of my friends, and I had found a used bicycle. I was bringing that home, and when I was crossing the street I was struck by a car."

"Was this in Seattle?" I asked.

"Yes. When I was crossing the street, I was sort of excited because of the bicycle, and I didn't see the car until I looked up and saw the grill. Then it hit me—I was directly in front of my house.

"Everything went black, and I remember thinking to myself: *I'm dead. This must be what it's like to be dead; I'm dead.*"

A Light, Love, and a Message

"I felt myself separated from my body—I didn't see my body, and it was black. But I remember being conscious and thinking about what was happening. And . . . and I had a feeling—not just my mind—that there was something to me. There was something tangible to me.

"After awhile I recall a sense of motion, or a feeling that I was moving. And it was like . . . it was like there were walls, or there was something confining me. I recall moving, at first not very fast, but then the speed began to increase. I saw a light, a very bright light; I could feel a very strong and powerful love that was coming towards me—filling me, from this light.

"The light, or the love, or something, was speaking to me with a very comforting voice. I was drawn closer and closer to it. Although I could sense this really compassionate feeling coming from the light, I realized that if I arrived at where the light was there was a point at which I would not be able to come back. And I wouldn't be with my family or my friends. That thought frightened me.

"I remember that the light was speaking to me, and I don't recall the exact words. It wasn't like a voice that you hear, it was more like . . . it was like speaking to my heart. And it was telling me that there were still things in life for me to experience.

"I drew very close to the light, and I could feel that power, and that . . . the love flowing through me. I don't have a recollection of going back. It was black, and at some point I opened my eyes and there was a paramedic and some other people standing over me.

"My mother was there. I think the first thing out of my mouth, I was screaming, was that I was dead. I thought that I was dead.

"I was taken to the hospital where I stayed for awhile with a severe concussion. I don't know how close to death I was, but the experience was definitely an out-of-body experience. That's essentially what happened."

Further Review of Joe's Experience

"Okay, Joe, let me ask you some questions. Can you describe the color of the light?"

"It was extremely white and brilliant."

"Could you look at it or did you have to shield your eyes?"

"I don't remember covering my eyes, but it was very bright. I imagine that I was looking at it, because I kept noticing how bright it was."

"And you had a feeling of moving towards it?"

"Yes, first at an imperceptible speed, but as I got closer I moved more rapidly."

"As you moved towards the light, were you conscious of your surrounding?"

"Not really the surrounding, except the feeling that I was being pressed in on the sides. It was as if I were moving towards a focal point, and I was being confined by actual walls—maybe like moving up in a pyramid."

"Could it be like a cone, if you were inside and moving towards the apex?"

"Yes, that's it. It was like a cone."

"Did you see a personage in the light?"

"No. I didn't see anyone. I just felt this love coming from the light. If you are talking about the characteristics that we associate with a person, I did feel that. But I didn't see the physical shape of a body or anything like that."

"You said that your own body felt as if it existed in some form?"

"Yes. I didn't spend a lot of time thinking about it, but it wasn't like a mind floating in space. I felt as if I had dimensions and a particular shape, moving my limbs, and those sorts of things."

"When the voice told you that you had more to experience yet in life, did you want to stay or to come back?"

"I was crying at that point. Being drawn to that powerful love is . . . it's hard to express the feelings that it invokes. I felt very torn. But, I'm here, and I realized as I was drawn close to the light that I desired to be with my family."

"Is that all there was to the experience?"

"That's all there was to that part of the experience, but it's connected to another experience I had."

LDS Missionaries

"I was 15 years old, and it occurred on January 14, 1977. It was in my room, and we were living off Peacock Hill Road in Gig Harbor, Washington. It was the result of my contact with some missionaries."

"These were Mormon missionaries?"

"Yes. As background, my mother and father were divorced when I was two or three years old. My father had lived sort of a reprobate life, and I was raised by my mother. I had visited my father shortly before this experience, and he had turned his life around. He had been meeting with the Mormon missionaries and had become a member of the church. I was very impressed with the differences I saw in his life, so I had the missionaries come and teach me.

"As the missionaries taught me, I was not impressed—to say the least, I was not impressed." Joe laughed as he thought back.

"What was it that caused you not to be impressed?"

"Well, the idea that some farm boy in upstate New York had been visited by God and his son Jesus Christ did not impress me as something that I could believe. I also didn't think that The Book of Mormon had much to give me in the way of instruction over the Bible."

"Did you tell the missionaries what you thought?"

"Oh yes, they knew how I felt. I don't know why they continued to come out, but they did. And they challenged me to be baptized on January 15, if I knew that the Church was true by that date. I told them: 'Sure, if I know it's true—but there's a fat chance of that happening.'

"By the fourteenth when the missionaries were to visit me I had decided that I wasn't going to be baptized. I told my mother and my step-father that I didn't know that the Church was true, and I didn't want to be involved with it. I felt that this would be the final meeting with the missionaries.

"They had someone with them to interview me. He had the regular flip charts and he showed me a picture of Joseph Smith. He asked me if I believed Joseph Smith was a prophet, and I told him no, I thought he was a fraud. He asked me if I thought The Book of Mormon was the word of God, and I told him no, I thought it was bogus. He showed me a picture of Spencer W. Kimball and asked if I thought he was a prophet of God. I told him that the man had a kindly face, but I didn't believe he was a prophet of God.

"The missionary then asked me if I wanted to know if these things were true—if I *really* wanted to know. And it wasn't what he said, it was the way he said it. I felt something inside of me that said: *Yes, that is why you have been speaking with the missionaries. That is why you have had them come.* I found myself saying: 'Yes, of course I want to know if it's really true.'

"He asked if I would like to pray about it right then. I responded: 'Certainly.' I had prayed before, but I hadn't been very serious—it had seemed so obviously fraudulent.

"We went into my room, this young missionary and I, and as I got on my knees, it was not a vocal prayer, I began to pray. I felt the Holy Ghost over me. It was a very powerful feeling.

"At that time I didn't know it was the Holy Ghost. The missionary opened his eyes and said to me: 'That feeling that you are feeling now is the Holy Ghost. If you ask the question you are going to ask, you will get an answer.' "

A Vision of Light—A New Church

"I was surprised that he knew what I felt. I closed my eyes and . . . and at that point it was as though the walls fell away from my room, and the floor fell from beneath me. I was just there. And it was that same intensely bright light. There was that same powerful feeling of love that I had known when I was hit by the car." Joe had difficulty holding back the tears as he remembered the event. He continued with some difficulty.

"It was more than viewing the light. It was like being totally enveloped. And it was reassuring me—again not with an audible voice—but it was speaking very powerfully to my heart, that the step I was about to take, I needed to do; that it was important for me to do that.

"I don't know how long that continued, but after awhile it was done. I became aware of my surroundings. The missionary was still praying beside me. Then he opened his eyes, and we went into the other room. He never asked me what I experienced, and I don't know what he saw or felt. But that was my experience.

"The other two missionaries were sitting at the kitchen table. They looked up, and I told them I was going to join the Church. I thought they were going to fall out of their seats.

"That was my experience, and it has fundamentally changed my perception of things. I have been exposed to much anti-Mormon literature and claims against the Church. But I'm always careful to separate those kinds of intellectual claims from my own experience. The judgment I made to join the Church is based on the experiences I had—and they are hard to refute. I can't say that they never happened, because I know they did.

"I had some serious questions, even after I joined the Church, that weren't totally resolved. Still, because of these and other spiritual experiences, I am a member."

"Has your feeling about death changed as a result of those experiences?"

"Certainly. It's not something that you are afraid of once you know what's on the other side."

"You say that you know what's on the other side. How do you know that your experiences weren't some kind of dream or hallucination?"

"It was my experience. I don't know how else to say it. I don't have the sense that I was dreaming or hallucinating."

"You felt that they were real experiences?"

"Most certainly. They were as real as now, when I hold my hand up and look at it, it's a real hand. Neither experience was like a dream."

Part II

The Meaning

For man is spirit. The elements are eternal, and spirit and element, inseparably connected, receive a fulness of joy; . . .

The glory of God is intelligence, or, in other words, light and truth.

Doctrine and Covenants 93:33, 36

Chapter Nineteen

The Light

Descriptions of the Light

Probably no part of the typical near-death experience (NDE) is so universally described as is "the light." A majority of the written accounts of people who have undergone an extensive NDE mentions some form of bright light, and most books written about NDEs spend some time discussing it. To most of those going through an NDE the light is not an ordinary light. It has properties which produce ethereal feelings: feelings of peace, joy, and love. It is often associated with some sort of superior being, and in some cases, with a different kind of world.

Derald Evans's Description of the Light

. . . the beautiful bright-white light. It gave me a feeling like . . . almost like soft music, or something that was one-hundred percent pure. It's hard to describe in words. I had never seen nor heard anything like it before. It was not frightening, though. More softening. And it kept coming closer, getting brighter and brighter. . . . I will never forget the feeling I got from the light.

Ann's Description

I noticed a light coming into the room. It was a beautiful golden-white light which seemed to appear in the wall to the left of my bed. . . . It was about three feet up from the floor and mid-length of the bed . . . . As the ball of light grew the pain and feeling of illness suddenly left me. I had no idea what was happening, but I felt at peace.

I sat up and watched the light grow. It grew rapidly in both size and brightness. In fact the light got so bright that it seemed to me that the whole world was lit by it.

Lois Clark's Understanding of the Light

At the time that I was in the place to see the light I thought it was real. The whole thing . . . oh, there was the light, and there seemed to be soft, soft, soft, . . . you couldn't really hear it, you more felt this music. It . . . it was soft, and immaculately beautiful. There was, I guess there's no way to really describe it, there was a feeling of peace, beauty, love, and . . . it just felt like this is what I want. This is the ultimate.

Kathleen Pratt Martinez's View of the Light

The room itself was illuminated with a light that I had never seen before. It was a goldish sort of color. But it was so bright that it was . . . it was awe inspiring. It was like something from another world. It was soft yet it was so illuminating. I have a hard time describing it because I have never seen anything like it in this world. The closest thing I can come to it is something like a sunset—but that wasn't it either.

None of these people knew each other, nor had they communicated with each other. They were unaware of the similarity of words that they used to describe the bright light. It was fascinating to watch them struggle for words as they attempted to portray the light.

Scriptural References to the Light

In view of the sublime feelings associated with the light, it might be expected that the scriptures have something to say about it, and they do. The light is associated with God and with Jesus Christ, as expressed in the New Testament and as discussed in particular detail in LDS scriptures.

The First Epistle of John says of God: "This then is the message which we have heard of him, and declare unto you, that God is light, and in him is no darkness at all."[1] James says that "every good gift and every perfect gift is from above, and cometh down from the Father of lights . . . ."[2]

From John, in the New Testament, the mission of John the Baptist is described as a forerunner of Jesus Christ. In this discussion Christ is referred to as the Light.

There was a man sent from God, whose name was John. The same came for a witness, to bear witness of the Light, that all men through him might believe. He was not that Light, but was sent to bear witness of that Light. That was the true Light, which lighteth every man that cometh into the world.[3]

Perhaps the best scriptural definition of what the light is can be found in Section 88 of the Doctrine and Covenants:

He that ascended up on high, as also he descended below all things, in that he comprehended all things, that he might be in all and through all things, the light of truth;

Which truth shineth. This is the light of Christ. As also he is in the sun, and the light of the sun, and the power thereof by which it was made.

As also he is in the moon, and is the light of the moon, and the power thereof by which it was made;

As also the light of the stars, and the power thereof by which they were made;

And the earth also, and the power thereof, even the earth upon which you stand.

And the light which shineth, which giveth you light, is through him who enlighteneth your eyes, which is the same light that quickeneth your understandings;

Which light proceedeth forth from the presence of God to fill the immensity of space—

The light which is in all things, which giveth life to all things, which is the law by which all things are governed, even the power of God who sitteth upon his throne, who is in the bosom of eternity, who is in the midst of all things.[4]

Beings of Light

The light is often associated with heavenly, or spiritual beings. Many of the respondents interviewed spoke of such beings.

Ann's Description of Her Guardian

There was this beautiful woman, and she was part of the light, in fact she glowed. . . . Her body was lit from inside in a way . . . it's very hard to explain what she looked like. It seemed as if she were a pure crystal filled with light. Even her robe glowed with light as if by itself.

. . . the robe was white, long-sleeved, and full length. She had a golden belt around her waist and her feet were bare. Not that she needed anything on her feet since she stood a couple of feet off the floor.

. . . I had never seen such kindness and gentle love on anyone's face such as I saw in this person.

Ruth's View of Beings of Light

. . . there were three beings of light. . . . They were composed of, let's say, tissues of light. I recognized them, I knew them, yet they didn't have faces, or names that I know now, but I knew them, and they knew me. . . . And each being had a somewhat different color. One was golden, one was kind of pinkish, and the other was a blue-blue.

Lois Clark's Description

I saw forms. I didn't see . . . recognizable faces, or anything, just forms . . . and the one was brighter than the others. . . . one seemed to just shine with brightness.

Marcia Anderson's Guardian Angels

They were rather translucent, I could see the outline of their bodies. I could kind of see through them, in a way. I couldn't tell you what their faces looked like. I knew that they had a body, and I knew that they had a face. They were smiling with a peaceful kind of aura that was there. There was a brightness about them, a white-light. I was totally awake and I wasn't frightened.

Forrest Hansen and a Being of Light

. . . This was a being, or an image of a being, constructed completely of light. It was not focused enought to make out distinct details but it was obviously a human-type image. . . . When I say constructed of light, I also mean that it was semi-transparent and had depth. The light seemed to be particles of light of which there were an innumerable quantity.

Scriptual Comparisons with NDE Accounts of Beings of Light

The scriptures often speak of angels appearing to individuals. In the tenth chapter of Acts[5] Cornelius describes an angel who visited him: ". . . Four days ago I was fasting until this hour; and at the ninth hour I prayed in my house, and, behold, a man stood before me in bright clothing, And said, Cornelius, thy prayer is heard, and thine alms are had in remembrance in the sight of God."

Undoubtedly the best description of the appearance of an angel is given by the prophet Joseph Smith in his description of the angel Moroni. In 1823, when he was about eighteen years of age, Joseph had retired to bed for the evening and was praying for forgiveness of his sins and for a manifestation that he might know of his status with the Lord. His account follows:[6]

> *While I was thus in the act of calling upon God, I discovered a light appearing in my room, which continued to increase until the room was lighter than at noonday, when immediately a personage appeared at my bedside, standing in the air, for his feet did not touch the floor.*
>
> *He had on a loose robe of most exquisite whiteness. It was a whiteness beyond anything earthly I had ever seen; nor do I believe that any earthly thing could be made to appear so exceedingly white and brilliant. His hands were naked, and his arms also, a little above the wrist; so also, were his feet naked, as were his legs, a little above the ankles. His head and neck were also bare. I could discover that he had no other clothing on but his robe, as it was open, so that I could see into his bosom.*
>
> *Not only was his robe exceedingly white, but his whole person was glorious beyond description, and his countenance truly like lightning. The room was exceedingly light, but not so very bright as immediately around his person.*

Joseph Smith also described the scene when the angel Moroni left, after communicating with him:

> *After this communication I saw the light in the room begin to gather immediately around the person of him who had been speaking to me, and it continued to do so until the room was again left dark, except just around him; when instantly I saw, as it were, a conduit open right up into heaven, and he ascended till he entirely disappeared, and the room was left as it had been before this heavenly light had made its appearance.*[7]

Compare that description with the explanation of Ann, in this book, of how she returned with her guardian from another world:

We came back through the darkness, as before, with the surrounding light making a sort of tunnel through it. . . . We emerged back in my bedroom. My guardian smiled at me and suddenly I was back in bed without the slightest idea of how I got there. . . . the light was diminishing. I waved at her and she smiled and waved back. Then the light sort of gathered around her and she was gone.

Derald Evans told of the disappearance of the individual who came in the light to see him in this manner:

As suddenly as it had come the light began to diminish. . . . he had been standing in the light, and when the light disappeared, he disappeared.

In May, 1829, Joseph Smith and Oliver Cowdery were given the Aaronic Priesthood with its authority to baptize by John the Baptist. Joseph described the event this way:[8] "While we were thus employed, praying and calling upon the Lord, a messenger from heaven descended in a cloud of light, and having laid his hands upon us, he ordained us . . . ."

The Doctrine and Covenants indicates that we all may receive the light.[9] "And if your eye be single to my glory, your whole bodies shall be filled with light, and there shall be no darkness in you; and that body which is filled with light comprehendeth all things." From this scripture it is clear that, as we obtain the light, we also obtain knowledge. A fourteen-year-old boy in a car which had been swept underwater described it this way: "It [the light] was all being, all beauty, all meaning for all existence."[10]

Under most mortal conditions humans looking at another human do not detect the light in that person. Under certain conditions this changes, however, as evidenced by the eight-year-old patient of Melvin Morse. Morse wrote a book on the experiences of some of his young patients. In this particular case[11] an eight-year-old girl fell from her father's boat into the Puget Sound. A family friend dove into the water, which was so murky as to disallow vision beyond a few feet. After several dives the friend found her, because she was "illuminated from within." The girl recovered.

A somewhat different type of incident was discussed in Chapter 10 when Stephanie LaRue described how, when she first saw her future husband in a bowling alley, "I saw this bright light around a man, . . ."

Sublime Feelings

Individuals exposed to the light, or to beings of light, often express feelings of sublimity. It was interesting to interview them and watch them grope for words as they tried to express the feelings they had about the light, about individuals they saw in the light, and sometimes about the new world which they visited. Frequently they were reduced to tears as they relived the experiences in their minds.

Ruth Describes Her Feelings

It was as if I were proceeding down a tunnel. Then I came to the end, and there were three beings of light. They were waiting to greet me, and they were so filled with love. It was the most pure, unselfconscious, beautiful experience of my life.

Ann Tells How She Felt

I felt thoroughly refreshed, enlivened and spiritually rejuvenated. I was filled with a zest for life. It is impossible to explain what it felt like to be lighter than air, with no pain, and totally at peace with everyone and everything around.

Lois Clark's Reaction

. . . all of a sudden I saw this bright light. I've never seen anything like it as long as I've lived, since. It was just beautiful. So I started walking towards this light to see . . . .

When Joseph Smith and Oliver Cowdery were visited by John the Baptist in 1829. Oliver Cowdery described the event in this manner:[12]

I shall not attempt to paint to you the feelings of this heart, or the majestic beauty and glory which surrounded us on this occasion; but you will believe me when I say, that earth, nor men, with the eloquence of time, cannot begin to clothe language in as interesting and sublime a manner as this holy personage. No; nor has this earth power to give the joy, to bestow the peace, or comprehend the wisdom which was contained in each sentence as they were delivered by the power of the Holy Spirit! Man may deceive his fellow-men, deception may follow deception, and the children of the wicked one may have power to seduce the foolish and untaught, till naught but fiction feeds the many, and the fruit of falsehood carries in its current the giddy to the grave; but one touch with the finger of his love, yes, one ray of glory from the upper world, or one word from the mouth of the Savior, from the bosom of eternity, strikes it all into insignificance, and blots it forever from the mind. The assurance that we were in the presence of an angel, the certainty that we heard the voice of Jesus, and the truth unsullied as it flowed from a pure personage, dictated by the will of God, is to me past description, and I shall ever look upon this expression of the Savior's goodness with wonder and thanksgiving while I am permitted to tarry; and in those mansions where perfection dwells and sin never comes, I hope to adore in that day which shall never cease.

Shortly after Joseph Smith completed the translation of the Book of Mormon, in June 1829, he was granted permission by the Lord to show the golden plates, from which the book was translated, to some witnesses. Three of the witnesses, Oliver Cowdery, David Whitmer, and Martin Harris, also saw an angel and a bright light. Joseph described the event in this manner:

> *. . . When presently we beheld a light above us in the air, of exceeding brightness; and behold, an angel stood before us. In his hands he held the plates which we had been praying for these to have a view of. He turned over the leaves one by one, so that we could see them, and discern the engravings thereon distinctly. . . . we heard a voice from out of the bright light above us, saying, "These plates have been revealed by the power of God, and they have been translated by the Power of God."*[13]

David Whitmer said of the same event:

> *We not only saw the plates of the Book of Mormon, but also the Brass Plates, the plates of the Book of Ether, and many other plates. The fact is, it was just as though Joseph, Oliver, and I were sitting just here on a log, when we were overshadowed by a light.*
>
> *It was not like the light of the sun, nor like that of fire, but more glorious and beautiful. It extended away around us, I cannot tell how far, but in the midst of this light there appeared, as it were, a table with many records or plates upon it, . . .*
>
> *I saw them just as plain as I see this bed, and I heard the voice of the Lord as distinctly as I ever heard anything in my life.*[14]

The Meaning of the Light

Some researchers investigating NDEs try, in vain, to explain the light and other near-death events in terms of some known scientific phenomenon; or worse, as a parapsychological illusion conjured up by the person having the experience. Individuals who experience the light wonder at it and struggle to explain their feelings when exposed to it.

If the light is accepted as a spiritual phenomenon, then the scriptures cited above have special meaning. In that context the light is a characteristic of Deity. It originates with the Father and the Son. It is the power of creation, the power of life, the power of knowledge, the power of governing the earth and the stars, in short, it is the Light of God.

It is not surprising that words fail individuals as they attempt to explain the light. It is more, to most of them, than just a visual phenomenon—it is a heavenly experience. It is their contact with the influence and power of God, and it is overwhelming. They never want to leave it.

Similarly, individuals meeting with beings of light feel of the power, love, truth, and perfect peace of those beings. These spiritual beings carry with them the light and power of God. And that light and power are available to all mankind—by following the simple prescriptions detailed in the scriptures.

Occasionally someone who has encountered the light, or a being of light, is able to express his or her feelings eloquently. Oliver Cowdery did after his meeting with John the Baptist. A more recent description was given by a lady in a conference on NDEs. She described her feelings after being exposed to the light. Her description is recorded in a book by Carol Zaleski.[15] It is probably an excellent way to end this chapter.

> *It was a dynamic light, not like a spotlight. It was an incredible energy—a light you wouldn't believe. I almost floated in it. It was feeding my consciousness feelings of unconditional love, complete safety, and complete, total perfection . . . It just POWED into you. My consciousness was going out getting larger and taking in more; I expanded and more and more came in. It was such rapture, such bliss. And then, and then, a piece of knowledge came in: it was that I was immortal, indestructible. I cannot be hurt, cannot be lost. We don't have anything to worry about. And that the world is perfect; everything that happens is part of a perfect plan. I don't understand this part now, but I still know it's true. . . . Later, when I was saying the Lord's prayer, and I got to the part that says "thine is the kingdom, and the power, and the glory," I thought that nothing could describe this experience any better. It was pure power and glory.*

Chapter Twenty

Life's Purpose

Why They Came Back

Individuals who have undergone a near death experience repeatedly express their feeling that they came back for a purpose. They do not always have a complete understanding of the specific reasons behind the purpose, but they cling to a belief that they came back because they had something more to accomplish before they left this life. In many cases they identify this purpose as having to do with children.

Stephanie LaRue—Her Life's Purpose

I felt that there were things that I still had to do on this earth. . . . I could be wrong, but I had the feeling that I'm supposed to have two children. I felt that there would be a special spiritual person coming into my life. And I knew that I had to be there for that person or persons.

Derald Evans—Future Children

For some reason I seemed to know that there would be more children in the future that would be dependent upon me. It puzzled me that I would know about some, as yet, unknown children, but I did.

Later in his life Derald became responsible for many more children through some unexpected events.

Norma—Not Her Time

After the experience I knew that it was not my time to go. There would have been no family or anyone to greet me. I'm not afraid to die, but it wasn't my time. . . . I was to have more children, especially Jonathan, my youngest child—and then there was Amanda.

Maureen Daniels—More Children

[My purpose was to] have my baby. I would have thirteen of them if I could. I feel I have a lot to accomplish here—with a family—and to leave behind.

Karl Muecke—To Bear Testimony

Well there was my family, of course. But there was even . . . it was a more important thing. I was supposed to tell people . . . I was chosen to bear testimony that Jesus is the Christ, the son of God—when I was in a situation where people would listen with the right spirit.

Sometimes it is just a general feeling that life is not yet complete, there are more things still to be accomplished.

Elizabeth Vorwaller—Life Unfinished

We were having a conversation, and I remember being asked if I wanted to go with him or to stay. I was frantic at the thought; I told him that I wanted to stay on earth, because I felt that I had something more to prove. I felt that my life wasn't finished yet.

Do They Have a Choice of Life or Death?

Frequently those experiencing a NDE have a clear choice concerning whether they leave this life or return to it. Typical are these experiences:

Marcia Anderson—Given A Choice

Also, at that moment, I thought of my children and as the awareness of motherhood, my stewardship, and my place with them, filled my mind I made a conscious choice. I had a choice to stay there, with them, or to proceed to some other place . . . .

Janet McClellan—It's Okay to Die

A voice said, 'It's okay if you want to die.' . . . Because I had really wanted to die—I was in so much pain. And I was dying, I knew I was dying. The voice also said, 'It's okay, there's work for you to do if you choose to stay [in this life].'

Sometimes the individual having the out-of-body experience actually argues with another being in making a case to go or to stay.

Derald Evans—An Argument to Live

. . . [the personage] said, 'You know why I'm here—we've got to go. . . . I told him that I couldn't go. He responded that I didn't have anything to say about it. He said I had to go with him and it would be all right.

I argued as strongly as I had about anything in my life. . . . I knew I was arguing for my life.

To make his case Derald actually used information about future children, which he had no knowledge of prior to the experience, and the individual he was arguing with was sympathetic to the argument. It appears, in fact, that the individual provoked Derald into the argument and provided him with new information to help him better understand the reasons why he needed to continue living.

Ann, and Karl Muecke—A Limited Choice

Ann, who visited with an individual who identified himself as Jesus Christ, pled and argued to stay in the spirit world, but she lost the argument. In losing, however, she extracted a promise that her physical pain would be removed, and she would be cured of spinal meningitis, *if* she would return. She was still given the choice.

Karl Muecke, who communicated with a Presence in a new and wonderful spirit world, felt that he didn't have a choice. He was told that he must return because his mission was not yet complete. David Herard, the Vietnam veteran, also felt that he had to come back because he had things to do. It may have been that if Karl and David had argued for a different result, as Derald and Ann did, their options would have been presented.

The outcome seems to have proceeded as it did in Karl's case because he agreed with the decision to return. In David's instance, he didn't want to return, but he seemed to understand the reasons for his continuing in this life when he felt the presence of God. Indeed, after he returned he was frightened by the prospect that he might not have come back.

Jean, and Joy Melvin—Possibly No Choice

Of all the people I interviewed, the preponderant majority appeared to have a choice. Some may not, such as Jean, who wanted to stay in the spirit world because of the opportunity to study and learn in the extensive libraries that were there. She returned, screaming that she didn't want to come back. Also, however, she identified the fact that if she didn't return there would be no one to care for her children.

Joy Melvin, like Jean, may not have had a choice. She said:

> *I knew that's why I was being pulled [because of her life's purpose]. When I felt this pulling, I resisted, because I wanted to stay. But I had this knowledge, or feeling: 'Sorry, you've got to go back. There's too much to do.' . . . there was no fighting it, I was going back.*

It appears that usually individuals are given a choice as to whether they continue in this life or not. It is interesting that even Forrest Hansen, who was not persuaded that there is a life after death, felt that he was given a choice of terminating or continuing his physical existence.

Knowledge

One of the most fascinating aspects of interviewing people who had undergone NDEs was to watch them as they struggled with their emotions and attempted, sometimes unsuccessfully, to put into words what they had experienced in the new world. Carol and I often felt our own emotions involved in a sympathetic reaction to the person we were listening to, and in some cases to the astonishing information which was being presented.

There was an issue which came up, directly in a few cases, and indirectly in others, which always caused me to react with wonder. This was when individuals talked of the interrelationship of the world they had been to with the present world, and when they spoke of unusual knowledge. Often this special knowledge which the persons professed to have related to their life's purposes, as they understood them.

Jenette—Knowledge of a Bleeding Heart

When Jenette had three operations on her heart within 22 hours and experienced unusual bleeding behind the heart, she knew, even before the doctors did, where the problem was:

I could see them—it's like I came out of my body and was two feet above them. And I could see what they were doing, and I could see the heart, and I could . . . I just knew where the bleeder was before I even rose up from my body. It just came to my mind . . . I just knew where it was.

Jenette knew that she had further work to do in this life, but that purpose was being thwarted because the doctors couldn't solve her physical problem. It frustrated her.

Marcia Anderson—Knew What She Had to Do

When Marcia Anderson came out of her body she had complete knowledge of the carbon-monoxide, which had caused her incident, and she knew what she must do to get rid of the deadly fumes. She accomplished this despite great physical distress, and in so doing she was able to continue pursuing her life's perceived purpose—that of being a wife and a mother.

David Herard—Knowledge of Things as They Are

David Herard knew, several days before his experience, that he would be killed in Vietnam. He also described one of the significant events that happened to him during his out-of-body experience:

I had the feeling that I knew why things are as they are, why all the problems on the earth were as they were. . . . it was an overwhelming feeling of knowing, but I couldn't tell you now what I knew.

Stephanie LaRue—Had Total Knowledge

Stephanie LaRue stated that she had intuitive feelings of significant events in her life, including premonitions of the death of loved ones. Then, when she had her out-of-body experience, she said that this happened:

About this time I had an experience that I'll never forget. . . . a feeling of total, total knowledge without asking. It's like you and me sitting here, now, and wondering how far the universe expands, or . . . just questions we have on earth about the geography of the earth, craters, or anything. This feeling I had of total knowledge was just that, I knew everything without asking. It was an incredible feeling.

The Plan of Salvation

Fundamental to The Church of Jesus Christ of Latter-day Saints is the belief that Jesus Christ and his Father developed a Plan of Salvation for all humans. In that plan the purposes of life were defined; indeed, the purpose of existence was designated. Briefly stated the purpose of existence, as given in the Book of Mormon, is: ". . . men are, that they might have joy."[1]

Obviously people have been seeking joy, without much success, for millennia. The plan for achieving it, however, has been available wherever the Lord's word has been available.

Many people who have had an NDE report feelings of perfection, knowledge—and some describe the existence of a plan. To quote again, from Carol Zaleski, the lady who expressed her feelings at an NDE conference:[2]

> *And then, and then, a piece of knowledge came in: it was that I was immortal, indestructible. I cannot be hurt, cannot be lost. We don't have anything to worry about. And that the world is perfect; everything that happens is part of a perfect plan. I don't understand this part now, but I still know it's true.*

It is beyond the scope of this book to provide a detailed exposition of the Plan of Salvation, but to properly understand some of the comments made by those undergoing NDEs it is essential that the rudiments of the Plan be outlined.

To understand the Plan it is important to know that, in LDS doctrine, people have existed in one form or another forever, and they will continue to exist throughout eternity. They started as individual intelligences and at some point were born as spirit children of our Father in Heaven, with spirit bodies having the same appearances as human bodies. They continued in that form until they were born into this life, on earth, as mortal beings with both a physical body and a spirit.

Numerous individuals having NDEs have stated that they felt that they had lived forever, and as the lady from Zaleski's book said: "I was immortal, indestructible." Joe Geraci, who hemorrhaged following an operation, described how he felt after he left his body. His story is told in more detail in Kenneth Ring's, "Heading Toward Omega."[3]

> *. . . You just know. You're all-knowing—and everything is a part of you—it's—it's just so beautiful. It was eternity. It's like I was always there and I will always be there, and that my existence on earth was just a brief instant.*

The Plan of Salvation was ordained by our Father in Heaven and accepted by Jesus Christ. The basic elements of the Plan, as detailed in LDS scriptures, are as follows:

1. An earth would be created upon which we could have a variety of experiences.[4] This earth would be filled with life, including humans, beginning with Adam and Eve. Adam, after being tempted by Satan, would fall from a sinless, childless, paradisiacal state in order that other humans might be born and die.[5]

2. We would take upon ourselves physical bodies by being born, and we would live a physical life on this earth. These bodies would be after the image of Jesus Christ and our Heavenly Father.[6] We would have children and be responsible for their physical and spiritual welfare.[7]

3. All memory of our previous existence would be removed from us while we were mortal and on this earth. This forgetfulness, or lack of complete knowledge of a previous life, would enhance our ability to make free choices.[8]

4. We would be allowed to choose the kind of life we live within the constraints of physical mortality.[9] Freedom of choice would be guaranteed by providing for opposition in all things. That opposition would include suffering from illnesses, accidents and other events, some of our making and some not.[10] Our relationships with others, how we reacted to and how we treated our fellow humans would be tested.[11]

5. We would be given information about good and evil, through prophets speaking for our Father in Heaven, by both the written word and by oral instruction.[12] Satan would be allowed to tempt us to do evil.[13] We would benefit by gaining knowledge while in this world.[14]

6. A Savior, Jesus Christ, would be provided who would atone for our sins, and who would make it possible for the resurrection of all individuals.[15] All would ultimately live again as resurrected beings, with their body and their spirit reunited—a gift from Jesus Christ.[16]

7. Means would be provided for saving ordinances to be performed on this earth for all persons, living or dead.[17]

8. At the end of mortal life we would die: our spirit and our body would separate, with the spirit continuing to live and the body being temporarily discarded into the tomb. The spirit would pass to another sphere, the spirit world, and would reside there until the time of the resurrection. In this spiritual sphere, those who had not been taught the gospel during earth life would be given the opportunity to hear it.[18]

9. At some future time there would be a general resurrection, and we would again obtain a body which would never be lost nor destroyed.[19]

10. There would be a final judgment; and, depending upon how we lived and whether we repented of our sins or not, we would live eternally with our Father in Heaven and his son Jesus Christ.[20] In this state we would live with our families and would have immense knowledge. We would participate with our Father in Heaven in the creation of new worlds. We would experience eternal growth and happiness.[21]

11. Even those who do not live a very good life would find the new life rewarding and one which provides for growth. It would be much superior to the previous life on earth.[22]

These, then, are the main elements of the Plan of Salvation. All elements are not necessary for discussion in this chapter; some of them will be referred to in later chapters.

Comparison with Elements of the Plan of Salvation

The feeling that there is a purpose in life, which most of those undergoing NDEs had, derives directly from the Plan of Salvation. The strong feelings that so many had concerning having to return for their family or for their children relates to one of the most important elements of the Plan; namely, raising children and being responsible for their physical and spiritual welfare.

Those being interviewed outlined other purposes which are also part of the Plan. Both Karl Muecke, the German soldier, and Janet McClellan, the critical care nurse, felt that they were to love *all* people. Many of the respondents felt that they should help others. As Elizabeth Vorwaller put it, "The main thing is to do unto others as you would have them do unto you."

Stephanie LaRue—A Reason for Everything

The fact that there *is* a plan was mentioned by the lady in Carol Zaleski's book.[2] That the Plan involves coping with opposition and unpleasant experiences was detailed beautifully by Stephanie LaRue, who underwent terrible pain after a serious operation. She said:

> *I'd like people, who are struggling, to know that when life gets really difficult it is only temporary. They shouldn't give up, and they should know that there is a reason for their suffering. There is a reason for everything. And if they believe in themselves and listen to their intuition, no matter how despairing things get their problems will work out.*

Freedom of Choice—Part of Plan of Salvation

A fundamental element of the Plan is that we have freedom of choice. Apparently that freedom carries over, within limits, to the choice of whether certain individuals may continue to live or pass on to another sphere. In some instances, as with Ann, the choice was agonizing. Only after reassurance from the Savior was she willing to continue in this life. Many of those having experienced NDEs made the choice to alter their life style after they returned. Kathleen Pratt Martinez, who was on trial for her life, altered her life dramatically after her experience.

Forgetfulness of Former Life—Part of Plan

The emphasis on knowledge by those interviewed is interesting. The Plan calls for us to increase our knowledge at each stage of eternal life's journey. Even though we have forgotten what we knew before this life, many respondents had a brief period in which they again remembered, and it was exhilarating. Then they forgot what they knew, in accordance with the Plan, and they returned to earth.

This forgetfulness aspect of the Plan was especially interesting to watch in action. Tracie, who had an apparent diabetic coma, said of one event which she knew happened, but couldn't remember the details of:

> *No, it's . . . it's sort of like I'm not supposed to remember it. I just get the feeling that I'm not supposed to recall what went on there. It was sort of withheld from my memory.*

As David Herard said: ". . . it was an overwhelming feeling of knowing, but I couldn't tell you now what I knew."

The loss of memory of *certain* events was despite a sharpened memory of much of the near-death experience. Almost pervasively, those having NDEs spoke of how real their experience seemed, even years after the event. They could remember many details of the experience—except for particular events, which they apparently were supposed to forget.

John Stirling likened the whole experience to Paul's teachings in Corinthians where he speaks of seeing through a glass darkly. John said that during the experience he had expanded consciousness and knew more than he knew on earth, but since returning he again saw through a glass darkly.

Gaining Knowledge in This Life

Concerning the element of the Plan that we are to seek knowledge, Joseph Smith said:

> *. . . A man is saved no faster than he gets knowledge, for if he does not get knowledge, he will be brought into captivity by some evil power in the other world, as evil spirits will have more knowledge, and consequently more power than many men who are on earth. Hence it needs revelation to assist us, and give us knowledge of the things of God.*[23]

Also, from the Doctrine and Covenants, we read:

> *Whatever principle of intelligence we attain unto in this life, it will rise with us in the resurrection; and if a person gains more knowledge and intelligence in this life through his diligence and obedience than another, he will have so much the advantage in the world to come.*[14]

Jean—Educational Buildings

The experience of Jean illustrated beautifully the need for continuing education. She said:

> *. . . I suddenly found myself in this beautiful patio garden area. There were a group of buildings around, and the buildings were—I just knew they were libraries. They were educational buildings.*
>
> *I got so excited, because I recognized the buildings as 'The Libraries.' That's what I called them: 'The Libraries.' I knew that every single building was a different subject. All the knowledge in the universe was stored in those libraries. I was excited because I wanted to go and study and read everything. Since I had just been in college it made it all the more exciting; to be where all that knowledge was available.*

Life's Purpose from Plan of Salvation

The Plan of Salvation allows us freedom of choice, including freedom to choose good or evil. One element of the plan which enhances freedom provides for opposition in all things, including opposition by accident, illness, hunger, pestilence, and war. John the revelator saw, in vision, a latter-day apocalypse in which war, pestilence, hunger, and other natural calamities were meted out to human-kind in order to purge us of our wickedness.[24]

Many of those who have gone through an NDE had the feeling that even these extreme forms of opposition were part of a perfect plan. Stephanie LaRue put it this way: "Even poor children that die of cancer at a young age, somebody's life that is taken; everything has a reason."

Professor Howard Storm, who had an extensive NDE, said: "I then asked them [the angels] how come there had been so many wars. They said that they allowed those few to happen, out of all the wars that mankind tried to start. Out of all the wars that humans tried to create, they allowed a few, to bring people to their senses, and to stop them."[25]

In his book "Opening the Seven Seals," Richard Draper analyzes much of the Book of Revelation. In his review of John's vision of the seventh seal, Doctor Draper writes:[26]

> *The Lord is perfectly prepared to allow thousands to die in order to protect his people. Some may have trouble with this idea, but the Seer has a very realistic understanding about death. From John's perspective, all must die. The question is when and how. Ultimate destiny is not determined by the moment and manner of death; it is by the manner of life. Those who are destroyed are not annihilated. They have further existence.*

As Carol and I listened to those who had undergone, for a moment, a glimpse of eternity, it was thrilling to share, albeit vicariously, their feelings of joy and wonder. We were spellbound as they outlined elements from the Plan of Salvation—frequently without knowing what they were doing.

The Plan of Salvation answers one of life's most frequently asked questions: Is there a purpose in life? It resoundingly answers: Yes, and what a beautiful purpose in a grand plan. The people we interviewed sensed that overall purpose in their own existence, and they were awed as they struggled to explain the specific purposes behind their return to this life.

Chapter Twenty-One

Spirit Bodies and Physical Bodies

In or Out of the Body?

Scientists studying near-death phenomena have sometimes questioned whether the individuals have actually left their bodies.[1] Those persons that Carol and I interviewed who had gone through the experience were completely convinced that they left their bodies. Even Forrest Hansen, who wasn't sure that there was a life-after-death, felt that he left his physical body as a sort of mental being. Some of those we interviewed had sufficiently unique experiences that it would be difficult to explain the phenomenon in any other way than an out-of-body experience.

Jackie—Saw Doctors Explaining Her Death

Jackie, whose heart stopped for ten minutes while she was undergoing emergency treatment, including two unsuccessful attempts to restart her heart with electric paddles, left the emergency room where her physical body was and found herself in the waiting room. There, she witnessed detailed conversations with the doctor, her friend, Len, and her sister. When I asked her if she later told anyone of her experience, she said:

> *Yes, I told Len after it happened. At first he didn't believe me, he just said, 'oh sure.' Then I told him of the detailed conversation he had with the hospital people about signing papers and the later conversation with the doctor and my sister. That convinced him. He said there was no way that I could have known what he said unless I had been there.*

Dee—Out-of-Body; Visited Distant Friend

Dee, in the first of two out-of-body experiences, was living in Indiana and found herself back on an army base in Virginia where she had previously lived. While there, she visited the house of her friend, Janey. She described what she saw:

I walked down the street, going south, toward Jane's house. I was going fast, it was like a floating walk. I walked right up to Janey's house, and I walked through the closed screen door.

I could see Janey sitting there with a cigarette, drinking coffee, and rubbing her temple. When she rubbed her head I always knew she was depressed. I knew, looking at her, that she had had the baby. She had shorts on, and she never wore shorts. I gave her a pair but she would never wear them, no matter how hot it got, because her husband made fun of her legs.

She seemed super-depressed and I decided I didn't want to bother her. I wanted to see the baby, though. That was the most important thing in my mind. So I went upstairs, floating up the stairs, right into the baby's room. I looked around and it seemed so sweet. When I looked at the baby I knew it was a boy. I just knew. I remember thinking that it looked more like her husband than her.

In a later telephone conversation with her friend, Dee confirmed the details of what she had seen.

Many Saw Their Bodies When Out of Them

Numerous individuals that we talked to saw their physical bodies while they were out of them. It was interesting to hear them explain that they had no emotional attachment to their body which, in some cases, was broken, bruised, or ill. In some instances they were even repulsed by it. Many of those going through an NDE were able to recount details of the medical resuscitation effort, which they later verified by conversations with the doctors and nurses.

Perhaps the best way to summarize the feelings of those having an NDE concerning whether or not they were out of their bodies is to quote one of them on the subject. I asked Stephanie LaRue: "Do you feel that the experience was truly out-of-body, and that it was a real experience and not a dream or a hallucination?" Her response was short and to the point. She said: "I'd bet my life on it."

What is the Spirit Body Like?

I asked many of those who had an out-of-body experience what their spirit body felt or looked like. Their responses were not always the same, but there were elements which were repetitive. Some examples will illustrate similarities and differences.

Jennette—Body Had No Weight

"Did your body feel like it was a body . . .?" I asked.

"Myself?" she said.

"Yes, yourself. What was it like?"

"It was an amazing thing, it was . . . there was no weight of a body. It was like floating on water, only there was no water around."

"Did you have arms and legs?"

"Oh, as far as I know I did. I really didn't look at myself. I was getting places somehow; now whether I was floating, or walking, I'm not sure."

Forrest Hansen—A Mental Experience

Forrest Hansen said: "Now this was a . . . I wasn't aware of any body whatso-ever. It was strictly a mental experience. Even the sensation of motion was not one you'd have where you could feel wind or something like that. It was only motion that you'd feel, like . . . like your equilibrium, or something. Only a mental experience."

No Pain—A Body of Energy

A comment that most of the respondents made was that all pain had left them. Many spoke of increased sensitivity to colors. Margaret Amodt was a particularly interesting case, because of the interaction of her spirit body with that of the physical body of her child. She also observed a release from pain when she was out of her physical body. Her response was as follows:

"What do you remember next, Margaret?"

"I knew I was . . . I felt so good. And I thought: *Wow, this is beautiful.* I really liked it, I liked it, the feeling I had."

"The pain was gone?"

"Yes, the pain was gone."

"Did you see yourself—your body?"

"No, the first thing I saw was my kids. They had been taken to my parents' house. They were running around, laughing."

"How many children did you have?"

"Two little girls. They were playing and I was in my parents' house. I remember, I wasn't standing, I was, like, floating. And then my oldest daughter ran right through me."

"Did that surprise you?"

"Yes. I tried to hold her and I couldn't. And she started screaming . . . I could hear her scream, 'Mamma.' Shortly after that I was back in the hospital and I felt pain. It was awful . . . ."

"When you were in your parents' home did your body feel like a body?"

"No."

"What did it feel like?"

Margaret thought for a moment. "It didn't feel like air either . . . energy!"

"Did this energy have arms and legs?"

"Just like me."

"As far as you can tell it was just like your present body?"

"Well, okay, I didn't look down. It was as if I were hovering, and I could see my children."

"And you actually tried to embrace your child?"

"Yes, my daughter. She was running and I reached out to hold her, and she ran through me. I saw her just run through me."

John Stirling—Body Defined as an Energy Field

Margaret's comment about energy is interesting. John Stirling mentioned an energy field. He said:

". . . All the emotional pain that I had been feeling was gone. I looked at my hand, and I saw a hand, but . . . but it had an aura around it. It wasn't the same hand as an earthly hand. There was an energy field that defined its shape. . . ."

"You say that you saw an aura around your hand when you looked at it," I said. "Was that aura all over your body as far as you could tell?"

"Yes."

"How did your spirit body feel when you were out of your physical body?"

"Peaceful, calm, real, existing . . . ."

A Beautiful Body

Two individuals were conscious of a spirit body that resembled, in all details, their physical body—except that it was more beautiful. Katrina said of her body:

When I went into the garden I was in a different body than the one I had left. I was not overweight, I was maybe even a little on the thin side. I seemed to be a young woman; not adolescent, but not the 35 years old that I was at the time. I had long black hair and my body was perfect. Just as beautiful as it could be. And I had more senses than the five senses we have on this earth. I had more perception. My body wasn't heavy, it wasn't cumbersome, it wasn't burdensome. It was beautiful and I didn't want to leave it.

Deceased Relatives Appeared Youthful

Several respondents described deceased grandparents, and others, as having bodies that were restored to youthful vigor.

Maureen Daniels's description of her grandparents is typical:

Approaching me from the front were my grandparents, and I recognized them immediately. My grandfather had died in 1968, and my grandmother had died three months before the incident in May, 1983. We grew up in a duplex with them, and I was very close to them. It really hurt when my grandmother died.

They approached me. I knew that it was them, but they weren't old as my grandparents had been. They walked very upright with no arthritis, and with no wrinkles—but I could tell that they were my grandparents. They came, and they didn't physically embrace me, but I felt embraced by them.

Spirit Bodies Had Increased Abilites

A few individuals observed that they were able to smell and feel while in their spirit bodies. Many people felt as if they had increased mental and visual capacities. Communication was usually by thought transference, but not always.

The common elements, from studying the above quotations and from reviewing other elements from the previous chapters, were: loss of physical, mental, and emotional pain; feelings of euphoria; increased mental and visual abilities; a feeling of weightlessness, and an ability to travel by "floating"; an ability to go through solid objects; an increased spiritual and emotional sensitivity; and an ability to direct oneself to other locations, and even other worlds, solely through mental or spiritual processes—sometimes at enormous speeds.

Less common, and sometimes contradictory descriptive elements, were: a spirit body consisting of arms, legs and other entities similar to a physical body, but made up as though it were an energy field with an observable glow; a spirit body similar to a physical body, but without the infirmities brought on by age, illness, or disability, and without the limitations of a physical body; a strictly mental entity with no body; a spirit body with an ability to smell, and to feel; and a spirit body with no sense of smell or feel.

The contradictory elements will be discussed in a later chapter. For the moment it is useful to review the LDS teachings concerning a spirit body.

LDS Teachings About a Spirit Body

Spirit Leaves Physical Body at Death

The Plan of Salvation was outlined in the previous chapter. Two of the elements are important to this chapter. They are:

> *At the end of mortal life we would die: our spirit and our body would separate, with the spirit continuing to live and the body being temporarily discarded into the tomb. The spirit would pass to another sphere, the spirit world, and would reside there until the time of the resurrection. In this spiritual sphere, those who had not been taught the gospel during earth life would have the opportunity to hear it.*
>
> *At some future time there would be a general resurrection, and we would again obtain a body which would never be lost nor destroyed.*

The Prophet Joseph Smith, and later LDS Prophets, have much to say about these two elements of the Plan of Salvation, and much is included in LDS scriptures. From the Book of Mormon we read:[2]

> *Now, concerning the state of the soul between death and the resurrection—Behold, it has been made known unto me by an angel, that the spirits of all men, as soon as they are departed from this mortal body, yea, the spirits of all men, whether they be good or evil, are taken home to that God who gave them life.*
>
> *And then shall it come to pass, that the spirits of those who are righteous are received into a state of happiness, which is called paradise, a state of rest, a state of peace, where they shall rest from all their troubles and from all care, and sorrow.*

This scripture makes clear that between death and the resurrection the spirit leaves the body and returns to God. Those spirits of righteous individuals go to a place of peace and happiness.

Spirit Body Resembles Physical Body

In Ether in the Book of Mormon, the Brother of Jared, because of his great faith, is permitted to see Jesus Christ, *before* the Lord had been born on this earth and before his resurrection. Christ says to the Brother of Jared:[3]

> *. . . Seest thou that ye are created after mine own image? Yea, even all men were created in the beginning after mine own image.*
>
> *Behold, this body, which ye now behold, is the body of my spirit; and man have I created after the body of my spirit; and even as I appear unto thee to be in the spirit will I appear unto my people in the flesh.*

The Lord thus appeared in the form of a man while still in his Spirit body, and he indicated that he would, at a later date, take upon himself a physical body. Moreover, he told the Brother of Jared that men, also, were created in a form like him.

One of the latter-day apostles of The Church of Jesus Christ of Latter-day Saints, B. H. Roberts, had this to say about spirit bodies—before they are born into this life:[4]

> *. . . We know for instance that the form of the spirit in outline, at least, is like the form of the human body of flesh and bone, which subsequently the spirit inhabits in the earth life, that he meets in the assemblies of spirits; that he exercises agency, that he is obedient to law, or rebels against it, as he chooses; that he is righteous or unrighteous as he wills; that he is capable of receiving or imparting intelligence. In a word, he is capable of participating in a very wide range of activities.*

Viewing Spirit Bodies

Normally we cannot see spirits—unless our faith is great enough, or unless the Lord prepares us so that we can. In the Pearl of Great Price, Book of Moses, the Lord speaks to the Prophet Enoch:[5]

> *Anoint thine eyes with clay, and wash them, and thou shalt see. And he did so.*
>
> *And he beheld the spirits that God had created; and he beheld also things which were not visible to the natural eye . . . .*

Joseph F.Smith, the sixth president of the Church, described the stature of spirits. He said:[6]

> *The spirits of our children are immortal before they come to us, and their spirits, after bodily death, are like they were before they came.*

They are as they would have appeared if they had lived in the flesh, to grow to maturity or to develop their physical bodies to the full stature of their spirits. If you see one of your children that has passed away it may appear to you in the form in which you would recognize it, the form of childhood; but if it came to you as a messenger bearing some important truth, it would perhaps come . . . in the stature of fullgrown manhood . . .

Composition of Spirit Bodies

In April, 1842, the Prophet Joseph Smith wrote an editorial entitled, "Try the Spirits," in the *Times and Seasons*. It is a long exposition which explores the nature of good and evil spirits. In one part of the editorial he discusses the physical body of man and the spirit of man. He says:[7]

. . . we shall find a very material difference between the body and the spirit; the body is supposed to be organized matter, and the spirit, by many, is thought to be immaterial, without substance. With this latter statement we should beg leave to differ, and state that spirit is a substance; that it is material, but that it is more pure, elastic and refined matter than the body; that it existed before the body, can exist in the body; and will exist separate from the body, when the body will be moldering in the dust; and will in the resurrection, be again united with it.

Spirit Matter

Joseph also said: "There is no such thing as immaterial matter. All spirit is matter, but is more fine or pure, and can only be discerned by purer eyes. We cannot see it, but when our bodies are purified we shall see that it is all matter."[8] Joseph taught that the spirit was eternal and could not be destroyed.[9] He said of matter:[10]

. . . Hence we infer that God had materials to organize the world out of chaos—chaotic matter, which is element, and in which dwells all the glory. Element had an existence from the time he had. The pure principles of element are principles which can never be destroyed; they may be organized and re-organized, but not destroyed. They had no beginning and can have no end.

Joseph made these comments decades before Einstein discovered the equivalence of matter and energy, in which Einstein observed that matter could not be created nor destroyed—only transformed from or into energy.

Summary of LDS Teachings About Spirit Bodies

From the quoted scriptures and teachings, and from others which have not been quoted, the following points are derived:

•Our spirit bodies are eternal; they cannot be destroyed. We have always existed, first as intelligences, and then as spirit bodies created by God.

•Spirit bodies are made up of matter, but it is matter in a different form than we are accustomed to.

•Our spirit and physical bodies are created in the image of God and his son, Jesus Christ.

•Spirit bodies normally cannot be seen by mortal beings—except when the Lord transforms us, or when our faith becomes strong enough so that we can see.

•Spirit bodies are usually in adult form. They may appear, however, in child form in order to be recognized by the person viewing them.

•When we die our spirit bodies leave our physical bodies and continue to live. They have capabilities that our physical bodies do not have. They do not suffer pain.

•Between death and the resurrection our spirit bodies return to that God who created us. There, a temporary judgment occurs and the righteous spirits go to a world of peace, beauty, love, and growth.

•Our physical bodies deteriorate after death—until the resurrection when the spirits of all beings who lived physically on this earth will again be reunited with a perfect physical body, one which cannot be destroyed.

Some Observations Concerning the Spirit

I shall now comment on some phenomena which I observed as we interviewed the respondents. In so doing, it should be noted that not all of my observations can be validated by scriptural or scientific references. Rather, these are tentative deductions based upon the sometimes peculiar circumstances described by those having had an unusual NDE or other spiritual experiences.

Basic Elements of a Near-Death Experience

Generally, in a "normal" Near-Death Experience (NDE), the person having the experience has undergone a traumatic physical event; one serious enough to bring the individual to the boundary, or beyond the boundary, of clinical death. Under such circumstances the spirit of the traumatized individual physically separates from the body and is free to leave the vicinity, sometimes traveling great distances and at enormous speeds—apparently, in many cases exceeding the speed of light. During this departure the spirit has little, if any, control of the physical body which it has left.

While away from the physical body the spirit has enormous abilities to sense and understand what is happening around it. Trauma and pain are removed. Often, knowledge of past and prospective future events are unfolded in spectacular detail, including a review of the person's life. Knowledge of the reasons behind cosmic, historic, and philosophic events is sometimes given, although memory of what it knew is usually taken away upon return to this world.

The spirit has a sense of deja vu—it knows that it has been there before and it understands that it is returning to a place which is familiar. It realizes why it had been on earth, that it had a mission to accomplish, and that everything that happens in the world has a purpose. While in the spiritual realm the individual may see a beautiful world of light with colorful flowers, ethereal music, and beings of light. The spirit often desires to stay in this new spiritual realm, but, because of an understanding of its mission in life consents to return to the earth.

Sometimes, while in the other world, and while thoroughly involved in activities of that world, the spirit is allowed to see its physical body on earth. Under these circumstances the spirit can view medical teams working on the body, grieving relatives, and emergency crews attempting to address physical problems. These circumstances occasionally bear on the decision of the individual to return.

Upon returning to the vicinity of the body the spirit either enters immediately, with little knowledge as to how it got in, or it views the body and hesitates. In the latter case, it enters, sometimes with difficulty, through the head region. Feelings of pain, which may have been there before the spirit left, return, often with a vengeance. This, then, is the so called normal NDE, albeit a rather extensive one.

Unusual Out-of-Body Experiences

I first became aware of variations on this theme as I interviewed James Niitsuma. During the interview James said that he was out of his body, yet his lips moved and he talked to the nurse who was treating him. His spirit observed this from a distance, and he had no idea how his body was able to respond while his spirit was out of it. Later his spirit departed for another world and he lost all contact with his physical body.

As James explained the situation, I suggested that he must have been mistaken, his spirit was probably still in his body while he was talking to the nurse. James insisted that it was as he described it and not as I wished it to be. I typed the experience as he gave it, even though I was uncertain that it happened as he said.

Doris—Out of a Body That Continued to Walk

The most startling confirmation of James's experience came when Carol and I interviewed Doris. Doris had stopped eating for eleven days, in an attempt to get out of the navy, when her experience happened.

> *. . . On the eleventh day, after I finished my duty with the spuds, I was walking back to my bunk and as I passed a cinder-block wall, all of a sudden, within the snap of a finger, I found myself high above my body. My body continued to walk below me.*
>
> *Naturally, I went into shock. I never had expected anything like that. I had never even heard of it. It took me at least a minute to get hold of myself. In the meantime my body kept right on walking below me.*
>
> *When I got hold of myself I figured I had to do something about it. I thought: I just can't stay up here in the air with my body below me. I came down to my body which was walking, and I hovered in front of it.*
>
> *As I hovered there, with my body walking toward me, I studied the head and shoulders to try and figure out a way to return to my body. I almost despaired because I couldn't see any way to get back in. Suddenly, like the snap of a finger, I was back.*

Doris said that her body never missed a step while she was out of it. She apparently had control but had no idea how.

Joy Melvin—Emotional Trauma

Two other confirmations of this type of experience occurred, and both had other peculiar similarities. Joy Melvin described the emotional trauma she felt after the death of her husband, her father, and her brother. As she was lying on the couch, in great distress, her spirit left her body and went to what she described as a way station. There she was able to see, feel, smell and communicate with her deceased loved ones.

Upon completion of her communication she felt as though she were pulled back by a tugging in her stomach area. Indeed, this tugging was sufficient to make her feel as if she were being pulled into a V-shape during the return.

While she was out of her body, Joy was aware of noises in her house, even though she was no longer there. Furthermore, in the beginning of the experience she could feel her head, stationary on the couch, while her spirit head was moving from side to side. She appeared to have partial control of her physical body while her spirit was leaving or had left.

Dee—Attached to Body by a "Thread"?

An analogous experience to Joy's was that of Dee when she was out of her body and being chased by an evil spirit. Although she didn't seem to have control of her physical body while her spirit was away, still, there was apparently some type of attachment between the spirit and physical bodies. Dee described it as a thread similar to a spider's web attached in the stomach area. She was terrified, when she was being chased, over the thought that she would get too far from her physical body and the thread would break.

Tentative Conclusions

From these, and other, experiences I came to some tentative conclusions—some hypotheses which should be tested by further research. I deduced that under certain circumstances the spirit body can separate from the physical body, retain some connection with it and still maintain a degree of control over it. I also hypothesized that spirit separation is triggered either by severe physical trauma, or by severe emotional trauma.

I became aware, also, of another type of spirit separation from the physical body. During the period that Carol and I were interviewing respondents to our advertisements, we got numerous calls from individuals who had different kinds of experiences. A common call was from individuals who had developed an ability to leave their body at will. I received a sufficient number of these calls to suspect that they may also have been real experiences. If they were, then I further suspect that the individuals who willingly left their bodies were playing a dangerous game—for reasons discussed in a later chapter on evil spirits.

We Are Children of Our Father in Heaven

Let me end this chapter with the observation that we are, literally, children of our Father-in-Heaven. He created our spirit bodies and set up a system whereby we could be born with our spirits enclosed in physical bodies during our sojourn on this earth. We are here to gain experience, physically and spiritually, and then to return to that spiritual realm from whence we came. Thanks to the Savior of the world, Jesus Christ, we will all be resurrected after death, and we will again have both a spirit body and a perfected physical body. To that end, perhaps we should let Job have the last word: "And though after my skin worms destroy this body, yet in my flesh shall I see God."[11]

Chapter Twenty-Two

The Other World

What They Saw and Heard

One of the most fascinating aspects of interviewing people for this book was to listen to their descriptions, often hesitatingly given with awe and wonder, of the strange and fabulous world they had seen. My first exposure to this wondrous world was when my father attempted to explain what he had seen. He described a world with a variety of plants, bushes, trees, flowers and grasses which extended beyond what we know on earth. The colors were of a wider range and more intense than anything we know here.

As Carol and I listened to those who had gone to the other world, I heard again the familiar words which my father had used, years before, to tell of this strange world. Here are a few examples:

Karl Muecke—A Colorful World

It wasn't this world—it was beautiful. It's hard to describe . . . the colors, they were clear colors . . . I was walking in a field and there were trees and flowers like I had never seen in this life. Everything was bright, and the flowers and trees . . . I had seen some of the trees in this life but many were different from this world. It was very colorful, more so than in this life.

Ann—A World of Peace and Love

. . . And then I saw . . . there was this astonishingly beautiful world before me. It was like nothing else I have since seen on earth. Somehow I knew, inside of me, that the earth had been left behind. I had no idea where I was, and I didn't care. I felt a deep, profound peace . . . no, it was more than that. It was a world of peace and love.

The new world looked sort of like the world I had left behind, but it was also very different. Everything glowed from the inside with its own light. The colors were beyond anything on earth—they were more vibrant, brilliant, and intense. And there were colors I had never seen before—don't ask me what they were. There were shrubs, trees and flowers, some of which I had seen on earth, like evergreens, and others which I hadn't seen before, and I haven't seen since. They were beautiful, beautiful.

Katrina—A Beautiful Garden

I remember leaving the void and entering a garden. The garden was similar to a wooded, or forest area, but it had plants that were tropical in nature, sort of like you would find in Florida.

There was the most beautiful music. It was not something I heard with my ears. Rather, it was something I felt with my soul.

There were animals; birds, butterflies and small furry creatures, one resembling a fawn.

Joanne Jones—More Beautiful Than Yosemite

Joanne Jones didn't tell of the new world until I prompted her with some questions. She responded in this manner:

"What did the surroundings look like in the other place?" I asked.

"Well, okay, there were mountains, beautiful mountains, trees."

"Were there flowers?"

"It was mostly foliage, more beautiful, all kinds of beautiful stuff. Not necessarily from any one region, just gorgeous . . . it was beautiful. That's all I can say. The water was . . ."

"There was water there, too?"

"It seems to me, I can't remember exactly, there was either a river, or a fall. . . ."

"What were the colors like?"

"They were vivid. Not like here; if you imagine the most beautiful place you can think of here."

"Yosemite?"

"It's . . . it's a hundred times more vivid, more wonderful than that. You can't believe it, the colors were magnificent—you can't describe it."

Other Descriptions—Music

Several people attempted to tell of music, or something like music, on the other side. In attempting to recreate the music she heard, Katrina listened to hundreds of hours of classical music—which she normally didn't listen to. She never found exactly what she was looking for. She said of the piece which she finally selected as being most representative: "It is Daniel Kobialka's version of 'Pachelbel's Kanon.' It's classical and it's pretty soft, but it's still too harsh."

The word *soft* seems to be characteristic of music in the other world. Derald Evans, in describing how he felt when he first saw the bright light, said: "It gave me a feeling like . . . almost like soft music, or something that was one-hundred percent pure." Maureen Daniels characterized it this way: "Then there was . . . I wouldn't say there was music, but there was a knowing of . . . of a calm sound. Not unlike waves, or a seashore, which I frequently went to. It was as if there were a beach kind of sound."

Cities of Light

My father, from his experience, also talked of a "city of light." He depicted buildings, roads and pathways, and other structures, all constructed of materials which had the appearance of gold, silver, marble, and other precious substances—except they glowed as if from an internal source. Dad talked of people in this city busy working on spiritual matters and learning new things. He met Peter the Apostle, who was overseeing some of this work.

During the interviews that Carol and I carried out, of all our respondents, only two people mentioned any buildings. Tracie said that she entered a building, but she did not see the exterior nor much of the interior of the building she was in. Jean described grounds and buildings in this manner:

> *The garden areas were so gorgeous. I had never seen such a well kept garden. And the colors of the flowers were so vivid. I can remember exactly, and even the cement was pure white. The sidewalks, and the benches, and the patios were beautiful. There were people all over the place, and I just stood there in the middle of the garden looking around. . . .*
>
> *I followed them into one of the buildings. It was beautiful inside, with mahogany, and cherry wood, and . . . just a beautiful interior.*
>
> *We walked up a winding staircase which was crowded with people. At the top of the staircase we entered a room that was similar to a*

courtroom, or a high-council room. In the center of the room there was a large elongated oval table with chairs all around it. In the corner there was a fenced off area with a beautifully engraved fence. There was a platform behind the fence in a sort-of closed circle.

The near-death literature, although not frequently, does identify people who saw buildings and a city of light. Raymond Moody has a section in one of his books entitled: "Cities of Light." In that section he included one woman's description of such a city:[1]

> *. . . There was the most beautiful, brilliant light all around. And this was a beautiful place. There were colors—bright colors—not like here on earth, but just indescribable. There were people there, happy people. . . . People were around, some of them gathered in groups. Some of them were learning. . . .*
>
> *Off in the distance . . . I could see a city. There were buildings—separate buildings. They were gleaming, bright. People were happy in there. There was sparkling water, fountains . . . a city of light I guess would be the way to say it. It was wonderful. There was beautiful music. Everything was just glowing, wonderful. . . . But if I had entered into this, I think I would never have returned. . . . I was told that if I went there I couldn't go back . . . that the decision was mine.*

Another account of a city is included in the book "Beyond Death's Door," by Doctor Maurice Rawlings. An elderly accountant who had a heart attack said:[2]

> *I . . . saw on the other side this beautiful, brilliantly lit city, reflecting what seemed to be the sun's rays. It was all made of gold or some shiny metal with domes and steeples in beautiful array, and the streets were shining, not quite like marble, but made of something I have never seen before. There were many people all dressed in glowing white robes with radiant faces. They looked beautiful. The air smelled so fresh. I have never smelled anything like it.*

Even Stranger Experiences

These narratives of beautiful gardens and cities, although not common to all near-death experiences, occur frequently enough so that similarities between experiences can be detected. Occasionally, however, individuals tell of some unusual scene or experience which falls outside the range of normality—if any near-death experience can be called normal. These different experiences, when they occur, are especially interesting because they have the potential for expanding our understanding of this strange and fascinating world.

Forrest Hansen—A Giant Geometric Shape in Space

My first exposure to a uniquely different experience was when I interviewed Forrest Hansen. I expected some differences even before the interview, because Forrest had told me over the phone that he did not believe, or had strong doubts, about a life after death. That, in itself, was unusual among those having had an out-of-body experience; they are usually certain that there is a life after death.

Forrest had two rather extensive out-of-body experiences. In the one, he traveled beyond the stars and saw a being of light who asked him if he wanted to terminate his existence. Forrest chose to continue and returned to earth. This particular experience was somewhat similar to that of John Stirling, who also traveled through the stars, saw his life's review, and chose to return to this life.

The really unusual experience of Forrest occurred during a later illness, in which he left his body, saw, in a black field, an enormous geometric shape being formed before his eyes. The shape consisted of, roughly, two cones on congruent axes with their apexes together. A plane, with a point of light, was perpendicular to the axis of the cones. There were two concentric spheres intersecting the cones and circumscribing the point of light, and there was a larger cone encompassing the whole.

Forrest understood this rather complex geometry to be a symbolic representation of the birth and growth of the universe, with his place in it represented by the point of light. All life experiences in the universe were symbolically represented in the cones. He entered one of the cones and traveled toward the light, and he was able to see portions of his life reviewed as he traveled up the cone. He said that as he traveled towards the light it resembled a giant tunnel of light.

If Forrest had just described his trip through the tunnel of light, his life's review, and his seeing a point of light at the end of the tunnel, then his experience would have been similar to many others who left their bodies. Forrest never got to the light, though, and his description of the geometries was unique—at least I thought it was. Then I read Phyllis Atwater's book, "Coming Back to Life."

Phyllis Atwater—A Giant Geometric Shape in Space

Phyllis Atwater is one of the few near-death researchers who have gone through such experiences. Phyllis had several out-of-body experiences as a result of a severe illness, physical and emotional. In one of the experiences, an extensive one, she traveled through the stars, entered a bright light which she characterized as "divine," and then saw an enormous geometric shape. She said:[3]

> *Further movement on my part ceased because of the shock of what happened next. Before me there loomed two gigantic, impossibly huge masses spinning at great speed, looking for all the world like cyclones. One was inverted over the other, forming an hourglass shape, but where the spouts should have touched there was instead incredible rays of power shooting out in all directions. The top cyclone spun clockwise, the bottom counter-clockwise, . . .*

Phyllis indicated that she saw herself in one of the cyclones, in which the past and future were represented. Other people could also be viewed in the cyclones, and the lower cyclone seemed to be a mirror image of the upper one. She headed toward the energy spouts in the middle, where she felt she would find God, but before she could get there she was called back to life by her son.

Although there are differences between the experiences of Phyllis and Forrest, the similarities are striking. Phyllis's hourglass shaped cyclones are almost replicates of Forrest's two gigantic cones expanding in opposite directions. Moreover, both Phyllis and Forrest saw these geometric shapes as a symbolic representation of the universe with their place in it. Both also felt that the past, present and future were depicted.

Joy Melvin—Colorful Glass-Like Mountains

There were two other experiences that I became aware of that were sufficiently different as to warrant discussion. Joy Melvin, whom Carol and I interviewed, described this situation:

> *. . . it was kind of like mountains, but they weren't mountains. See, I have to describe things that you can picture, but it's not how it was. They were sort of, like mountains, but you could see through them, and they had colors in them. Colors like pastels. Colors that . . . there's just*

no colors that I've ever seen. Pinks and . . . kind of like pinks, I don't know how to describe it, oranges and . . .

They were almost . . . they almost looked like glass. You know, I just don't know how . . . they were shiny.

There was light behind them, like before the sun comes up in the morning, and you can see the mountains with light behind them. That's how it was. It was sort of a pinkish-yellowish color.

Joy met her deceased relatives with these mountains as a backdrop. She understood the location to be some sort of *way* station—not heaven. Maureen Daniels, who saw her grandparents, also used the words *way station* to describe where she was.

A Prefab Building and Nasturtiums

Another different type of experience is recorded in the book "Return from Death" by Margot Grey, a British researcher who also had an NDE in 1976.[4] She tells of an elderly English lady who suffered a heart attack and then found herself in another world. The lady saw a prefab building (similar to those used in England in World War II to shelter bombed-out victims) in which her deceased mother was living. There were nasturtiums around the building. She commented that this was the type of building and flower arrangement that her mother always wanted. She found her mother inside making a dress. She felt at peace and communicated with her mother, who told her it was not her time—then she returned to life.

LDS Teachings about the Spirit World

Teachings of Brigham Young

Brigham Young, who succeeded Joseph Smith as president of the Church, said of the spirit world:[5]

I can say with regard to parting with our friends, and going ourselves, that I have been near enough to understand eternity so that I have had to exercise a great deal more faith to desire to live than I ever exercised in my whole life to live. The brightness and glory of the next apartment is inexpressible. It is not encumbered so that when we advance in years we have to be stubbing along and be careful lest we fall down. We see our youth, even, frequently stubbing their toes and falling down. But yonder, how different! They move with ease and like lightning. If we want to visit Jerusalem, or this, that, or the other place—and I presume we will be permitted if we desire—there we are, looking at its streets. If we want to behold Jerusalem as it was in the days of the Savior; or if we want to see the Garden of Eden as it was when created, there we are, and we see it as it existed spiritually, for it was created first spiritually and then temporally, and spiritually it still remains. And when there we may behold the earth as at the dawn of creation, or we may visit any city we please that exists upon its surface. If we wish to understand how they are living here on these western islands, or in China, we are there; in fact, we are like the light of the morning, or, I will not say the electric fluid, but its operation on the wires. God has revealed some little things, with regard to his movements and power, and the operation and motion of the lightning furnish a fine illustration of the ability of the Almighty. . . .

When we pass into the spirit world we shall possess a measure of his power. . . . Here, we are continually troubled with ills and ailments of various kinds . . . in the spirit world we are free from all this and enjoy life, glory, and intelligence; and we have the Father to speak to us, Jesus to speak to us, and angels to speak to us, and we shall enjoy the society of the just and the pure who are in the spirit world until the resurrection.

It would be difficult to improve upon this description based upon those individuals Carol and I spoke with concerning their venture into another world. Brigham Young's description of traveling as if by light or electricity would fit John Stirling's explanation of how he could travel at enormous speed where he wished, or Dee's narrative of her spirit body's trip from Indiana to Virginia and return.

His discussion of how we will be free from illnesses could be reiterated by any number of people we talked with who were overjoyed because they were free from pain and illness in the other world. His description of the brightness, power, glory, and intelligence that we will enjoy mimics much of what we heard.

His comment that we might visit places on the earth and see what they were like decades, or thousands of years earlier, is fascinating. The life's review, which many having an NDE went through, is, in effect, a detailed examination of a microscopic part of the earth's history—as it pertained to the individual. Moreover, Forest Hansen's geometric shape, as he understood it, contained all of the history of the world and the universe.

Brigham Young also speaks of a spiritual creation before the temporal or physical creation. That is basic LDS doctrine. From the third chapter of the Book of Moses in the Pearl of Great Price it says:[6]

> *And every plant of the field before it was in the earth, and every herb of the field before it grew. For I, the Lord God created all things, of which I have spoken, spiritually, before they were naturally upon the face of the earth.*

Brigham Young said that when we pass into the spirit world we shall possess a measure of God's power. He is speaking in particular of those spirits who have lived righteously on this earth, in accordance with God's laws, when they leave and go into the next life. That power will consist of the ability to teach others, as God and Jesus Christ have—and ultimately—the power to create other worlds.

Joseph F. Smith—Vision of the Dead

One of the most comprehensive scriptures on the spirit world is given in the Doctrine and Covenants and is known as the "Vision of the Redemption of the Dead." It was a vision received on October 3, 1918 by Joseph F. Smith, the sixth president of The Church of Jesus Christ of Latter-day Saints (and not to be confused with Joseph Smith, Jr., the first president of the Church). The vision provides unusual detail on what happens to spirits after they leave this life. As such, it is particularly pertinent to those who have had an NDE. The entire vision is too long for inclusion, but applicable portions are reproduced below.[7]

> *11. As I pondered over these things which are written, the eyes of my understanding were opened, and the Spirit of the Lord rested upon me, and I saw the hosts of the dead, both small and great.*
>
> *12. And there were gathered together in one place an innumerable company of the spirits of the just, who had been faithful in the testimony of Jesus while they lived in mortality; . . .*
>
> *15. I beheld that they were filled with joy and gladness, and were rejoicing together because the day of their deliverance was at hand.*
>
> *16. They were assembled awaiting the advent of the Son of God into the spirit world, to declare their redemption from the bands of death.*
>
> *17. Their sleeping dust was to be restored unto its perfect frame, . . .*

19. And there he preached to them the everlasting gospel, the doctrine of the resurrection and the redemption of mankind from the fall, and from individual sins on conditions of repentance.

20. But unto the wicked he did not go, and among the ungodly and the unrepentant who had defiled themselves while in the flesh, his voice was not raised; . . .

29. And as I wondered, my eyes were opened, and my understanding quickened, and I perceived that the Lord went not in person among the wicked and the disobedient who had rejected the truth, to teach them;

30. But behold, from among the righteous, he organized his forces and appointed messengers, clothed with power and authority, and commissioned them to go forth and carry the light of the gospel to them that were in darkness, even to all the spirits of men; and thus was the gospel preached to the dead. . . .

32. Thus was the gospel preached to those who had died in their sins, without a knowledge of the truth, or in transgression, having rejected the prophets.

This particular scripture explains what happens to spirits after they leave this life, and before they are resurrected. It implies that there is a separation of the righteous from the other spirits, and it tells how the righteous spirits teach the others. The revelation goes on to say that there is unique work being done to tie families together.

All of these concepts, namely: the separation of the righteous from the wicked, the joy of the righteous spirits, the work that they are to do, the teaching and learning that takes place, and the tie to families, can be found in the various events reported by people having had near-death experiences. The concepts are a part of the Plan of Salvation (elements 7 and 8 in Chapter 20).

A Resurrection and a Final Judgment

Part of the Plan of Salvation calls for a resurrection and a final judgement, after which the righteous and unrighteous are separated into three different kingdoms (elements 9 and 10 from Chapter 20). Even the least of these kingdoms will be much greater than we can imagine. A discussion along these lines was given in a publication by Melvin J. Ballard who was an Apostle in the Church.[8]

We must not overlook the fact that those who attain to the higher glories may minister unto and visit and associate with those of the lesser kingdoms. While the lesser may not come up, they may still enjoy the companionship of their loved ones who are in higher stations. Also we must not forget that even the least degree of glory, as the Lord has expressed it, is beyond all our present understanding. . . .

John Taylor—Different Degrees of Glory

John Taylor, who succeeded Brigham Young as president of the Church, said this about the three degrees of glory:[9]

Some of our sectarian friends think that we have curious ideas about them. I tell you what it arises from. We are aiming at what we term a celestial glory. They do not understand this. Will they get a glory: Yes, they will get all that they are looking for, just as much as they can abide, as much as it is possible for God to confer upon them under the circumstances. And will the heathen be saved? Yes, all the children of God, no matter by what name they are called, will be saved, receiving as high a glory and salvation as they are capable of receiving. But are all going to inherit the celestial glory? No, but the degree of their glory will altogether be ahead of their ideas with regard to it. It may doubtless be said of them, as it was said of others, that "eye hath not seen, nor ear heard, neither have entered the heart of man, the things which God hath prepared for them that love him."

These ideas, that the degree of glory *ultimately* achieved in the next life—after the resurrection and the final judgement—will be beyond belief, even for those who fall short in their spiritual achievements, is comforting. The idea that each individual will receive as much glory as he or she feels comfortable with agrees completely with the view of most of those having had an NDE. More will be said about this in a the next chapter, which deals in some detail with evil spirits.

Some Postulations

Why People See Different Things in an NDE

A key to understanding why people having NDEs see and experience what they do is given if we understand the ways of God and his son Jesus Christ. The scriptures teach us that the Lord is merciful, with infinite love for his children. He will allow us to advance in this world and in the next—both of which are part of his kingdom—just as fast as we are willing. He will not abridge our free agency, however, in order to force us into a higher kingdom; to do so would defeat the Plan of Salvation, and in-turn, this would lead to a self-defeating lesser achievement and glory by us, his children.

Why, then, does one person who has an out-of-body experience view a world with a beautiful garden, another view a city with beautiful buildings, another see her mother in a prefabricated building with nasturtiums, and still another see a gigantic geometric shape in the sky?

Why does one person see little children playing, another see children who died presented in form as adults, another see relatives in their earthly clothes, and still another see them in white robes? Why does one person see the light, or have a life's review, and another not?

These different experiences stem from the Lord's knowledge of us, and his understanding of our needs. John Stirling commented after his experience that we see through a glass darkly in this life, but in the next we are known by Jesus Christ, and we know him. John said it was a comfortable feeling, one which he was familiar with. He was amazed at the review of his life, and at the complete knowledge of him shown in the review—in the presence of himself and his God.

Thus we are known by Jesus Christ far better than we know ourselves. When individuals leave this earth, even temporarily from some sort of trauma, the Lord understands them. He is able to tailor a view of the spirit world according to their particular needs. What to one person might be complete nonsense, to another is a tremendous spiritual experience.

And these experiences, in my view, are real. It is a real world that those having NDEs are visiting, albeit a spiritual one. Many whom we interviewed said that the other world was more real to them than this one.

We understand from latter-day scriptures that the Lord created this world and everything in it spiritually before he created it physically. It is, surely, a small matter for him to create—or allow us to view—a portion of a spiritual world tailored to the needs of each of us. Those privileged to view this world see that which will give them the greatest growth. Many feel of the great love and compassion of the Savior. They also get a glimpse of his power and glory.

It is also clear from the scriptures and from the experiences of those who have gazed into the other world that it is a busy place. The stereotype of our spirits languishing on a cloud and playing harps couldn't be farther from the truth. There is continual work by those righteous spirits already there to bring others to a knowledge of the truth. It is, therefore, a place of study, a place of teaching, and a place of learning. The teaching and learning, for the most part, takes place in family groups—extending back for generations.

Howard Storm—Angels Respond to Our Needs

After I wrote the material directly above, I received a tape recorded by Howard Storm who had an unusual experience.[10] I will say more about Professor Storm's experience in the next chapter. Some of what he had to say, however, is directly pertinent to this chapter. His comments are reproduced below:

> *I asked my friend, and his friends, about death—what happens when we die? They said that when a loving person dies, angels come down to meet them, and they take them up. . . .*
>
> *The angels know what's inside of every person. They don't have to prove anything by showing off. They know what each of us needs, so they provide that. In some cases it may be a heavenly meadow, and in another, something else. If a person needs to see a relative, they will bring that relative. If the person really likes jewels, they will show the person jewels. We see what is necessary for our introduction into the spirit world. And those things are real in the heavenly, the divine sense.*
>
> *They gradually educate us as spirit beings, and bring us into heaven. We grow and increase, and grow and increase, and shed the concerns, desires, and base animal stuff that we have been fighting much of our life. Earthly appetites melt away. It is no longer a struggle to fight them. We become who we truly are, which is part of the Divine.*
>
> *This happens to loving people; people who are good and love God, however they may understand that. . . .*

The Fate of Righteous Individuals Who Die

Righteous individuals who die, then, become part of the host of righteous spirits working to bring us closer to God. The goal of this work is to expand the knowledge of each individual so that he or she will accept the truths taught by Jesus Christ and, in so doing, become more like him. Each individual in this environment has the opportunity to grow to the maximum extent possible and to share in the glory and power of God.

Chapter Twenty-Three

Evil Spirits

The NDE Accounts

Only a few of those Carol and I interviewed felt that they had an encounter with evil spirits. Nyk Fry, on two occasions, felt that some evil influence was trying to change the direction of his life. Katrina, after her suicide attempt, may or may not have had a brush with some evil force. She felt that she was fighting something, but she wasn't sure what.

Dee's Encounter With an Evil Spirit

The most dramatic account from those that we interviewed was that of Dee, who left her body during a period of great emotional trauma. As she told us of her experience, her hands shook, and she appeared to be in a state of agitation. She actually relived the terror of her experience. Some of what she saw and felt is repeated below:

> *The next thing I knew was . . . there was something behind me, and I was afraid. I felt this awful presence—and I knew that it was after me. I looked back and I saw that my string, which I was hooked to, was getting tight. I was afraid, and I was thinking: What is this thing behind me? I started to circle, because I knew I had to get back to the house.*
>
> *The thing was coming after me fast, and I had the feeling it could kill me. I was moving through the tops of the trees, and I was thinking that I couldn't break my string, and I had to get back quick. . . .*
>
> *This . . . this thing, this awful, this terrifying thing—I could feel it on me. It was pushing me away from the house, and I could see the string getting tighter. I was sure I was going to die. . . .*
>
> *Every time I would circle and try to get back to the house the thing would come up behind and push me. I knew I was going to die. I could feel the tug at my string. I was being chased by something that was the*

personification of evil. And it wanted me. It wanted to destroy me. I was terrified and I was crying, and I remember thinking: Oh God, help me, help me God. I got all my strength to go as fast as I could—I could actually feel this thing on the back of my neck.

The next thing I can remember was: SLAM! I was in my body and I was screaming.

Dee also said of the evil spirit:

I thought that it was the Devil, or a spirit that was trying to get my body. . . . As soon as I felt this presence behind me I knew that this was ugly, this was terror, this was the worst . . . it was the most ugly, the most horrible thing that I had ever encountered. It was going to get me—it was going to destroy me—it was after my body.

Other Accounts of Evil Spirits

There are several accounts of evil spirits, and a world of evil, in the near-death literature. Margot Grey tells of a lady, in London, who went out of her body during an operation:[1]

. . . I became aware that I was hovering above my body looking down at myself on the operating table. I felt very frightened and began to panic. I wondered why I was no longer in my body and thought I must be dead. I next found myself in a very frightening place, which I am sure was hell. I was looking down into a large pit, which was full of swirling grey mist and there were all these hands and arms reaching up and trying to grab hold of me and drag me in there. There was a terrible wailing noise, full of desperation. Then suddenly I found myself rushing back through this dark tunnel and I found myself back in my body in the hospital bed.

Dr. George Ritchie described several instances of seeing evil spirits while he was out of his body and being led by a being of light to various places on this earth. In one instance he described entering a bar with many service men and, as individuals drank themselves into a stupor, seeing evil spirits enter the bodies of those who became unconscious.[2]

In a separate incident he saw innumerable spirits involved in various acts of debauchery. He said of that incident:[3]

At first I thought we were looking at some great battlefield: everywhere people were locked in what looked like fights to the death, writhing, punching, gouging. . . . [There were] no weapons of any sort, I saw as I looked closer, only bare hands and feet and teeth. . . . They could not kill, though they clearly wanted to, because their intended victims were already dead, and so they hurled themselves at each other in a frenzy of impotent rage. . . .

Even more hideous than the bites and kicks they exchanged, were the sexual abuses many were performing in feverish pantomime. Perversions I had never dreamed of were being vainly attempted all around us. It was impossible to tell if the howls of frustration which reached us were actual sounds or only the transference of despairing thoughts.

Howard Storm—An Extensive Experience

One of the most complete descriptions of evil spirits in another world is given by Professor Howard Storm, from Northern Kentucky University. Professor Storm became ill while on a trip to France with his wife and some students. While in a hospital in Paris he had an extensive out-of-body experience.[4]

Prior to the experience, Professor Storm explained, he had lived a rather material life, and he didn't believe that there was a life after death or that there was a God. During the experience he saw both evil spirits, and, similar to Dr. Ritchie's extensive experience, he enjoyed the presence of beings of light. These beings of light taught him much about the other world. A portion of Professor Storm's experience follows:

. . . But I felt really strange, and I opened my eyes. To my surprise I was standing up next to the bed, and I was looking at my body lying in the bed. My first reaction was: This is crazy! . . .

Then I heard my name. In French there is no equivalent to Howard, and they messed it up when they tried to use it. But someone was saying my name correctly. I heard: "Howard, Howard—come here."

I wondered where it was coming from. I discovered that it was coming from the doorway, and there were different voices calling me. I asked who they were, and they said: "We are here to take care of you. We will fix you up. Come with us."

I asked, again, who they were. I asked them if they were doctors and nurses. They responded: "Quick, come see. You'll find out."

As I asked them questions they would give evasive answers. They kept giving me a sense of urgency, that I should step through the doorway. With some reluctance I stepped into the hallway. And in the hallway—I was in a fog, or a haze. It was a light colored haze. It wasn't a heavy haze, I could see my hand, for example, but the people who were calling me were 15 or 20 feet ahead; I couldn't see them clearly. They were more like silhouettes, or shapes, and as I moved towards them they would back off into the haze. . . .

I walked for what seemed to be a considerable distance, with these beings all around me. They were leading me through the haze. I don't know how long—

As we traveled, the fog got thicker and darker. And the people began to change. At first they seemed rather playful and happy. As we traveled, though, some of them began to get aggressive. Then, others would seem to caution the aggressive ones. I seemed to hear them warn the aggressive ones to be careful or I would be frightened away.

I continued to ask questions, and they repeatedly urged me to hurry and to stop asking questions. I felt very uneasy, especially since they continued to get more aggressive. I would have returned, except I didn't know how to get back. I didn't know where I was. There were no features that I could relate to. There was just the fog and a wet, clammy ground. I had no sense of direction.

I finally told them that I wouldn't go any farther. At that time they changed completely. They became much more aggressive and insisted that I was going with them. They began to push and shove me, and I responded by hitting back at them.

It seemed to be, almost, a game for them, with me as the center-piece of their amusement. My pain became their pleasure. They seemed to want to make me hurt—by clawing at me and biting me. Whenever I would get one off me, there were five more on me. By then it was almost complete darkness, and I had the sense that instead of there being 20 or 30, there were an innumerable host of them. Each one seemed set on coming in for the sport they got from hurting me.

I fought well and hard for a long time, but ultimately I was spent. I lay there amongst them, and they began to calm down since I was no longer the amusement that I had been. People were still picking at me, occasionally, and I just lay there all torn up, unable to resist.

Exactly what happened was . . . and I'm not going to try and explain this. From inside of me I felt a voice, my voice, say: " Pray to God." My mind responded to that: "I don't pray. I don't know how to pray." The voice again told me to pray to God. I was in a dilemma since I didn't know how. The voice told me a third time to pray to God.

I started saying things like: "The Lord is my shepherd, I shall not want . . . God bless America," and anything else that seemed to have a religious connotation. And these people went into a frenzy, as if I had thrown boiling oil all over them. They began yelling and screaming at me, telling me to quit, that there was no God, and no one could hear me. While they screamed and yelled obscenities, they also began backing away from me—as if I were poison.

I screamed back at them: "Our Father who art in heaven," and similar ideas. This continued for some time until, suddenly, I was aware that they had left. I was alone in the dark, yelling things that sounded churchy. And I was pleased that these churchy sayings had such an effect on those awful beings.

I lay there for a long time. I was in such a state of hopelessness, and blackness, and despair, that I have no way of measuring the time. I was just lying there in an unknown place—all torn and ripped. And I had no strength; it was all gone. I felt as if I were sort of fading out, that any effort on my part would expend the last energy I had. My conscious sense was that I was perishing, or just sinking into the darkness.

Then a most unusual thing happened. I heard, very clearly, once again in my own voice, something that I had learned in nursery Sunday School. It was the little song: "Jesus loves me, yes I know, . . ." and it kept repeating. I don't know why, but all of a sudden I wanted to believe that. I didn't have anything left, and I wanted to cling to that thought. And . . . and I, inside, screamed: "Jesus, please save me." I screamed that with every ounce of strength and feeling left in me.

When I did that, I saw, off in the darkness somewhere, the tiniest little star. I didn't know what it was, and I thought it was a comet or a meteor, because it was moving rapidly. Then I realized it was coming toward me. It was getting very bright, rapidly.

As it came up to me, and its radiance was all over me, I just rose up—not with my effort—I just lifted up. Then I saw . . . and I saw this

> *very plainly, I saw all my wounds, all my torn spots, all my brokenness, just melt away. And I became whole in this radiance.*
>
> *What I did—was to cry uncontrollably. I was crying, not out of sadness, but because I was feeling things that I had never felt before in my life.*
>
> *Another thing happened. All of a sudden I knew a whole bunch of things. I knew things . . . I knew that this light, this radiance, knew me. I don't know how to explain to you that I knew it knew me, I just did. As a matter of fact, I understood that it knew me better than my mother or father did.*

I shall comment, shortly, about these different experiences with evil spirits. For the moment it is useful to turn to some LDS teachings.

LDS Teachings and Scriptures

The New Testament is replete with examples of evil spirits occupying the bodies of susceptible beings. One of the best known stories involves Christ's encounter with the man who could not be bound with chains, and who cut himself with stones. When challenged by Christ, evil spirits in the man identified themselves as "Legion." Christ ordered them to leave the man and they entered a herd of two thousand swine nearby. The swine then ran off a cliff into the sea.[5]

The scriptures also make clear that even the elect will be tempted by Satan and by his legions. This is especially true if the work the individual is doing threatens Satan's work, or if the individual is weakened from emotional, physical, or other causes. Christ, himself, was tempted by Satan after he had completed his forty day fast.[6] Similarly, the Prophet Joseph Smith found himself bound by an evil power just before he saw the Lord. (The entire account is given in Chapter 26.)

Heber C. Kimball—Legions of Evil Spirits

One of the best descriptions of the effort of evil spirits trying to stop the work of the Lord is provided by Heber C. Kimball, an early Apostle in The Church of Jesus Christ of Latter-day Saints. In July, 1837, Heber Kimball, in the company of Orson Hyde, Isaac Russell, and Willard Richards, were in Preston, England, beginning missionary work in that land, when they were attacked by evil spirits. Heber Kimball's description of the event follows:[7]

I saw legions of wicked spirits that night, as plain as I now see you, and they came as near to me as you now are, and company after company of them rushed towards me; and Brother Hyde and Brother Richards also saw them. It was near the break of day, and I looked upon them as I now look upon you. They came when I was laying hands upon Brother Isaac Russell, the wicked spirits got him to the door of the room, I did not see them till after that took place, and soon afterwards I lay prostrate upon the floor. . . . and they struggled and exerted all their power and influence. . . . I saw their hands, their eyes, and every feature of their faces, the hair on their heads, and their ears, in short they had full-formed bodies.

Where Do Evil Spirits Come From?

It is clear from these teachings that evil spirits attempt to terminate the spiritual well being of humans on this earth. They are especially active against those about to enjoy success in the work of the Lord—although usually with no success. They have more success against those individuals who put themselves in harm's way through hatred, fear, despair, greed, ambition, hypocrisy or through the use of drugs.

Where do these evil spirits come from? Some were with Satan from the beginning, when a third of the host of heaven followed him after he rebelled against the plan presented by our Heavenly Father and by Jesus Christ.[8] These spiritual minions of the devil are consigned to his realm. They will never receive a physical body, since they will not be born into this world, as will the rest of our Father's children. They will be joined by those other pitiful souls, known as the sons of perdition, who, having known the truth, and having had it confirmed by the Holy Spirit, deny it. For all of these there is no forgiveness in this world nor in the world to come.[9]

Many of the devil's followers, though, come from those hapless individuals who, during their mortal life, fall prey to the enticements of Satan and his legions. These poor souls, after they die physically, also become spiritually dead; that is, they are cut off from the presence of the Father and the Son.

What Happens to Spirits of Those Who Lived Wickedly?

Alma, in the Book of Mormon, describes their fate thus:[10]

And then shall it come to pass, that the spirits of the wicked, yea, who are evil—for behold, they have no part nor portion of the Spirit of the Lord; for behold, they chose evil works rather than good; therefore the spirit of the devil did enter into them, and take possession of their house—and these shall be cast out into outer darkness; there shall be weeping, and wailing, and gnashing of teeth, and this because of their own iniquity, being led captive by the will of the devil.

Now this is the state of the souls of the wicked, yea, in darkness, and a state of awful, fearful looking for the fiery indignation of the wrath of God upon them; thus they remain in this state, as well as the righteous in paradise, until the time of their resurrection.

It is interesting to read of the darkness, and of the weeping, wailing, and gnashing of teeth, in light of the descriptions presented by those having been exposed to these satanic forces in a near-death experience. The outer darkness thus described is hell, where the wicked remain until the resurrection. Then, they along with the rest of our Father's children who have lived on the earth, will be judged according to how they lived, and they will be accorded an appropriate glory.

Man's Free Choice—Evil or Good

What is the goal of Satan and his followers? It is to gather other followers for Satan, and thus, to make the new followers miserable like they are. What is the goal of our Father in Heaven? It is, through granting us freedom of choice, to provide for our growth so that we might, with him, have eternal joy and become co-creators. These thoughts are expressed well by Lehi in the The Book of Mormon:[11]

Adam fell that men might be; and men are, that they might have joy.

And the Messiah cometh in the fulness of time, that he may redeem the children of men from the fall. And because they are redeemed from the fall they have become free forever, knowing good from evil; to act for themselves and not to be acted upon, save it be by the punishment of the law at the great and last day, according to the commandments which God hath given.

Wherefore, men are free according to the flesh; and all things are given them which are expedient unto man. And they are free to choose liberty and eternal life, through the great mediation of all men, or to choose captivity and death, according to the captivity and power of the devil; for he seeketh that all men might be miserable like unto himself.

The Lesser Glory

In the preceding chapter we observed that even those souls who lived a miserable life, and who did not sin against the Holy Spirit, would be granted a final glory (the Telestial) after the resurrection which exceeds anything we now know. This will be a glory, however, which God and his son Jesus Christ do not visit. Only the angels will minister to those in this glory. The Doctrine and Covenants describes the beings who inherit this glory in these terms:[12]

> *These are they who are liars, and sorcerers, and adulterers, and whoremongers, and whosoever loves and makes a lie.*
>
> *These are they who suffer the wrath of God on earth.*
>
> *These are they who suffer the vengeance of eternal fire.*
>
> *These are they who are cast down to hell and suffer the wrath of Almighty God, until the fulness of times, when Christ shall have subdued all enemies under his feet, and shall have perfected his work.*

So, even these pitiful creatures, after the resurrection and the final judgment, will receive all the glory that they want, and all that they are comfortable with.

The Book of Mormon makes clear that people who live unrighteous lives and who deny Christ will not be comfortable, later, in his presence:[13]

> *Then will ye longer deny the Christ, or can ye behold the Lamb of God? Do ye suppose that ye shall dwell with him under a consciousness of your guilt? Do ye suppose that ye could be happy to dwell with that holy Being, when your souls are racked with a consciousness of guilt that ye have ever abused his laws?*
>
> *Behold, I say unto you that ye would be more miserable to dwell with a holy and just God, under a consciousness of your filthiness before him, than ye would to dwell with the damned souls in hell.*
>
> *For behold, when ye shall be brought to see your nakedness before God, and also the glory of God, and the holiness of Jesus Christ, it will kindle a flame of unquenchable fire upon you.*

Further Thoughts on Hell

A Personal Observation Concerning Satan

From the scriptures, and from the experiences of those who have endured an encounter with evil spirits, it is abundantly clear that Satan, his followers, and hell, are real. In the book "In Search of Angels," I had this to say about Satan and his followers:[14]

I struggled for some time with the reality of Satan and whether he could directly influence how I acted and thought. In time I came to recognize Satan's influence in some of our most precious institutions. Music, movies, TV, and even books were not beyond his intervention, usually in ways so subtle as to escape attention. Entertainment was often presented as a counterfeit for joy, and offered prescriptions which, if followed, tended to destroy the family and a belief in God.

Hollywood, in particular, seemed obsessed with debasing the institution of marriage and presenting extramarital sex as the ultimate joy. Rock music added its sexual overtones, and later its overt depiction of sex, to the litany of counterfeit joy offered by Satan's ambassadors. For dessert, I and my friends were offered alcohol in a variety of attractive packages—and later narcotics—to supposedly make us really free from the inhibitions which would restrict our fun. Violence was also presented by Hollywood in escalating orgies designed to assure titillation of our already overused senses, and all this in the name of art and freedom of expression!

To assure that we did not fall back into any archaic religious teachings which might identify the reality of Satan's obfuscation, Satan attacked the very elect. He did this by influencing the thinking of thought leaders in our community.

Some of our best teachers, for example, helped us to rationalize our improper behavior. This was particularly true at the University of California, [which I attended] and the city of Berkeley, where bizarre behavior was often looked on as a badge of honor. I observed, also, that numerous professors at the university doubted the existence of God, and they considered Satan to be an absurd fiction created by religionists to keep their flock in line.

My own observations and other experiences convinced me that Satan was horrifyingly real. Moreover, I determined that he and his followers were clever beyond belief in presenting counterfeits for joy and happiness.

How to Avoid Satan

How, then, may we avoid the snares left by Satan and his followers? Answers may be found by listening to those who have seen, though briefly, the other side. And, more importantly, by reading the scriptures prayerfully—and then acting upon that which the Spirit tells us to do.

Let me, first, illustrate what some of those having had an NDE have to say.

Advice from Dee

I believe that people should do more good with their lives, to guard their souls against the ugly things that are out there. After my experiences I did change.

One of the ugliest things is hate. It takes a long time to get rid of hate—and it is so ugly—it's like that thing that was chasing me. When I was in a depressed state, I hated, and when I finally let go of it . . . wow, it was like a clean slate.

Hate was making me ugly; hate and loathing for my husband were destroying me. So, when I was out of my body, I was ripe for the thing that was chasing me. It could easily have taken over. The only thing that saved me was my love for my daughter and my appeal to God. Love can destroy hate if we let it.

Jackie—Concerning Anger

Well, it's like I said about my friend. He was angry with the whole world. I think if you are angry, and if you are hateful, you might not be able to separate yourself from this material world. I think you really have to be able to separate yourself to go on to a higher plane.

Katrina on Wanting to Do Right

Instead of being so worried about condemnation I feel as though I have been set free from that. Now I'm **wanting** *to do what is right by my family. And I* **want** *to have a relationship with Christ—out of a desire inside me, not because if I don't I'm afraid I will go to hell. I just want to. I've been changed inside.*

Howard Storm on Prayer

Howard Storm, who was asked, after his experience, if he thought we should try and get in touch with the spirit world through channeling had this to say:[15]

I think there is a lot of abuse in that area . . . They [the angels] are into non-interference. They want us to do the work. It would be pointless, since they can to do it effortlessly, for them to do it for us. They have, therefore, kind of a hands-off attitude about this world.

I also think that there is a lot of potential for demonic forces to weasel their way in, and play games with people, for the sake of their own mindless amusement. I strongly believe in speaking to the spiritual world, and in being open to its response. But one has to be very circumspect, and careful, as to how one does that.

I pray, frequently, and I sometimes anticipate and enjoy responses to my prayers. I try to do that with clarity, with goodness, and with a pure heart. I tend to be highly, highly, highly suspect of anyone who does it for personal gain. That could be a pretty good clue as to whether it was an improper way to seek communication with the spirit world. Or, someone who is trying to do it for ego enhancement, and is pretending to have this elite, esoteric knowledge.

Key Scriptural Messages

These are but a few thoughts of those who have had a glimpse of eternity. The scriptures deliver similar messages. Perhaps the scriptural messages can be summarized by three quotations from the New Testament. Paul, in Colossians, says about preparing for Christ's coming:[16] "But now ye also put off all these; anger, wrath, malice, blasphemy, filthy communication out of your mouth. Lie not to one another, seeing that ye have put off the old man with his deeds; And have put on the new man, which is renewed in knowledge after the image of him that created him."

Matthew quotes Christ, in helping us to set priorities, as saying:[17] "But seek ye first the kingdom of God, and his righteousness; and all these things shall be added unto you."

The third scriptural message, also appearing in Matthew, occurred when a lawyer asked Christ, thinking to trap him, "Which is the great commandment in the law?" Jesus answered:[18]

Thou shalt love the Lord thy God with all thy heart, and with all thy soul, and with all thy mind.

And the second is like unto it, Thou shalt love thy neighbour as thyself.

On these two commandments hang all the law and the Prophets.

If there is a single message that would characterize the near-death experience, this last scriptural passage is it. Carol and I heard, repeated many times, that the other world, the good one, was filled with love, the love of

God and of Jesus Christ. This love was tangible to those experiencing it—it engulfed them. And they reciprocated. Upon returning to this life they felt that the most important message they brought back with them was that we should all love everybody else—all the children of God—with an unconditional love.

The corollary experiences from the evil world were just the opposite. That world was filled with hate, despair, terror, hopelessness, darkness, and with the animal passions of this world magnified many times—but with no satisfaction of those passions. It was, in short, hell!

Chapter Twenty-Four

The Power of God

Some Strange Patterns

When Carol and I started interviewing people for this book, I had no idea where it would lead us. I knew we would hear some unusual experiences, but I didn't know *how* unusual, nor did I understand that some patterns would develop which would lead to conclusions about the near-death experience which I had not anticipated.

In the Introduction I mentioned that I have frequently been asked how I knew that the people we were interviewing were telling the truth. I observed, there, that the demeanor of those being interviewed was often as though they were reliving their experiences. Even to retell what they had experienced was an intensely moving event to them—and one which brought back memories of a real experience.

There were other reasons, however, why I became convinced that they were telling the truth; at least those whose stories we accepted for this book. One of those reasons had to do with patterns which I saw develop while they were telling their stories. The patterns in some instances were astonishing. And they came from individuals with different educational, cultural, and religious, backgrounds.

Usually the people granting the interviews were not aware that they were exposing a pattern of thought or behavior that someone else had also exposed. They were intensely interested to know if others had had similar experiences. When they recounted their stories they were merely expressing, oftentimes with difficulty, something that they didn't fully comprehend. In many instances, as they repeated a pattern of thought that we had previously heard, it was as if some other power were directing their words, thoughts, and actions.

Words

One of the initial patterns that became evident was that certain words kept appearing repeatedly. One word in particular appeared so often that it almost appeared as though the people were under compulsion to use it. That word was: *peace*. Its synonyms also appeared frequently. A few examples will illustrate the point.

Karl Muecke said: "It was all around me, the most peaceful, the most beautiful feeling . . . ." Ann said: "Suddenly I felt this tremendously powerful . . . it's beyond the words of powerful, it's . . . I was suddenly enveloped in this deep, deep peace." Jennette described it this way: "The serenity . . . there are no words that can explain . . . the peace, the calm . . ." Pauline, while she was drowning, said this about her feelings: "And then, the peace, the unbelievable peace." Lois Clark, describing beings she saw, said of them: "The others seemed at peace—sort of idyllic." Chris Walker said of his very brief out-of-body experience: "It was just total peace." Marcia Anderson, who left her body when her home was filled with carbon monoxide, said: "I was really calm, and I felt completely at peace."

Kim, the 15-year-old who left her body after an operation, said: ". . . and I saw this brilliant light—not like heat warmth, more peace-warmth." Tracie, the other 15-year-old who left her body during a diabetic coma, said: "It was very peaceful and it felt safe." By the time we interviewed Tracie it was apparent that the word peace, and its derivatives, were used repeatedly by those having an NDE, so I asked Tracie why she used it. Her reply was: "I don't know, it just seems like the right word."

Because of the repeated use of the word peace, I used my scripture search computer program to determine how many times it appears in the standard scriptures used in The Church of Jesus Christ of Latter-day Saints (*Bible, Book of Mormon, Doctrine and Covenants*, and *Pearl of Great Price*). The word appears in 545 verses, and is among the more frequently used words in the scriptures.

Jesus, when he was nearing the end of his ministry and was trying to prepare his disciples for that event, told them that they would receive the Holy Ghost. And then he said:[1] "Peace I leave with you, my peace I give unto you: Not as the world giveth, give I unto you. Let not your heart be troubled, neither let it be afraid."

The people whom we were interviewing, apparently, were using a word that is special to the Lord, and one that is used in the scriptures in that special sense. The peace which the people were talking about was not the kind of peace that we usually think of. One of the definitions given in the dictionary is: "quiet, calm, peace of mind, freedom from anxiety," and it certainly was all of that. But, as the people used the word, it was more than that. In fact, it was peace "not as the world giveth," but as Christ gave it.

The peace that the people spoke of seemed to include calmness, peace of mind, and freedom from anxiety, but it also included power and love—the power and love of God. Joe Swick described it in this manner: "I grew very close to the light, and I could feel the power, and that . . . the love flowing through me."

Joseph Smith, in 1839, after spending months in prison, prayed to the Lord and asked how long the saints must endure such suffering. The responding revelation was one of the most beautiful pieces of scripture ever recorded. The opening verse of the Lord's response is pertinent to this discussion. The Lord began:[2] My son, peace be unto thy soul; thine adversity and thine afflictions shall be but a small moment; . . ."

It appears that when people are suffering from severe physical or emotional distress, as with an NDE, and when they are righteous individuals, then the Lord blesses them with his peace. That peace has the power to heal the troubled soul, and the individuals emerge feeling refreshed and rejuvenated. The peace is not as the world giveth, but as the Lord giveth.

Love is another word that kept appearing in the language of those having had an NDE—but not as frequently as the word peace. Moreover, on several occasions when people used the word love, they quickly qualified what they meant. Stephanie LaRue, when I asked her if she felt love in the other world, put it this way: "Oh definitely love, definitely. It . . . there are no words in the English language to describe it. It's more than love; the word love is just the tip of the iceberg, so to speak."

Several individuals made similar comments. Tracie mentioned, also, that it wasn't translatable into English. It was almost as if the word love had the wrong connotation in the divine sense, but it was the best word they could come up with to describe their feelings.

Joy was a word which was frequently used without qualifications. It appears to be used in the scriptures, particularly The Book of Mormon, in the same sense that the NDEers used it.

Several individuals spoke of an extra, or fourth, dimension in their perception. That was the only way they could describe their additional sensitivity.

I have already covered the many words used to describe the *brightness of the light*. Words often failed them in this cause.

It was also interesting to watch people grope for words as they tried to describe the *colors* of the other world. There was universal agreement that the colors were beyond anything in this world. Howard Storm, who was Chairman of the Art Department of Northern Kentucky University when he had his experience, said:[3]

> *As an aside, I'm an artist. There are three primary, three secondary, and six tertiary colors in the visible light spectrum. I was seeing a visible light spectrum with at least 80 new primary colors. I was, also, seeing this brilliance. It's disappointing for me to try and describe, because I can't—I was seeing colors that I had never seen before.*

Many people spoke of increased *knowledge* and *power*—the power of expanded knowledge. They also spoke of the power to travel at unheard of speeds.

Several used the word *warm*, but in an unusual way. Joy Melvin expressed it this way: "I was walking, and . . . and when I was walking I felt really warm. It wasn't temperature warm, it just was warm." This, also, seems to be a word that is used in a special spiritual sense. In the same section of the Doctrine and Covenants where Joseph Smith is promised peace, he is told: "Thy friends do stand by thee, and they shall hail thee again with *warm* hearts and friendly hands."[4] This seems to be the sense in which warmth was used by those having an NDE.

There are numerous other words which kept appearing in interesting ways in the vocabulary of those having an NDE. It was not surprising that the people we listened to struggled to find the right words as they expressed their feelings about the spiritual world. What was surprising, though, were the parallels that we found in their expressions. The parallels were more than mere coincidence. They were manifestations of the spirit and power of God touching the minds of men and women who were striving to describe the majesty of God.

Healings—and Suffering

A totally unexpected pattern concerned healings. I expected to find people who had returned to this life after an NDE more-or-less healed after their bout with death. And this was the case. Indeed, with several, in addition to the miracle of the NDE, there was a miraculous healing upon their return to this life. This was true of Ann who had leukemia prior to her childhood

NDE and was healed; then, as an adult, she contracted spinal meningitis, had another NDE, and was healed again upon her return.

Ruth—A Bad Lung is Healed

These kinds of healing experiences, although spectacular in their own right, were not unexpected. The really unexpected pattern, though, I came upon almost by accident. Carol and I had largely finished our interview with Ruth, the lady who, when she took a birth-control pill that caused her heart to stop, had an out-of-body experience. We were ready to leave and I asked her, almost in passing, if there were any other events she would like to talk about. She responded that another event, a year later, but not an NDE, helped her considerably.

> With our encouragement, she told us the following story: *About a year later my left lung started giving me trouble again. I mentioned that I smoked—not very much, maybe ten or twelve cigarettes a day, but it was too much. I went to a doctor and he did a number of tests including an x-ray. I had had flu, pneumonia, pleurisy, and other related problems. His x-ray showed that I had a spot on my lung.*
>
> *I went to another doctor and he told me that eventually the lung would have to come out. He asked me if I smoked, and when I told him I did he told me to quit. The doctors had scared me enough that I stopped instantly.*
>
> *Anyway, during this period I went to a church in San Diego that someone had recommended. It was the Self Realization Church, and it was based on spiritual precepts. I was sitting in the back of the church and I felt this tremendous peace, and . . . and I had a spontaneous healing. I didn't know it was a spontaneous healing—it felt like electricity, and it came from my neck and spread down over my back. It was so powerful that, inside, I was thinking that I wasn't ready for this, whatever it was. In fact, I hoped it would stop.*
>
> *I went in for a chest x-ray, a month later, and I didn't expect anything different. The doctor came out; he was just beaming, and he said, 'This is perfect, your lung is completely healed.'*

Ruth's experience was so similar to that of DeAnne Anderson Shelley, whom I had known years before in California, that I included both of their experiences in the same chapter. I thought their experiences were so unique that I wouldn't find another one. Then it happened again—with Lois Clark.

Lois Clark—Healing of Breast Cancer

Lois told how, as the result of a car accident in 1965, she had left her body during an NDE. Then, in 1989, she developed cancer of the breast, which the doctors weren't sure could be halted even with a complete mastectomy.

Prior to the operation to remove the breast she invited an LDS missionary to give her a blessing. During the blessing she felt as though waves were passing through her body. Then she was wheeled to x-ray for a last examination prior to the operation. The doctors decided that the x-ray machine was out of order when it didn't show what they knew was there—until a second machine also showed no evidence of cancer. The operation was cancelled.

Lucy—Walks Again

By the time another respondent, Lucy, told her story I was accustomed to the unusual. She told of how her father, of Jewish background, became a convert to the LDS Church prior to his death. Lucy was also baptized into the church and became an active member. Many years later while crossing the street she was struck by a car. She had an out-of-body experience and then returned to a body racked with severe physical problems.

For two years Lucy was unable to walk. A few days before they were to surgically remove her leg, she prayed desperately for help—and she saw Christ. He told her to have faith.

She was scheduled to get some preliminary tests prior to the operation, and while she was being wheeled to the doctor's office she had the following experience:

> *On the way to the doctor's office there was another building, and something beckoned me to it. I had my mother push me up there. There was a Naturopath—a natural doctor. When I was in there, the doctor was in back . . . . He said that he felt he had to come forward, he didn't know why. I had not . . . I had just come in the door.*
>
> *He rushed me into a room, and he told me that something was stuck in my leg. He told me to wait a moment, and he called another doctor. Another doctor came over, a woman, and they removed something from my leg. Anyway, I walked out. . . . I had not been able to walk for two years. I walked for the first time in two years.*

A Pattern of Healing—For a Purpose

The pattern that became evident from these experiences was the following:

•The individuals were good people, who, as the result of an illness or an accident had an out-of-body experience.

•They came back to this life with an even firmer resolve to live a righteous life. They were more spiritually attuned than they previously had been. They had a sense of purpose about life.

•An illness or injury developed (or lingered) which threatened their ability to carry out their perceived purpose.

•A healing occurred which defied medical knowledge.

Admittedly, the four experiences are hardly enough to suggest that they represent a universal paradigm. The parallels were strong enough and the events so unusual, however, that, at least for these cases, there appeared to be a pattern.

From these experiences I reached a tentative conclusion or hypothesis. The hypothesis is:

> *When an individual undergoes an NDE and returns to this life, that return is for a purpose. If the individual, after return, has some illness or injury that threatens to thwart the person's life purpose, then the Lord intervenes and removes the threat.*

This hypothesis should be tested by further research of persons having NDEs.

The very fact that a person has an out-of-body experience and comes back indicates the Lord's interest in the person. I have already discussed how the majority of the people felt that they came back for a purpose. To allow the person to return to this life and then not be able to fulfill his or her purpose would seem a fruitless exercise.

This is not to suggest that each person returns with a strong and healthy body. Just the opposite is often true—and the people having had an NDE understand that they may have to live under difficult circumstances when they return. David Herard, the Vietnam veteran, for example, couldn't remember when he had last been without pain. Several others we interviewed were in similar circumstances. The difference between them and the four cases, was that they were still able, despite their physical disabilities, to carry out their perceived life's purpose.

Stuart—A Modern Job

There is an interesting case in a publication of the International Association for Near-Death Studies (IANDS).[5] Doctors Surdahely and Walker describe an individual, whom they call Stuart, who had spent the majority of his life unable to speak in a normal fashion, and who had limited physical abilities because of spastic quadriplegia. He could communicate in a crude fashion through the use of programmed messages and by responding "yes" or "no" to those messages. At the time of Stuart's interview he was 39 years old.

As a result of some interesting circumstances, it became clear that Stuart had undergone an NDE as a child, and subsequently had experienced other occasions—three before he was 21 years old, and three after that—when he left his body.

Stuart had extensive experiences out of his body. On the first occasion, among other things, he saw a bright light that he identified as God. He also saw a future time, which he knew to be after this life—and not as a reincarnation—when his body would be restored with normal functions. After viewing several scenes he was told that he had to return to this life.

In later experiences, as the pain of his illness became too much for Stuart to withstand, he left his body and met with Jesus and God. Jesus loved and nurtured him, even embracing and holding him, during these occasions. He was informed that one of the purposes for his coming back was to serve as an example for other disadvantaged people. It was also to witness to able-bodied persons that there is more to the individual than the outer-body, and that people should be less concerned with how they look.

On his last out-of-body experience, in February, 1989, he met with numerous of his deceased relatives, including a glowing woman who had died a century ago. His grandfathers and grandmothers were present, along with two deceased stepbrothers. He characterized it as a "big reunion," with much love.

Stuart is under considerable pain much of the time. During the interview process, for example, the researchers observed the pain that he suffered. They wondered, since he got such relief when he left his body, whether he could leave at will. Stuart made it clear that we should not seek such experiences as a relief from pain; rather, the experiences occurred as a spontaneous gift from God. Stuart was completely fearless concerning death.

Apparently, for Stuart, a portion of his life's purpose is, in effect, to suffer, and in so doing to demonstrate to others how to handle disabilities; even painful disabilities. Stuart, as a modern Job, must be a choice child of our Father in Heaven to be chosen for such a role.

Healings—Examples of God's Power

The scriptures, particularly the New Testament, are full of examples of miraculous healings. The Doctrine and Covenants speaks of special gifts given to people:[6]

> *And again, to some it is given to have faith to be healed;*
> *And to others it is given to have faith to heal.*
> *And again, to some is given the working of miracles; . . .*

If it is the Lord's will, and if the individuals have sufficient faith, then a healing can occur. That, apparently, was what happened in the NDE cases cited. Unusual healings of this type are among the more dramatic ways that God's power is made manifest to humans.

The Importance of Families

A pattern of family affiliation which extends beyond the grave was clearly evident in the experiences of numerous individuals that we interviewed. On several occasions these reunions occurred together with similar features to those that usually happen with an NDE, except that the nearness of death was not present.

Joy Melvin—Two Family Experiences

Joy Melvin had two unusual experiences. She first described this incident from her childhood:

> *When I was about five or six years old, on a fishing trip with my family to Flaming Gorge, it was really late at night, and my mom told me to run over to the bathrooms they have at the campground. I was running with my shoe laces untied, and I tripped on my shoe. I got down to fix my shoe, and . . . and there was this really, really bright light.*
>
> *The light was very bright and I looked up. It was my grandma. I knew it was her—from her pictures—and, I just knew it was her.*
>
> *. . . I remember her brown curly hair, she had naturally curly hair. I kept looking at her feet because they weren't touching the ground, and I asked her what she was standing on. She talked to me—I think—it's just like I felt her words inside me. She told me that she loved me so much, and to tell my mother that she was okay.*
>
> *She said that she was fine, she would be waiting for my mother, and everything was okay. I think the whole thing was more for my mother.*

I don't know why she didn't go to her, but she kept emphasizing that I should tell my mom that she was really happy where she was.

She was wearing a white robe, and there was a glow behind her. Her feet were bare, and she wasn't standing on the ground.

Joy's grandmother had committed suicide, and Joy's mother had continued to worry about her. When Joy told her mother what she had seen, her mother sobbed her relief.

Later in Joy's life she had an out-of-body experience (but not an NDE) where she saw her brother, her husband and her father, all of whom had died within a short time of each other. They reassured her and gave of their love, so that she could recover from the anguish she felt from their deaths.

Shirley James—Saw Deceased Relatives

I lay down on the couch—I was just lying there thinking about dying. I felt that I couldn't go on. Then a light, and I can't say it was a bright light, it was an indescribable light, appeared in the room. It just lit up.

I was watching the light when . . . I can't say they floated, they appeared—my husband who had died, my two sisters-in-law, and my grandfather and grandmother who had passed on. . . .

Each of these people came toward me and then passed me. As this was happening, I felt overwhelmed by love. I was not frightened. I felt warm. They didn't speak to me; it was like telepathy. It came from their heads to my head. And they each said: 'It'll be okay.' . .

Each spirit that appeared before me during this episode was absolutely glowing with health. Their skin—they looked happy, and there were no differences in age. Although my husband was only twenty years old when he died, and my grandparents were in their seventies, there didn't seem to be an age difference between them.

Numerous NDEs Involving Relatives

Balladeers often sing of a love which endures forever. They are more right than they know. These two experiences indicate that our spouses and other relatives continue to be concerned about us and to feel love for us long after they are gone.

Several others we interviewed who underwent NDEs spoke of seeing relatives and feeling of their love and concern. Maureen Daniels, who had an NDE due to a nerve disorder, told of seeing her grandparents and of the great love she felt while in their presence.

Kathleen Pratt Martinez, who went through an NDE during childbirth, saw several of her relatives who participated in a discussion as to whether she should return to this life or not. They were concerned that she might not be able to fulfill her life's mission. Jean saw her deceased husband during a difficult pregnancy she underwent, and then later, at a missionary farewell, she saw many of her relatives.

Several others talked of the love they felt from relatives they saw while on the other side. Apparently our Father in Heaven desires that family ties be maintained, and even reinforced, when we leave this life.

Ordinances Which Tie Families Together

Baptism—For Whom?

If it is true that, as those having NDEs observed, there is a continuation of family ties after death, then there must be some way—guaranteed by the power of God—that marriage vows and family affiliations can be sustained in the next life. God must arrange for earthly ordinances to be binding in the next life as well as this one. But what are those ordinances and how do they work?

Chapter 20 outlined the main elements of the Plan of Salvation. Element 7 stated that: "Means would be provided for saving ordinances to be performed on this earth for *all* persons, living or dead." There are several ordinances that allow families to be tied together. One of those ordinances is baptism, for which Christ himself set the example. In Mark we are told: "He that believeth and is baptized shall be saved; but he that believeth not shall be damned."[7]

The Book of Mormon makes clear that little children, under the age of eight, are automatically saved in the Celestial Kingdom if they die—there is no necessity for baptism.[8] All others—being accountable for their sins—must repent and be baptized.

Baptism for the Dead

But what about those who have died and never heard of baptism, how are they saved? Are they damned simply because they never had the opportunity to be baptized?

In First Corinthians, Paul, in making an argument that there is a resurrection, asks, "Else what shall they do which are baptized for the dead, if the dead rise not at all? why are they then baptized for the dead?"[9] Clearly there was an ordinance in which baptism for the dead was practiced during Paul's time. This practice, about which more will be said in a moment, is one of those ordinances which are vital for the salvation of those who never had the opportunity during life. Baptism is required before individuals can be tied together as families.

The Authority to Act for God

In Chapter 19, I mentioned that John the Baptist appeared on May 15, 1829, and bestowed upon Joseph Smith and Oliver Cowdery the Aaronic Priesthood with its authority to baptize. Later, Peter, James and John restored the Melchizedek Priesthood to Joseph and Oliver with its increased authority.[10] These two priesthoods, again, gave man the ability to act in the name of and with the power and authority of God.

Elijah—Ties That Bind

In the last two verses of Malachi, the Lord tells us: "Behold, I will send you Elijah the prophet before the coming of the great and dreadful day of the Lord: And he shall turn the heart of the fathers to the children, and the heart of the children to their fathers, lest I come and smite the earth with a curse."

On April 3, 1836, in the Kirtland, Ohio Temple, Joseph Smith, the Prophet, and Oliver Cowdery were visited by a series of heavenly beings, including Elijah, who restored the heavenly keys necessary to bind families for eternity—in short, to turn the heart of the fathers to the children, and the heart of the children to their fathers. These heavenly keys made it possible for *all* individuals to have an equal opportunity to partake of saving ordinances and to be bound as eternal family units.

The Doctrine and Covenants sheds further light on the scripture from Malachi:[11]

> *It is sufficient to know, in this case, that the earth will be smitten with a curse unless there is a welding link of some kind or other between the fathers and the children, upon some subject or other—and behold what is that subject? It is the baptism for the dead. For we without them cannot be made perfect; neither can they without us be made perfect. Neither can they nor we be made perfect without those who have died in the gospel also; for it is necessary in the ushering in of the dispensation of the fulness of times, which dispensation is now beginning to usher*

> *in, that a whole and complete and perfect union, and welding together of dispensations, and keys, and powers, and glories should take place, and be revealed from the days of Adam even to the present time.*

In LDS temples, baptism for the dead is performed where living persons, acting as proxy for the dead, are baptized for individuals who never had that opportunity during life. Similarly, husbands and wives (both living and dead) are sealed together for eternity, with their children bound to them in family units.

Genealogy With a Purpose

The LDS Church has the largest genealogical effort in the world. The purpose of this work is to identify family ties as far back as possible, and to perform the vicarious ordinance work for those individuals which will tie them together. In order for that work to be efficacious, though, the individuals must accept it. They still have their free agency in the spirit world and can accept or reject the work being performed on their behalf.

When Earthly Ordinances Become Binding

In Chapter 22, I discussed the work that righteous spirits could perform—teaching others who were less-advanced than they. This effort was mentioned by many who had an NDE, and it was amply illustrated by numerous scriptural references. The purpose of this work is to bring people closer to Christ. If the less advanced spirits accept those teachings, then the earthly ordinance work, which Christ himself said was necessary, becomes effective and binding.

Summary

This chapter is about the power of God. That power manifests itself in innumerable ways, a few of which were discussed. It was noted that certain words seemed to fall into a pattern of repetition which was beyond the recognition of those using them. The word *peace*, for example, appeared to represent a type of peace that was different from the peace we normally think of. It was used in a Godly sense. One which invoked divine feelings.

Certain patterns of healing became evident. Carol and I joined in the joy of those we interviewed as they told of the miraculous events leading up to their being healed. They described how they came back from the door of death, were healed from the cause that sent them there—and in several instances had a later miraculous healing from a second life-threatening disease. In many cases the healings defied scientific medical explanation.

Carol and I witnessed the happiness, relived again, as our people told of family reunions. Few words were exchanged in these reunions. Instead of words there was an exchange of celestial love. Those whom we interviewed described the meetings as healing moments of peace, love, and joy. They returned from these encounters refreshed and enlivened, ready to resume life knowing that they would, again in the future, be with their righteous loved ones.

All of these events can be explained by the scriptures. Scriptures which tell of a loving Father who has provided a plan for the succor, growth, and development of his children. A plan which ties righteous families together forever. A plan which permits the use of His power—and the sharing of His glory—for righteous purposes.

Chapter Twenty-Five

Judgment and Revelation

Introduction

This chapter is about two seemingly different subjects: judgment and revelation. Actually, they are both gifts of God and as such are related to the power of God. They are of interest because so many of those who had an NDE were exposed to both of these gifts.

The Plan of Salvation, as discussed in Chapter 20, has two elements which make mention of judgments.

Element 9 states that at some future time there will be a general resurrection in which we will all regain a body that will never again be destroyed. Element 10 indicates that there is a final judgment, and depending upon how we live, and whether we repent of our sins or not, we will live eternally with our Father in Heaven and with Jesus Christ.

Revelation, as the term is used here, is about God's communication to humans. In particular, in this book it is about God's communication to those who have had an NDE. The very nature of an NDE is such that it is a form of personal revelation. Revelation can take many forms, and several examples will be illustrated.

A Life's Review

The life's review, as many who had an NDE underwent it, was both a form of judgment and a teaching experience. During the review most individuals were not aware that it was a teaching experience, since it was not clear at that point that they would return to this life. Moreover, most of those who went through a life's review would probably argue that it really wasn't a judgment—there was only love involved. I believe, nevertheless, that both judgment and teaching were involved.

About ten percent of those I interviewed claimed to have had a life's review. My father, in his out-of-body experience, had a review in the presence of the Savior. He characterized it as a loving experience.

James Niitsuma said that he saw his life of twenty years flash by. He emphasized that the review wasn't about material things; instead, it concentrated on previous incidents involving his friends and family. Ray Berg, who had his review during a swimming pool incident, never left his body. His review flashed before him while he was trying to escape from drowning.

John Stirling—A Detailed Life's Review

John Stirling gave the most detailed account of a life's review of anyone I talked with. He said the review was the ultimate movie—in color, in three-dimensions, and with feeling. John felt that his review was carried out in the presence of Jesus Christ, and that ultimate love was shown during the review. Some of his comments follow:

> *Then the voice said: "Well, let's look at your life." And I saw . . . I saw my life flashed before my eyes. Everything from when I was a child up to the present time. And every emotion that I had during my life, when I saw the scene, I felt the same emotion. I could feel the reasons that I did things as I saw the scenes unfold.*
>
> *. . . The life's review came as a shock. When I heard the voice say: "Well, let's see your life," I didn't know how it would happen. It was totally unexpected, and it was right there in my view. It was as if both the voice and I were viewing it—and both of us could feel it as well as visually see it.*
>
> *. . . It was the same feeling you would get in a heart-to-heart conversation with a loving father about anything that concerned you. Not that judgment would be involved, but that you would both view the circumstances, see the way things were, and go on from there.*
>
> *. . . I felt, inside, that we both felt the emotions. As I recall, the life review started when I was two or three years old. The review, starting from that time, showed all the daily events, all the people involved, as I lived through the events. There were the funny times, the sad times, and my concerns at the time—for my age.*

Howard Storm—An Extraordinary Life's Review

Howard Storm, the art Professor from Kentucky, had an extensive life's review in the presence of several beings of light. He described it this way:

> *Then, they wanted to talk about my life. And my life played out before me, maybe six or eight feet in front of me, from beginning to end. The life review was very much in their control, and they showed my life, but not from my point of view. I saw me in my life—and this whole thing was a lesson—even though I didn't know it at the time. They were trying to teach me something, but I didn't know it was a teaching experience, because I didn't know that I would be coming back.*
>
> *We just watched my life from the beginning to the end. Some things they slowed down on, and zoomed in on, and other things they went right through. They showed me my life in a way that I had never thought of before. All of the things that I had worked to achieve, the recognition that I had worked for, in elementary school, in high school, in college, and in my career, they meant nothing in this setting.*
>
> *I could feel their feelings of sorrow and suffering, or joy, as my life's review unfolded. They didn't say that something was bad or good, but I could feel it. And I could sense all those things they were indifferent to. They didn't, for example, look down on my high school shot-put record. They just didn't feel anything towards it, nor towards other things which I had taken so much pride in.*
>
> *What they responded to was how I had interacted with other people. That was the long and short of it. Unfortunately, most of my interactions with other people didn't measure up with how I should have interacted; which was, in a loving way.*
>
> *Whenever I did react during my life in a loving way, they rejoiced. Most of the time I found that my interactions with other people had been manipulative. During my professional career, for example, I saw myself sitting in my office, playing the college professor, while a student came to me with a personal problem. I sat there looking compassionate, and patient, and loving, while inside I was bored to death. I would check my watch under my desk as I anxiously waited for the student to finish.*
>
> *I got to go through all those kinds of experiences in the company of these magnificent beings. When I was a teenager, my father's career put him into a high-stress, twelve-hour-a-day job. Out of my resentment towards his neglect of me, when he came home from work I would be*

cold and indifferent toward him. This would make him angry, and it would give me a further excuse to feel hatred toward him. He and I would fight, and my mother would get upset.

Most of my life I had felt that my father was a creep and I was the victim. When we reviewed my life I got to see how I had precipitated so much of that, myself. Instead of greeting him happily at the end of a day, I was continually putting thorns in him—in order to justify my own hurt.

I got to see, when my sister had a bad night one night, how I went into her bedroom and put my arms around her. I didn't say anything. I just lay there with my arms around her. As it turned out, that experience was one of the biggest triumphs of my life.

I feel strongly that the whole life's review would have been emotionally destructive, and would have left me a psychotic person, if it hadn't been for the fact that my friend, and my friend's friends, while we watched the whole thing, were loving me. I could feel that love. Every time I got a little upset they turned it off for awhile and they just loved me. Their love was tangible. You could feel it on your body, you could feel it inside of you; their love went right through you. I wish I could explain it to you, but I can't.

The therapy was their love, because my life's review kept tearing me down. It was pitiful to watch, just pitiful. I couldn't believe it. And the thing is, it got worse as it went on. My stupidity and selfishness as a teenager only magnified as I became an adult—all under the veneer of being a good husband, a good father, and a good citizen. The hypocrisy of it all was just nauseating. But through it all was their love.

Teaching and Judgment During the NDE

These examples should be sufficient to make the point. Clearly they were teaching experiences. It is less clear that judgment was involved—unless judgment is considered in a different sense than we normally think of it. The harshest part of the judgment was the self-judgment rendered by the individuals involved.

Judgment from the beings of light who were present during the reviews was more an understanding type of judgment. It was a judgment tempered by love. Indeed, love was the overwhelming feature of the review. It was only when the individual being reviewed could feel the pain of those superior beings viewing it that the nature of their judgment became apparent.

Other Types of Judgment

Kathleen Pratt Martinez—Judgment by Relatives

The Experience of Kathleen Pratt Martinez, who had an out-of-body experience where she was on trial for her life is interesting from two points of view. First, because of the judgment involved—by her extended family—and second, because the judgment presupposed that she had a life's mission which was assigned before she was born. A few of her comments follow:

> *Through thought transference I knew that I was on trial for my life. The trial was to determine whether or not I would be allowed to continue in this life—based upon whether I would do the things I was supposed to do, and cease transgressing.*
>
> *My grandfather felt that I probably would not be able to continue. Evidently there was some mission I was supposed to perform. He felt that they might have to select someone else, because I wouldn't be able to carry it out. I apparently was not a strong enough character to follow through with whatever I was supposed to do.*
>
> *My grandmother took my defense and said that she thought that I would, and she said I should be given the chance to prove that I could do this. I, of course, didn't understand fully what they were talking about, except that I wanted to go on living. I told them that I had planned to continue with my schooling. I mentioned what I wanted to study, and I said that I would live my life uprightly from this point on. I asked them to give me another chance.*
>
> *So, it was decided—my grandfather looked at me, and at this other person in the chair, and they kind of viewed each other—and it was unanimously decided among them, through thought transference, that I would be given this chance.*

This particular experience illustrates several LDS points of doctrine. The tie to deceased ancestors is clearly evident, as is the concern of those ancestors for the living descendant. A judgment is rendered, and it is a loving one in which Kathleen is given another chance to live up to her potential; a potential which was recognized in her pre-mortal life. The scriptural significance of these points will be covered shortly.

Katrina—A Non-Judgmental Judgment

One of the most touching examples of a non-judgmental judgment was that of Katrina, who attempted suicide. Katrina, before her experience, was convinced that she was going to hell. She found, instead, the following:

> *I was amazed at the mercy, understanding and love given to me while in the Savior's presence. There was such total acceptance and love—no condemnation whatsoever.*
>
> *Standing in His presence I received a new perception of myself and of my worth. I had left the earth thinking of myself as human garbage. In a few moments in His presence, and feeling for myself what he felt for me, I totally reevaluated my worth. I did matter; He did care. Even more than that—he loved me, he forgave me.*
>
> *I was so overwhelmed by the utter love and peace and mercy that I did not want to leave.*

Katrina's non-judgmental judgment (an oxymoron) was really a judgment tempered by the Lord's mercy. It was a judgment that took into consideration the totality of Katrina's life, and one which tempered that judgment with God's love.

The Experiences Measured Against LDS Teachings

Measures of Judgment

These experiences indicate that there are measures of performance in this life which are used to judge us, but they are different measures than we often feel are important. And we are in no position to judge other people concerning their spiritual performance. Howard Storm put it this way:

> *. . . They [the angels] made it clear to me that we don't have any knowledge or right to judge anybody else—in terms of that person's heart relationship to God. Only God knows what's in a person's heart. Someone whom we think is despicable, God might know as a wonderful person. Similarly, someone we think is good, God may see as a hypocrite, with a black heart. Only God knows the truth about every individual. God will ultimately judge every individual.*

The scriptures deliver this same message in many different ways. The Sermon on the Mount as given by Luke makes the point in this way:[1]

> *Be ye therefore merciful, as your Father also is merciful.*
>
> *Judge not, and ye shall not be judged: condemn not, and ye shall not be condemned: forgive, and ye shall be forgiven.*

> *Give, and it shall be given unto you; good measure, pressed down, and shaken together, and running over, shall men give unto your bosom. For with the same measure that ye mete withall it shall be measured to you again.*

The measures of performance, then, have to do with keeping the Lord's commandments. Since all of us break some of those commandments from time to time—none of us is without sin—it is essential for us to repent of those sins. Having thus repented, we are washed free from the effects of the sins by the atoning sacrifice of our Savior. As recorded in the Doctrine and Covenants, the Lord says:[2] "Behold, he who has repented of his sins, the same is forgiven, and I, the Lord, remember them no more. By this ye may know if a man repenteth of his sins—behold, he will confess them and forsake them."

Justice and Mercy

Many of those who have had a life's review, or have otherwise experienced the Lord's judgment, speak of his mercy. How justice and mercy are reconciled in the judgment of God is best explained in the Book of Mormon where, in Chapter 42, Alma explains to his son Corianton how the principles of justice and mercy interact. The entire chapter is devoted to that subject. I shall quote but a brief portion:[3]

> *And now, the plan of mercy could not be brought about except an atonement should be made; therefore God himself atoneth for the sins of the world, to bring about the plan of mercy, to appease the demands of justice, that God might be a perfect, just God, and a merciful God also. . . .*
>
> *Now, how could a man repent except he should sin? How could he sin if there was no law? How could there be a law save there was a punishment?*
>
> *. . . And if there was not law given, if men sinned what could justice do, or mercy either, for they would have no claim on the creature?*
>
> *But there is a law given, and a punishment affixed, and a repentance granted; which repentance mercy claimeth; otherwise, justice claimeth the creature and executeth the law, and the law inflicteth the punishment; if not so, the works of justice would be destroyed, and God would cease to be God.*
>
> *But God ceaseth not to be God, and mercy claimeth the penitent, and mercy cometh because of the atonement; and the atonement bringeth*

to pass the resurrection of the dead; and the resurrection of the dead bringeth back men into the presence of God; and thus they are restored into his presence, to be judged according to their works, according to the law and justice.

These scripture make clear that there is such a thing as sin—breaking the laws of God—but, through the atonement of Jesus Christ, and through his infinite love and mercy, we can be reclaimed from the demands of justice if we truly repent. For those who lived and died without hearing the laws of God, they still have the opportunity to repent—through the teachings in the spirit world after they die, and through vicarious ordinances performed for them in this life.

Foreordination

The idea that certain individuals are pre-selected for unique missions in this life is also part of LDS doctrine. In the Pearl of Great Price, the book of Abraham, it says:[4]

Now the Lord had shown unto me, Abraham, the intelligences that were organized before the world was; and among all these there were many of the noble and great ones;

And God saw these souls that they were good, and he stood in the midst of them, and he said: These I will make my rulers; for he stood among those that were spirits, and he saw that they were good; and he said unto me: Abraham, thou art one of them; thou wast chosen before thou wast born.

And there stood one among them that was like unto God, and he said unto those who were with him: We will go down, for there is space there, and we will take of these materials, and we will make an earth whereon these may dwell;

And we will prove them herewith, to see if they will do all things whatsoever the Lord their God shall command them . . . .

This scripture does not mean that those who have an assigned mission prior to this life are predestined to accomplish it. They still have their free agency—freedom to succeed or to fail. That, in fact, was the point of the trial of Kathleen Pratt Martinez.

Personal Revelation and Testimony

Strength of LDS Church—Individual Testimonies

There is nothing more fundamental to the teachings of The Church of Jesus Christ of Latter-day Saints than is the idea that each individual may receive personal revelation from God. Indeed, each individual has a responsibility to seek such revelation concerning his or her responsibilities, problems, challenges, needs, and, most importantly, concerning their understanding of the Gospel. Upon receiving such revelation, the individual is under obligation to bear testimony of the truthfulness of what he or she knows—particularly concerning the fact that Jesus is the Christ, the living son of God.

The necessity to seek revelation from God is illustrated well in the Book of Mormon. Moroni, the last chronicler of the book, and the individual who later appeared to Joseph Smith as an angel, gave this challenge to those who would read the Book of Mormon:[5]

> *Behold, I would exhort you that when ye shall read these things, if it be wisdom in God that ye should read them, that ye would remember how merciful the Lord hath been unto the children of men, from the creation of Adam even down unto the time that ye shall receive these things, and ponder it in your hearts.*
>
> *And when ye shall receive these things, I would exhort you that ye would ask God, the Eternal Father, in the name of Christ, if these things are not true; and if ye shall ask with a sincere heart, with real intent, having faith in Christ, he will manifest the truth of it unto you, by the power of the Holy Ghost.*
>
> *And by the power of the Holy Ghost ye may know the truth of all things.*

Arguably, the strength of the LDS Church is in the individual testimonies of the members—those that testify that they know, through revelation from God, that Jesus is the Christ and that the Church teachings are true. In this, as well as in other aspects, the Church is similar to the primitive Church established by Christ during his earthly ministry. The early Christian church grew rapidly because there were numerous individuals who claimed, through personal knowledge, that Jesus was the son of God, had been resurrected, and lived again.[6]

Testimonies of Those That Had NDEs

Although not all persons having had an NDE agree that God is the author of all that they saw, the predominant majority do feel that such was the case.

Moreover, the predominant majority also feel that they had a unique experience—a revelation—of a marvelous new world. Their accounts—testimonies—of what they saw stir primal feelings of joy, love, happiness, and of a forgotten glory, in those of us fortunate enough to talk with them.

In addition to the "normal" NDE with its inherent personal revelation to the recipient, Carol and I observed some unusual examples of revelation. Kathleen Pratt Martinez and Jean, for example, both experienced a trial for their lives—unusual forms of personal revelation.

Several individuals indicated a knowledge of events that could occur at some future date. Both John Stirling and Gary Gillum, before their NDE, couldn't explain the feelings they had that they were going to leave for someplace unusual; someplace they didn't understand. David Herard knew several days before he was wounded in Vietnam that it was going to happen. Numerous individuals were aware that they were going to have more children, even identifying the sex of the children. Lucy told how her father knew he was going to meet two unusual men and then die shortly thereafter.

Gary Gillum and Joe Swick—Similar Revelations

The experiences of Gary Gillum and Joe Swick, though, were the most unusual examples of personal revelation that I heard. Both men called me from the Brigham Young University campus within a few days of each other; I interviewed them on the same day. Neither was acquainted with the other, and neither knew of the experience of the other individual.

Both men started as members of the same Protestant sect. Both had an out-of-body experience which resulted from an automobile accident. Both saw the light and had feelings of intense love. They both understood that there was more they could accomplish if they returned to this life. As a result of a combination of circumstances, later, both men listened to LDS missionaries present discussions about The Church of Jesus Christ of Latter-day Saints.

During the discussion with the missionaries, both men were skeptical. Both were challenged to read the Book of Mormon and to pray about whether or not it, and the Church, were true. Upon praying, both men again experienced the light that they had originally seen in their out-of-body experience, and both knew that they should join the Church.

There were differences, of course. Joe's experiences took place at a much younger age than did Gary's. Before his experience Gary had prayed that something would direct him to the truth. Gary also saw something in his future life, which, at the time, he didn't understand. He saw a building with spires and with people inside dressed in white. Eight years later, when he went to be sealed to his wife in the Manti Temple, he recognized the events as scenes he had viewed during his out-of-body experience.

Both men recognized their experiences as personal revelations directed so as to help them in their lives. Joe, in commenting on his second experience with the missionaries, provided an excellent definition of the essence of personal revelation:

> *I haven't shared this experience with many people. It is too sacred to me. But whenever I have shared it, I have always told people that the experience has taught me that God is willing to reach out and talk with us. I'm nobody special, I don't have a . . . all I do is translate languages. Nobody knows my name—but I do know that God knows my name. And that he was willing to reach out and talk with me. If he would talk to somebody like me, then he would do it for anybody.*
>
> *That was a realization that profoundly influenced my joining the Church. God didn't just talk to Joseph Smith, a farm boy in New York. He talked to me too. And he would talk to anybody, it seems to me, if he would talk to somebody like me.*

Chapter Twenty-Six

Deity

A Personage of Love

In my father's out-of-body experience he told how, as his guide took him on a path in a beautiful field, he saw a being of light ahead of him. When the guide asked him if he knew who the being was, he responded: "Yes, it's Jesus Christ."

As they got closer to the Savior my father was overwhelmed by his magnificence, and by his love. On the few times that Dad told of his experience he was, again, overwhelmed when he talked of the Savior. He characterized Jesus as a personage of love.

Several of those we interviewed felt that they had been in the presence of the Savior. John Stirling, during his life's review felt that it occurred in the presence of Jesus. He had difficulty with his emotions when he told of his feelings about that portion of his experience.

David Herard, after he left his body during a war-time experience in Vietnam, felt the hand of God on his shoulder—then he felt as if he were embraced by God. He said of this experience: "When I was embraced, I felt a warmth all through me. And there was a feeling of love. It was all the love there is. . . . it was like that was all the love there was, everywhere. It was like . . . I can't explain the feeling. It's beyond words."

A Personage of Light and Beauty

Several of those we interviewed spoke of seeing the Savior. In some instances he identified himself as such. Their descriptions of this magnificent being were consistent with each other, and they were mesmerizing. In most instances the individuals were overcome with emotion as they described what they saw.

Joanne Jones Saw a Beautiful, Loving, Male Entity

There was an entity coming toward me. At first I didn't know whether it was a man or woman. The person was dressed as we've been led to believe men were dressed at the time of Jesus Christ, with a white robe. Anyway, soon we were face to face, and I've . . . I've never seen a more wonderful face in my life. It was the Lord Jesus Christ.

He was fairly young; I'd say around 35 or 40 years of age. He reached for me, embraced me, and said: 'I love you. Not yet my daughter.' . . I found him to be an extremely attractive person; beautiful, with a strong, gentle face. A man who . . . he was a man, you could feel it, yet he was something else. And the embrace—I could feel the strength, and the love, and the gentleness.

. . . He was dressed in a long robe. And he was this very gentle, beautiful, loving, male entity.

Jennette Saw a Being in White Robes

. . . It took a long time to get to the end where the brightness was greatest, and . . . and a figure stood there in a white robe with hands outstretched. In my heart I know it was my Christ. It was . . . it was the form of Jesus Christ. I felt a lightness of heart and easiness—it was as if in a dream state but more real. There was no pain, or anxiousness, just serenity and peace.

There were no vocal words, but there was no need for them. It was like my words went through my mind into the spiritual mind of my Christ and back to me, without hearing. There was no need to hear. So, definitely no need to speak, and yet a communion was there.

I was so happy to be in that place, so close to my Savior, and feeling such warmth and comfort as I'd never known on earth. And my Christ spoke to me and told me that I must go back, my work was not yet done.

Lucy Saw a Being of Light

Lucy, who had an out-of-body experience after being hit by a car, and later prayed to be relieved of the pain and suffering when she was crippled, explained what happened next in this manner:

I was praying, asking why. You know, there's got to be a reason. 'Cause I believed myself always to be a very good person. And I was asking, why?

While I was praying, instead of the voice I saw Christ. I saw him, like you, and he put his hands out to me and told me to trust, to have faith, and to believe.

. . . He was a being of light, mostly. And his robes were of a blue-tint light. He seemed to be a very strong man, very gentle, but very strong. I was on the floor, because . . . you know, I couldn't pray on my knees, so I was on the floor. And He was above me. It seemed that he was towering but it might not have been that.

. . . It just was a very calming feeling. He kept saying, have faith—he never said anything with his mouth. I just knew he was talking to me.

. . . most of Him was light.

. . . it wasn't gradual. He was there . . . he was not there, and then he was there. And the light sort of encompassed the room.

Ann saw a Beautiful Man

One of the most moving descriptions of an encounter with the Savior was that of Ann. She had two out-of-body experiences, one as a child when she had leukemia, and one as an adult when she contracted spinal meningitis. In the second experience she was under tremendous pain, more than she could cope with, when she left her body. She said of that experience:

> *. . . I traveled in the blackness—sort of like a tunnel—until I came to this person who blocked the way. . . . the person was standing in the way, and I couldn't go around so I stopped. The person was in this brilliant, brilliant light. I was fascinated. Even the hair was lit up, it was beautiful. In fact the person was beautiful, it was a man, he had this . . . oh, I didn't know that men could be that beautiful.*
>
> *I wondered who he was and he identified himself as my Savior, Jesus Christ. And I thought, WONDERFUL. I had this joy, that was, you know, welling up inside of me. It was like an explosion going on in me.*
>
> *Then he said, almost immediately, that I had to go back . . . I cried to him . . . 'No, please. I don't—*
>
> *At first I cried out, I, . . . I pleaded with him. I didn't want to go back. There was the pain I had just been in, the pain . . . it was far beyond anything I could handle.*
>
> *. . . I pled with him and he held me for a while. I don't know how long I pleaded and begged, it was a little bit of time, then . . . then I knew that he was feeling my sorrow and pain.*

> *Suddenly I felt this tremendously powerful . . . it's beyond the words of powerful, it's . . . I was suddenly enveloped in this deep, deep peace. It surrounded me, enveloped me, and he said: 'If you will go back I will put you immediately to sleep and when you awake you will be completely healed. And the pain will be gone.'*
>
> *Well I stopped crying, and I thought for a few moments. I looked at him and I knew that this was an absolute promise if I did what he said. I knew this was my Savior, and he was asking me . . . he was giving me the choice. I bowed my head and said that I would, and that very powerful peace stayed with me. It finally penetrated into my heart, I relaxed and turned around.*

These descriptions speak for themselves. They speak of a male personage who is a being of love, a being of compassion, a being of beauty, a being of light, a being of power, a being of godliness.

Scriptural Descriptions of Christ

There are, of course, numerous scriptural references to Christ during his earthly ministry in the old world. I shall confine myself to references of his appearance to people before and after his earthly ministry.

In Chapter 21, I described how the Brother of Jared, because of his great faith, saw Jesus Christ, and he was in the form of a man.[1] This event occurred approximately three thousand years before the birth of Christ.

Thomas, the Apostle, Sees Christ

Of the many descriptions of Jesus after his crucifixion his appearance to Thomas is one of the more interesting ones. John records it this way:[2]

> *But Thomas, one of the twelve, called Didymus, was not with them when Jesus came.*
>
> *The other disciples therefore said unto him, We have seen the Lord. But he said unto them, Except I shall see in his hands the print of the nails, and put my finger into the print of the nails, and thrust my hand into his side, I will not believe.*
>
> *And after eight days again his disciples were within, and Thomas with them: then came Jesus, the doors being shut, and stood in the midst, and said, Peace be unto you.*

Then saith he to Thomas, Reach hither thy finger, and behold my hands; and reach hither thy hand, and thrust it into my side: and be not faithless, but believing.

And Thomas answered and said unto him, My Lord and my God.

Jesus saith unto him, Thomas, because thou hast seen me, thou hast believed: blessed are they that have not seen, and yet have believed.

Stephen Has a Vision

Stephen, the first martyr for the testimony of the resurrected Savior, just prior to being stoned, had the following vision:[3]

But he, being full of the Holy Ghost, looked up stedfastly into heaven, and saw the glory of God, and Jesus standing on the right hand of God,

And said, Behold, I see the heavens opened, and the Son of man standing on the right hand of God.

Paul Has a Vision

Saul (later Paul), of the Pharisees, who persecuted Jesus, had a vision on the road to Damascus that is described in Acts in this manner:[4]

And it came to pass, that as I made my journey, and was come nigh unto Damascus about noon, sud denly there shone from heaven a great light round about me.

And I fell unto the ground, and heard a voice saying unto me, Saul, Saul, why persecutest thou me?

And I answered, Who art thou, Lord? And he said unto me, I am Jesus of Nazareth, whom thou persecutest.

Christ Appears to the Nephites

Undoubtedly the most dramatic account of Christ's appearance to people after his crucifixion is given in the Book of Mormon. Several Chapters in Third Nephi tell of Christ's appearance to people on this continent after his visit to those in the old world. Great destruction had been wrought because of earthquakes and other violent events after his death. Then, the people heard the voice of Christ explaining what had happened and why.

The people were confused as they heard the voice. The events which happened next are recorded as follows:[5]

And it came to pass that while they were thus conversing one with another, they heard a voice as if it came out of heaven; and they cast their eyes round about, for they understood not the voice which they heard; and it was not a harsh voice, neither was it a loud voice; nevertheless, and notwithstanding it being a small voice it did pierce them that did hear to the center, insomuch that there was no part of their frame that did not cause to quake; yea, it did pierce them to the very soul, and did cause their hearts to burn. . . .

And behold, the third time they did understand the voice which they heard; and it said unto them:

Behold my Beloved Son, in whom I am well pleased, in whom I have glorified my name—hear him.

And it came to pass, as they understood they cast their eyes up again towards heaven; and behold, they saw a Man descending out of heaven; and he was clothed in a white robe; and he came down and stood in the midst of them; and the eyes of the whole multitude were turned upon him, and they durst not open their mouths, even one to another, and wist not what it meant, for they thought it was an angel that had appeared unto them.

And it came to pass that he stretched forth his hand and spake unto the people, saying:

Behold, I am Jesus Christ, whom the prophets testified shall come into the world.

And behold, I am the light and the life of the world; and I have drunk out of that bitter cup which the Father hath given me, and have glorified the Father in taking upon me the sins of the world, in the which I have suffered the will of the Father in all things from the beginning.

Later Accounts of Christ's Appearance

Joseph Smith Sees the Father and the Son

Joseph Smith, the latter-day prophet who was the instrument through which the Lord restored his Church, saw the Lord on different occasions. The first instance was in 1820 when Joseph was in his fifteenth year. As a result of religious confusion which existed in the area of Manchester, New York (near Rochester), where the Smith family lived, Joseph sought solace in the scriptures. He read in James, the first chapter and fifth verse, where it states: "If any of you lack wisdom, let him ask of God, that giveth to all men liberally, and upbraideth not; and it shall be given him."

Joseph took this passage seriously, and on a spring day, retired to a wooded area adjacent to the family farm. His account of what happened next follows:[6]

> *After I had retired to the place where I had previously designed to go, having looked around me, and finding myself alone, I kneeled down and began to offer up the desire of my heart to God. I had scarcely done so, when immediately I was seized upon by some power which entirely overcame me, and had such an astonishing influence over me as to bind my tongue so that I could not speak. Thick darkness gathered around me, and it seemed to me for a time as if I were doomed to sudden destruction.*
>
> *But, exerting all my powers to call upon God to deliver me out of the power of this enemy which had seized upon me, and at the very moment when I was ready to sink into despair and abandon myself to destruction—not to an imaginary ruin, but to the power of some actual being from the unseen world, who had such marvelous power as I had never before felt in any being—just at this moment of great alarm, I saw a pillar of light exactly over my head, above the brightness of the sun, which descended gradually until it fell upon me.*
>
> *It no sooner appeared than I found myself delivered from the enemy which held me bound. When the light rested upon me I saw two Personages, whose brightness and glory defy all description, standing above me in the air. One of them spake unto me, calling me by name and said, pointing to the other—"This is My Beloved Son. Hear Him!"*
>
> *My object in going to inquire of the Lord was to know which of all the sects was right, that I might know which to join. No sooner, therefore, did I get possession of myself, so as to be able to speak, than I asked the Personages who stood above me in the light, which of all the sects was right—and which I should join.*
>
> *I was answered that I must join none of them, for they were all wrong; and the Personage who addressed me said that all their creeds were an abomination in his sight; that those professors were all corrupt; that: "they draw near to me with their lips, but their hearts are far from me, they teach for doctrines the commandments of men, having a form of godliness, but they deny the power thereof."*

The Lord Appears in the Kirtland Temple

In April 1836, after the Church had been established, and when the majority of the Saints were living in Ohio, a temple had been built in Kirtland. In the afternoon of April 3, the Prophet and Oliver Cowdery retired to the pulpit in the temple and began to pray. The account of what they saw is given in the Doctrine and Covenants:[7]

> *The veil was taken from our minds, and the eyes of our understanding were opened.*
>
> *We saw the Lord standing upon the breastwork of the pulpit, before us; and under his feet was a paved work of pure gold, in color like amber.*
>
> *His eyes were as a flame of fire; the hair of his head was white like the pure snow; his countenance shone above the brightness of the sun; and his voice was as the sound of the rushing of great waters, even the voice of Jehovah, saying:*
>
> *I am the first and the last; I am he who liveth, I am he who was slain; I am your advocate with the Father. . . .*
>
> *'For behold, I have accepted this house, and my name shall be here; and I will manifest myself to my people in mercy in this house.*

Other Accounts of Jesus

The Voice of the Lord

In chapter 19, a portion of the account by Oliver Cowdery is given in which he describes the visitation of John the Baptist. Both Joseph Smith and Oliver Cowdery witnessed this event in May, 1829. During the visitation they also heard the voice of the Savior. Oliver described the beginning of the event in this manner:[8]

> *On a sudden, as from the midst of eternity, the voice of the Redeemer spake peace to us. While the veil was parted and the angel of God came down clothed with glory, and delivered the anxiously looked for message, and the keys of the Gospel of repentance. What joy! what wonder! what amazement! While the world was racked and distracted—while millions were groping as the blind for the wall, and while all men were resting upon uncertainty, as a general mass, our eyes beheld, our ears heard, as in the "blaze of day"; yes, more—above the glitter of the May sunbeam, which then shed its brilliancy over the face of nature! Then his voice, though mild, pierced to the center, and his words, "I am thy fellow-*

servant," dispelled every fear. We listened, we gazed, we admired! 'Twas the voice of an angel, from glory, 'twas a message from the Most High! And as we heard we rejoiced, while His love enkindled upon our souls, and we were wrapped in the vision of the Almighty! Where was room for doubt? Nowhere; uncertainty had fled, doubt had sunk no more to rise, while fiction and deception had fled forever!

The Lord Appears in the Salt Lake Temple

Lorenzo Snow, the fifth President of The Church of Jesus Christ of Latter-day Saints, prayed to the Lord before the death of Wilford Woodruff in September, 1898, and asked, that if it be the Lord's will, President Woodruff's life be extended. Elder Snow offered the prayer in the recently completed Salt Lake Temple. He told the Lord that he had not sought the responsibility of being President of the Church, but if it was the Lord's will, he would accept it. The Lord Jesus Christ then appeared to him, and presented him with the procedures for reorganizing the First Presidency of the Church when the mantle of prophet of the church fell upon him.[9]

The Characteristics of Deity

Personality of the Godhead

Joseph F. Smith, the sixth president of The Church of Jesus Christ of Latter-day Saints said this about the Godhead:[10]

The personality of the Godhead is an absolute doctrine of the Church regarding which there can be no doubt or controversy. The Father, the Son and the Holy Ghost are three separate and distinct personages; the first two with glorified tabernacles of flesh and bone, the third a personage of spirit. If this fact is never lost sight of, there will be no difficulty in explaining any passage of scripture bearing on this subject.

But there is a oneness in the Godhead as well as a distinctness of personality. This oneness is emphasized in the sayings and writings of prophets and apostles in order to guard against the erroneous idea that these three may be distinct and independent deities and rivals for our worship. The stress laid upon this unity by the Bible has led to the error, so prevalent in the sectarian denominations, that this is a unity of personality—that there is only one personage, manifesting himself in three different ways. This error must be carefully guarded against.

God the Father and Jesus Christ, then, are two resurrected beings, and the Holy Ghost is still a personage of spirit. Jesus Christ is the only earthly begotten son of our Father (we are all the spirit children of the Father), and he came into the world from a virgin birth by Mary. We are in the same form as God the Father and Jesus Christ, so if we see them they will normally appear in the form of men—glorified personages of light.

Can they manifest their presence as a light or as a feeling? Of course they can, depending upon our needs and their wisdom. How, then, do we know that they are in the form of glorified men? Because they said so in the scriptures and because numerous prophets and others have seen them and recorded what they saw.

Many ask, though, isn't it arrogant for us to suppose that a supreme God would have the form of lowly man? An equally valid question would be, isn't it arrogant for us to assume that God is in any other form than what he tells us in the scriptures—and what the prophets say that they saw?

But, some people say, can we believe the scriptures? If not the scriptures, what? Should we believe in the wisdom of men? Or perhaps we should cast our lot on the sacred alter of science with it's pinnacle of achievement, the atomic bomb.

The Scriptures as a Way to Know God

Prophets for millennia have been urging us to prayerfully read the scriptures. Most recently, President Ezra Taft Benson has pled with us to again read the Book of Mormon.

Why the continued urgency to study the scriptures? Because there we can discover the nature of God, and we can learn for ourselves what he desires of us. An interesting discussion of the scriptures occurred in Howard Storm's out-of-body experience when he asked the angels about the Bible:

> *I asked, for example, "What about the Bible?" They responded: "What about it?" I asked if it was true, and they said that it was. I asked them why it was that when I tried to read it, all I saw were contradictions. They took me back to my life's review again—something that I had overlooked. They showed me, for the few times I had opened the Bible, that I had read it with the idea of finding contradictions and problems. I was trying to prove to myself that it wasn't worth reading.*
>
> *I observed to them that the Bible wasn't clear to me. It didn't make sense. They told me that it contained spiritual truth, and that I had to read it spiritually in order to understand it. I had to read it prayerfully.*

I was informed that it was not like other books. They also told me, and I later found out this was true, that when you read it prayerfully it talks to you. It reveals itself to you. And you don't have to work at it anymore.

We can get to know more about the Father and the Son by prayerfully reading the scriptures—and by listening to prophets—than by any other means. And it is important that we get to know them. Jesus, as he prayed to his Father, said this:[11]

And this is life eternal, that they might know thee the only true God, and Jesus Christ, whom thou hast sent.

I have glorified thee on the earth: I have finished the work which thou gavest me to do.

And now, O Father, glorify thou me with thine own self with the glory which I had with thee before the world was.

Later, in the same chapter of John, Jesus prays that we might be one with Him and the Father, and if we become one with them he indicates that we share in their glory. To have life eternal is to live eternally with our Father and his Son in celestial glory.

We can become one with the Father and the Son, then, by prayerfully reading the scriptures. In so doing we can gain, through personal revelation, a testimony which allows us to witness that Jesus is the Christ, the Savior of the world, and the Son of God. We can also know that he is our elder brother and that we, too, are children of God with the potential for future glory.

Lucy's Testimony About God

I shall end this chapter with the comments of Lucy when I asked her if there was any final message she would like to leave:

Only that there is a God, and it's a wonderful thing. And he knows better for us than we know. I feel I have a direct knowledge of God. A lot of people can tell you . . . they can give you a testimony that they borrow. With me, it's something I know. I remember asking if the Church was true—if it really was true. I was given the answer, an absolute answer, that it was. Also, there are things waiting for us that we don't understand.

Chapter Twenty-Seven

Human Destiny

Different Views of Human Destiny

Philosophers have been debating for centuries as to the ultimate destiny of humans. Most people during their lifetimes have wondered occasionally about the purposes of life and what their final destiny might be. Some of those having gone through an NDE have had feelings of a destiny beyond this life filled with joy, learning, knowledge, creation, and power—a destiny which embraces eternity; a destiny in the presence of God. Others, even some of those having had an NDE, disagree with this view of human destiny.

It is beyond the scope of this book to provide a comprehensive exposition of the diverse views of human destiny. Because of the relevance to what various individuals undergoing an NDE felt and saw, however, it is useful to briefly expose some of the different ideas of human destiny, relate them to near-death experiences, and compare them with LDS teachings on the subject.

In providing these brief expositions on human destiny it will become apparent that my biases favor a view buttressed by LDS teachings and scriptural explanations. Perspectives which deviate from these teachings, I believe, are fallacious. I will first discuss the ideas concerning human destiny which I think are false.

A Destiny of Extinction?

Existentialism and Humanism

One view of our destiny is that after this life we are extinguished as conscious beings—we become nothing. Truman Madsen, in his book "Eternal Man," describes two such positions: that of the Existentialists, and that of the Humanists.[1] He says of the first: "The existentialist attitude toward life is utter pessimism. Suicide is its most consistent outcome. Answerable to nobody and estranged from everybody, these people suffer through the disease of 'nihilism.'" Concerning the second group, he says: "For Humanists, man comes from something and returns to something. But this something is 'cosmic dust,' which is almost nothing."

Atheism

In chapter 23, I observed that in my early life at the University of California, in Berkeley, many of the professors at that institution were atheists. Professor Howard Storm, much of whose experience has been detailed in this book, indicated that prior to his out-of-body episode he was an atheist. He described how his bleeding ulcer felt when he recognized that he was dying:

> *By eight o'clock I felt that I was hanging on by my fingernails. Hanging on to life, that is. I had given up going unconscious. I had been hoping for that all day, [because of the pain] but to no avail. I was hanging on to life moment by moment.*
>
> *Sometime after eight the nurse came in and told Beverly, my wife, and me, that the doctor had gone home, and he would operate on me sometime the next day. I didn't say anything because I knew that was my death sentence.*
>
> *I wanted to say goodbye to my wife, but I couldn't—it was too painful. I told her that I loved her very much, which was as much of a goodbye as I could utter. She looked awful. She looked better after she had our children than she did then, because of the crying.*
>
> *I, kind of like, relaxed and closed my eyes. I felt that this was it, the end. This was the big nothing, the big blackout, the one you never wake up from, the end of existence. I had absolute certainty that there was nothing beyond this life—because that is how the really smart people understand it.*
>
> *While I was undergoing this stress, prayer, or anything like that, never occurred to me. I never once thought about it. If I mentioned God's name at all it was only as a profanity.*

Imagine Professor Storm's surprise to find himself, not extinguished, but alive and in another world. He found a world of infinite variety, and a world which he later came to recognize as one spoken of in the scriptures.

Near Death Experiences Do Not Prove Life-After-Death

Most near-death researchers argue that the NDE does not prove the existence of life-after-death. I agree with that position. If it were possible to prove life after death through the near-death experience then the Plan of Salvation would be compromised.

When we were born, we lost our memory of a previous life, and we lost our knowledge of a life to come. This forgetfulness was for a purpose—so that our free will might be more complete—to choose between right and wrong. It is a necessary part of our development that we move through this life with faith; faith in the ultimate goodness of our Father in Heaven, faith in the Lord Jesus Christ, faith that there is a life after death, faith that it does matter how we live.

Even though near-death experiences don't prove that there is a life after death they do add other witnesses to those included in the scriptures. Those witnesses are, for the most part, personal testimonies about a spiritual world of love—similar to the spiritual world of love described in the scriptures. It is a spiritual world which repudiates the nihilist view of human destiny.

Reincarnation?

Different Beliefs Concerning Reincarnation

Another view of human destiny is that our karma is to have repeated existences (reincarnation) on this planet until we get it right—when we reach a state of *Nirvana*, or perfection. After nirvana is achieved a hazy sort of life continuation occurs, but not as individual beings. Rather, we become part of an overall life force. Buddhists, Hindus, Sikhs and Jains (approximately one-third of the world's population) believe in reincarnation.

The reincarnation view has received much attention in the "New Age" literature. Researchers of the near-death experience also frequently mention the possibility of reincarnation.

The western concept of reincarnation (and that of most New Age writers) is one which normally restricts the repeated lives of an individual to existences in human form. In eastern belief the soul of an individual can be reincarnated in plant or animal form—until the soul learns from its previous lives how to improve so as to warrant being reborn into a higher level of existence.

The Prophet Joseph Smith taught that reincarnation was a false doctrine. On November 9, 1835, in Kirtland, Ohio, Joseph Smith was visited by Robert Mathias, who claimed to be a literal descendant of Matthias, the Apostle. He claimed further that the Apostle's soul was resurrected in him, Robert Mathias, and that this was the way of eternal life—the transmigration of soul or spirit from father to son (a specialized form of reincarnation).

Joseph Smith told him: "that my God told me, that his god was the devil, and I could not keep him any longer, and he must depart."[2]

One of the leading investigators of reincarnation is Ian Stevenson, born in 1918, and a psychiatrist at the University of Virginia. He began his investigations in 1958 and he has been widely quoted as providing substantial evidence on the validity of reincarnation. His writings are the basis for "scientific" discussions of reincarnation.[3]

Ian Wilson, a British historian and author, in writing on the near-death phenomenon investigated many of the widely known cases of reincarnation.[4] He showed that many of the cases which Stevenson cited as showing evidence of reincarnation were suspect. Wilson tabulated, for example, Stevenson's data on the most publicized Indian and Sri Lankan cases. In every case the child claiming to have been reincarnated from a particular family was born into a poor family—but the child was alleged to have reincarnated from a nearby rich family. The implications are obvious.

Bridey Murphy and Jane Evans—Publicized Cases

Numerous publicized cases of claimed reincarnation have resulted from the use of hypnotism on people who "regressed" to former lives, in some cases even speaking in a foreign tongue, or describing detailed experiences in a different era and culture. The most publicized event in the United States was that of "Bridey Murphy" in 1952. Her story was essentially discounted in subsequent investigations.[5]

A similar but more complex case occurred in England in 1976. It was the case of "Jane Evans," and it was featured on BBC television. Upon being hypnotized, the 30-year-old housewife regressed into six previous existences. Regressed back to Roman times, she recalled a life as "Livonia," wife of a tutor to the family of a Roman legate, Constantius, in the fourth century AD.

Jane knew substantial details of each life, but the most puzzling was her Roman experience. She gave details of individuals who could be, and were, checked historically for accuracy. She also named other Roman citizens who could not be found in historic documents of the period, but it was assumed these were lesser known figures who didn't make the history books.

One of those checking on the historic accuracy of Jane's story was Melvin Harris, a compulsive browser in second-hand bookstores. He stumbled upon Louis de Wohl's historical novel *The Living Wood*, published in 1947. The novel was devoted to the lives of Constantine, Constantius and Helena who lived in fourth century Rome. Moreover, Harris found the names of fictitious individuals whom Jane had named as being among her acquaintances in her previous life.[6]

Jane's story collapsed after these and other discoveries. It appeared that she had read and forgotten the novel some years before. It is interesting that under hypnosis she could withdraw from her subconscious memory the details of the story.

Why the Continued Reincarnation Interest?

Researchers' Interest in Reincarnation

The Buddhist, Hindu, Sikh and Jain religions in the East account for the reincarnation interest in that area of the world, but why such continued interest in the West? There is a certain glamour, of course, when Shirley MacLaine describes her previous existences (much of which Ian Wilson, has shown to be a confused dialogue).[7] But the persistence of the attraction goes beyond the glamour of Shirley MacLaine.

Many reputable researchers of the near-death experience report that those they interviewed mentioned the possibility of reincarnation. Kenneth Ring shows that numerous of his subjects reported being more inclined to a reincarnation perspective following their near-death experience than before.[8] Of all those Carol and I interviewed, two or three indicated that they thought reincarnation might be possible—one of those was quite certain about it.

I believe there are two reasons for this continued belief in the possibility of reincarnation. The first reason has to do with a feeling by many undergoing an NDE that they lived before, and that they will continue to live in some other type of future life. The idea that they existed prior to this life was new to them (unless they were LDS), and some of them considered their feelings as evidence of a cyclic life phenomenon. Researchers, themselves, are confused by these discussions of a previous life, and they sometimes succumb to the same type of thinking.

Hypnotic Regression Therapy

The second reason for the tenacity of reincarnation belief may have to do with a different type of research; namely, research associated with hypnosis. Psychologists have, for some years, used hypnosis for different therapeutic and experimental purposes.[9]

Psychotherapists using hypnotism have "regressed" patients into previous lives. This is particularly true of "New Age" therapists. Recent work by others in this field has proved interesting. Raymond Moody, Jr., in his book *Coming Back—A Psychiatrist Explores PastLife Journeys*[10] describes how he allowed himself to be hypnotized and regressed into nine previous lives. After that personal experience he conducted almost two hundred hypnotic regressions on other willing subjects.

As a result of Raymond Moody's work he neither argues for the reality of reincarnation nor against it.[11] He found regressive hypnotism to be useful as a method for revealing deepseated psychological problems in patients, but he was uncertain as to its usefulness as a method for discovering historically correct facts. He pointed out that "the mind likes to please and for that reason it is highly suggestible. When given the opportunity, it will fill in gaps with great aplomb. And when given the focused leisure time that hypnotism presents, it will often occupy itself with self-made fantasies."[12]

Hazards of Hypnosis for Retrieving Historic Facts

Numerous scholarly studies have verified the danger of using hypnotism as a tool for reconstructing memories, either memories of this life or memories of a presumed previous incarnation. The unreliability of such hypnotically derived memories is sufficiently great that "the AMA [American Medical Association] has indicated that previously hypnotized witnesses should not give testimony in court concerning the matters about which they have been hypnotized."[13]

One of the reasons hypnotic subjects are not reliable purveyors of historic facts is because "the inclination to confabulate [make up information] and to draw inferences to fill in missing information is apparently greater in hypnosis, and, as a consequence, can render the memory reports of hypnotized individuals deceptively more believable than normal recall."[14] This enhanced believability of the hypnotized subject can confuse even the therapist.

In addition to confabulating information under hypnosis, "there is evidence . . . that other exogenous sources such as books, movies, or special childhood and adult relationships may provide material that can be assimilated in a dissociated state and later be recalled under hypnosis as original material believed by the subject to be personal experience. The most publicized examples of this have been reincarnation stories elicited during hypnotic age regressions."[15]

These scholarly studies are unanimous in their advice that hypnotism be used solely as a therapeutic tool and not as a method for attempting to determine factual historic information—either recent or long-past historic data. Admittedly, all such studies, even the scholarly scientific type just cited, and their conclusions, are somewhat speculative.

Scriptural Teachings Concerning Reincarnation

Non-speculative information can be obtained from the scriptures. In the New Testament, Paul said: "It is appointed unto men once to die . . . ."[16] Reincarnation doctrine is, of course, that we die many times; each time that we are reincarnated. In the Book of Mormon, Amulek, in speaking of the resurrection said "that they can die no more; their spirits uniting with their bodies, never to be divided; thus the whole becoming spiritual and immortal, that they can no more see corruption.[17]

Numerous other scriptures attest to the fallacy of the doctrine of reincarnation. The atonement for example, holds out the promise that through our repentance, and through the mercy of Jesus Christ, we may obtain salvation in the Kingdom of God. Reincarnation doctrine would have us believe that there is no urgency in this life to repent of our sins since we can ultimately achieve nirvana simply by living enough lives. Such a scheme would contradict Amulek's admonition in the Book of Mormon that "this life is the time for men to prepare to meet God."[18]

A Celestial Kingdom

I have talked thus far in this chapter about what I think human destiny is not. I shall now comment on what I think human destiny is.

None of the individuals we interviewed told us that they were in heaven during their out-of-body experience. Most felt that they were in some wonderful spiritual realm, but it wasn't heaven. Howard Storm characterized it "as way out in the suburbs." Two others told us that they were at a spiritual "way station." Many felt that if they had proceeded into the other world and not come back they would have found an even more marvelous place.

One of the questions asked Howard Storm after his experience was: "There seems to be a hierarchy of order in the whole creative process, like an organization—is that true? Howard's answer was: "Yes, but everyone knows exactly where they stand, because one of the things about God's light is that only truth exists there. Nothing false can exist. So, when an angel begins to feel uncomfortable in that light, there is only one place to go—the darkness."

Three Degrees of Glory

In previous chapters I observed that at the final judgment everyone will receive a glory commensurate with how they lived—and according to the mercy of God.

Paul, in the same chapter of First Corinthians where he talks about baptism for the dead, talks about heavenly glory. He says:[19]

> *There are also celestial bodies, and bodies terrestrial: but the glory of the celestial is one and the glory of the terrestrial is another.*
>
> *There is one glory of the sun, and another glory of the moon, and another glory of the stars: for one star differeth from another star in glory.*
>
> *So also is the resurrection of the dead. It is sown in corruption; it is raised in incorruption:*
>
> *It is sown in dishonour; it is raised in glory: it is sown in weakness; it is raised in power: . . .*

Apparently, from this scripture, there are at least three glories which resurrected mortals go to. Paul names two of them: a celestial glory and a terrestrial glory. Actually, from a vision in 1832 to Joseph Smith and Sidney Rigdon all three are named: the highest glory is the celestial, likened to the glory of the sun; next is the terrestrial, likened to the glory of the moon; and the lesser glory is the telestial, likened to the glory of the stars.

The Highest Glory

Those who inherit the celestial glory, and their destiny, are described in this manner in the Doctrine and Covenants:[20]

> *And again we bear record—for we saw and heard, and this is the testimony of the gospel of Christ concerning them who shall come forth in the resurrection of the just—*
>
> *They are they who received the testimony of Jesus, and believed on his name and were baptized after the manner of his burial, being buried in the water in his name, and this according to the commandment which he has given—*
>
> *That by keeping the commandments they might be washed and cleansed from all their sins, and receive the Holy Spirit by the laying on of the hands of him who is ordained and sealed unto his power;*

And who overcome by faith and are sealed by the Holy Spirit of promise, which the Father sheds forth upon all those who are just and true.

They are they who are the church of the Firstborn.

They are they into whose hands the Father has given all things—

They are they who are priests and kings, who have received of his fulness, and of his glory;

And are priests of the Most High, after the order of Melchizedek, which was after the order of Enoch, which was after the order of the Only Begotten Son.

Wherefore, as it is written, they are gods, even the sons of God—

Wherefore, all things are theirs, whether life or death, or things present, or things to come, all are theirs and they are Christ's and Christ is God's.

And they shall overcome all things. . . .

And thus we saw the glory of the celestial, which excels in all things— where God, even the Father, reigns upon his throne forever and ever;

Before whose throne all things bow in humble reverence, and give him glory forever and ever.

They who dwell in this presence are the church of the Firstborn; and they see as they are seen, and know as they are known, having received of his fulness and of his grace;

And he makes them equal in power, and in might, and in dominion.

From these scriptures we may understand that a marvelous place is prepared for righteous individuals after this life. Christ, in talking to his Apostles, said of that place: "In my Father's house are many mansions: if it were not so, I would have told you. I go to prepare a place for you."[21]

Righteous Persons to Become as God

In this place of many mansions, righteous men and women will dwell with God and Jesus Christ in exultant joy. They will become co-creators with the Father and the Son, and they will share in their glory. As the scriptures say, "all things are theirs, whether life or death, or things present, or things to come, all are theirs and they are Christ's and Christ is God's." Indeed, they shall become gods.

Joseph Smith and later prophets in The Church of Jesus Christ of Latter-day Saints have discussed the potential godhood of righteous men and women.

Lorenzo Snow, the fifth President of the Church, expressed this thought in a couplet. The couplet which Lorenzo Snow received as a revelation was:

As man is, God once was;
As God now is, man may be.

It has become one of the most widely repeated LDS sayings. About three months before President Snow's death he said, about the couplet:[22]

> ... *Nothing was ever revealed more distinctly than that was to me. Of course, now that it is so well known it may not appear such a wonderful manifestation, but when I received it, the knowledge was marvelous to me.*

From these teachings we may understand that human destiny, for the righteous, is to become as God is and to share in his power. We can become teachers of spirits, organizers of worlds, creators of living beings, in short—Gods!

Will all share in this power and glory? Of course not—only those who kept the commandments, repented of their sins and "who received the testimony of Jesus, believed on his name and were baptized after the manner of his burial, being buried in the water in his name." But all will obtain a glory that is beyond what they expected, and one that is as much as they will feel comfortable with. And all will have had an equal *opportunity* to achieve the highest glory our Father has to offer.

Final Thoughts

As some of the final thoughts in this book I shall quote from a few of those who saw what, in my view, we are all destined to see upon the completion of this life. These comments were obtained as we completed our interviews when I asked each of them if they had any final thoughts to leave for others.

Janet McClellan—Found Love

He [Jesus Christ] wants me to love everybody. It doesn't matter what religion they profess, what their race or politics are, what their skin color is—I must love everybody. I must treat everybody as He would. I have to serve them as He would. And ... and the other thing that I have to do is gain all the knowledge that I possibly can, and use that knowledge to help others. That's the whole reason we are here, to help each other.

Pauline—Discovered What Matters Most

I've seen a lot of people in my life who have everything in a material sense, and in a split second they have nothing. I've decided it's not what you have which matters but what you've done for other people. . . .

I think we should talk about [death]—people should not be afraid of it. It's a personal experience, a very choice experience, so much like opening up, sort of like a panoramic view. Death is more of a beginning than an ending.

Forrest Hansen—Knows That Truth is Eternal

Truth remains the same regardless of human interpretation. I see a lot of these near-death experiences being interpreted in an attempt to understand some of the more difficult questions that humans have. And that's a proper thing to do, to look for those answers. Which, of course, is what this is all about. But humans make mistakes, and the real truth is always there regardless of how we interpret it.

Margaret Amodt—Discovered Purpose of Life

We all have a purpose here on earth.

Kerry—Learned What We Take With Us

We take with us into the next world the knowledge we gain here—nothing more.

Howard Storm—Found Out About Forgiveness

They [the angels] told me that when I made a mistake, I should ask for forgiveness. Before I even got it out of my mouth, I would be forgiven—but, I would have to accept the forgiveness. I would have to believe in forgiveness, and I would have to know that the forgiveness was given. I should confess, either in public or in private, that I had made a mistake, and then ask for forgiveness. After that, it would be an insult to them if I didn't accept the forgiveness. I shouldn't continue to go around with a sense of guilt. And they told me not to repeat mistakes; to learn from my mistakes.

Katrina—Got a Relationship with Christ

Death is so much different than . . . it's nothing to be feared. It's an awakening to the natural state that we're supposed to be in—this is the wrong state. The present life is the unnatural, the fallen state.

I am placing an emphasis now on a relationship with Christ. Christ is more important to me now than worldly things, and even church things.

It's like when I was in that garden. All the things that I thought were so important, and things that I was doing, just weren't important at all. The main thing is doing right by the ones we love and having a relationship with Christ.

I'm not so worried about sin now. I am not bound up in wondering: is this right, is that right? There is more of a feeling of mercy, non-judgment, and acceptance than I thought there would be. Instead of being so worried about condemnation I feel as though I have been set free from that. Now I'm wanting to do right by my family. And I want to have a relationship with Christ—out of a desire inside me, not because if I don't I'm afraid I will go to hell. I just want to. I've been changed inside.

Jean—Learned That Life Is a School

I know that there was life before this life, and I know that there is life after death. I also know that this life is a testing period, kind of a school. And that the people on both sides—in the life prior to this life, and those that are living in the spirit world after having died—are concerned about us and care about us. I think that the ones in the spirit world, after death, have more contact with us than those who have not yet been born.

I know that our deceased relatives are alive. I believe that when we pray and invite them to be with us they are allowed to come, if they are worthy. In order for them to visit us we must invite them, otherwise they can't come.

Finally, I know that the spirit world is so peaceful and calm, and we are all going to be so happy to be there, that if we knew what it was like . . . well, there is no way we would want to stay on the earth.

Joy Melvin—Learned that Life Has Many Risks

It's just that there are no guarantees in life. Things can change in a split second. I mean, it just took a phone call to tell me that my dad, my brother and my husband were dead. Life goes so fast you can't take anything for granted. You don't forget the "I love yous" and the flowers, and the letters. And you should try to be the best you can to people around you.

Gary Gillum—Learned About Personal Revelation

Death is a tragedy for those who are left behind. But death, as you indicated, is no big deal. What is important is living our lives so that we feel good about what we are doing for others and for our Heavenly Father. We should work to increase our faith in Jesus Christ, through personal revelation. We should obtain all the knowledge we can of the scriptures—and true theology—which presupposes that in order to know the truth we have to receive revelation.

Marcia Anderson—Found Answer to Prayer

My hope is that people will develop the love for our Father in Heaven and for his son Jesus Christ, the kind of love that they have for us. You see, he loved me, he loved my children. . . . He loved me enough, as involved as he is, to find us in our desperate time of need. And to extend that love to us in a very practical way. . . .

I asked [God] to please help us. I asked him and he listened. I knew it was from him—absolutely.

Carol and Arvin Gibson—What They Felt

Two of the reviewers of an early version of this book, and individuals whom I respect, commented that the book was a good analytical exposition of the new-death experience, but it didn't reflect enough of my feelings concerning the work. Two other reviewers commented that they would like to know how my wife felt during the interviews. As the final thoughts in the book, therefore, I would like to explain how the work affected Carol and me.

I asked Carol to respond to the two reviewers who asked about her. Carol's response was: "During the course of the interviews it became clear to me that Jesus Christ knows us far better than I had imagined. He knows of our struggles, he loves us, and he is there to help each of us. It doesn't matter who we are, we are each important to him. The incidents in the lives of these people verified his love. I felt of that love, through them, and knew that it was true because the Spirit bore witness to me. I further felt that we had made new friends, among these people, who would be part of our lives for all time—into eternity."

Carol and I, both, had a marvelous time getting to know and vicariously share the experiences of those who enjoyed a glimpse of eternity. The awe, wonder, peace, love—and power—that they felt spilled over into our own emotions. It was impossible to listen to them and not be touched.

To me, the work was more than an uncommon emotional experience, though. It became almost an obsession. As I became aware of unusual patterns described by different individuals with disparate backgrounds, and as some of those patterns mirrored the experience and teachings of early LDS leaders, I was enthralled. I was further entranced when I recalled scriptures I had previously read which gave meaning to some of the events described by those having had an NDE. In many instances, such as in the discussion of light in the 88th Section of the Doctrine and Covenants, I became convinced that the scriptures were more literal than I had ever supposed.

Another early reviewer said that this book was about God's love. If there was a single message I derived from the many people Carol and I talked with, that was it. And that love has been with me throughout the preparation of *Glimpses of Eternity*. My testimony of the truthfulness of the Gospel of Jesus Christ, and my knowledge of Christ's love, were strong before I began the book, and they have become stronger. It is not an overstatement to observe that my life has been changed forever as a result of this work.

I shall end with the thought left me by my father years ago as he told of his own near-death experience. "The other world is a magnificent place, Son. It is so filled with beauty and love—the love of Jesus Christ—that it is indescribable." My eyes fill with tears as I remember the tears in my father's eyes when he tried to reach out to me with that same love that he felt while on the other side.

May those of you who read this book also feel of that love, Christ's love, and in so doing catch a glimpse of eternity.

Notes

Introduction

1. Gibson, Arvin S. *In Search of Angels.* Horizon Publishers and Distributors, Inc., Bountiful, Utah 84011, 1990, pp. 107-112.
2. Moody, Raymond A., Jr. *Life After Life.* Bantam Books, New York, N.Y., 1988.
3. Ritchie, George G. with Sherrill, Elizabeth. *Return from Tomorrow.* Spire Books, Fleming H. Revell Co., Old Tappan, New Jersey, 1978.
4. Wilson, Ian. *The After Death Experience.* William Morrow and Company, Inc., N.Y., 1989.

   Grey, Margot. *Return from Death.* Arkana, London and New York, 1987.

   Murphet, Howard. *Beyond Death.* Quest Books, The Theosophical Publishing House, 306 West Geneva Road, Wheaton, IL 60187, 1990.
5. Zaleski, Carol. *Otherworld Journeys.* Oxford University Press, N.Y.; Oxford. 1987.

   Grosso, Michael. *The Final Choice.* Stillpoint Publishing, Walpose, New Hampshire, 1985.
6. Ring, Kenneth. *Heading Toward Omega.* William Morrow, Inc. N.Y., 1985.

   Gallup, G., Jr. *Adventures in Immortality.* McGraw Hill, N.Y., 1982.
7. Wilson, Ian. *The After Death Experience.* William Morrow and Company, Inc., N.Y., 1989.
8. Babb, Raymond C. "Hypnotic Induction of Experiences (Letter to the Editor)," *Journal of Near-Death Studies*, Vol 8, Number 1, Fall 1989, Human Sciences Press, Inc., 233 Spring Street, N.Y. 10013-1578, pp. 65-70.
9. Siegel, Ronald K. "Antimatter-Remembering Rogo." *Omni*, Magazine, Jan. 1991, p. 73.
10. Rawlings, Maurice, M.D. *Beyond Death's Door,* Bantam Books, N.Y., 1979.
11. Sorensen, Michele R.; Willmore, David R. *The Journey Beyond Life, Vol. One.* Family Affair Books, Orem, Utah 84057, 1988.

    Nelson, Lee. *Beyond the Veil-Volume I.* Cedar Fort Inc., Orem, Utah 84057, 1988.

    Nelson, Lee. *Beyond the Veil-Volume II.* Cedar Fort Inc., Orem, Utah 84057, 1989.

12. Crowther, Duane S. *Life Everlasting*. Bookcraft, Inc., Salt Lake City, Utah, 1967.
13. Ring, Kenneth. *Life at Death*. Quill, New York, N.Y., 1982, pp. 23, 24.
14. Storm, Howard. Taped experience recorded in 1989 at The NDE Research Institute, 702 North Fort Thomas Avenue, Fort Thomas, Kentucky 41705 (tapes are no longer available). Professor Storm indicated he sometimes can be available for lectures by writing him at 90 Hawthorne Ave., Fort Thomas, Kentucky 41075.

Chapter 3: Unusual Healings

1. Gibson, Arvin S., *op. cit.*, pp. 159-173.

Chapter 19: The Light

1. *The Bible.* 1 John 1:5.
2. *The Bible.* James 1:17.
3. *The Bible.* John 1:6-9.
4. *Doctrine and Covenants*. 88:6-13.
5. *The Bible.* Acts 10:30.
6. *Pearl of Great Price.* Joseph Smith, 2:30-33.
7. *Pearl of Great Price.* Joseph Smith, 2:43.
8. *Pearl of Great Price.* Joseph Smith, 2:68.
9. *Doctrine and Covenants.* 88:67.
10. Morse, Melvin with Perry, Paul. *Closer to the Light.* Villard Books, New York, N.Y., 1990, p. 120.
11. Morse, *op. cit.*, p. 127.
12. *Pearl of Great Price.* Joseph Smith, 2: Note at end by Oliver Cowdery.
13. *History of the Church.* Vol. I, pp. 54-55.
14. Evans, John Henry. *Joseph Smith an American Prophet.* Deseret Book, Salt Lake City, Utah, 1963; p. 386.
15. Zaleski, Carol. *Otherworld Journeys.* Oxford University Press, N.Y.; Oxford. 1987, p. 125.

Chapter 20: Life's Purpose

1. *The Book of Mormon.* 2 Nephi, 2:25.
2. Zaleski, *op. cit.*, p. 125.
3. Ring, Kenneth. *Heading Toward Omega.* Quill-William Morrow, N.Y., 1985, pp. 53, 54.
4. *Pearl of Great Price.* Abraham, 3:24,25.

5. *The Book of Mormon.* 2 Nephi, 2:25.
6. *Pearl of Great Price.* Moses, 3:26-28; *The Book of Mormon.* Ether 3:15-17.
7. *Doctrine and Covenants.* 68:25-28; 88:4.
8. *The Book of Mormon.* Alma, 42:7-10.
9. *The Book of Mormon.* 2 Nephi, 2:27.
10. *The Book of Mormon.* 2 Nephi, 2:11-16.
11. *Doctrine and Covenants.* 59:6.
12. *The Book of Mormon.* 1 Nephi, 22:1,2. *The Bible.* Amos, 3:7.
13. *The Book of Mormon.* 3 Nephi, 18:17-20.
14. *Doctrine and Covenants.* 130:18,19.
15. *The Book of Mormon.* Alma, 22:14.
16. *The Book of Mormon.* 2 Nephi, 9:21,22.
17. *The Book of Mormon.* Ether, 4:18. *Doctrine and Covenants.* 128:1-25.
18. *Doctrine and Covenants.* 138:1-36.
19. *The Book of Mormon.* Mormon, 9:13.
20. *The Book of Mormon.* Alma, 41:17; 3 Nephi, 26:4-5.
21. *Doctrine and Covenants.* 76:54-70.
22. *Doctrine and Covenants.* 76:81-90.
23. *History of the Church.* Vol. IV, p. 588.
24. *The Bible.* Revelation, 6.
25. Storm, Howard. Taped experience recorded in 1989 at The NDE Research Institute, 702 North Fort Thomas Avenue, Fort Thomas, Kentucky 41705.
26. Draper, Richard D. *Opening the Seven Seals—The Visions of John the Revelator,* Deseret Book Company, Salt Lake City, Utah, 1991, p.98.

Chapter 21: Spirit Bodies and Physical Bodies

1. Wilson, Ian. *The After Death Experience.* William Morrow and Company, Inc., N.Y., N.Y., 1987; pp. 124-128.
   Zaleski, Carol. *Otherworld Journeys.* Oxford University Press, N.Y. and Oxford, 1987, pp. 164-175.
2. *The Book of Mormon.* Alma, 40:11,12.
3. *The Book of Mormon.* Ether, 3:15,16.
4. Roberts, B. H. "The Immortality of Man," *The Improvement Era*, Vol. 13, Nov., 1909, pp. 401-423.
5. *The Pearl of Great Price.* Moses, 6:36.
6. Burton, Alma P. *Doctrines From the Prophets.* Bookcraft, Inc., Salt Lake City, Utah, 1970; p. 419.

7. *History of the Church.* Vol. IV, p. 575.
8. *History of the Church.* Vol. V, p. 393.
9. *History of the Church.* Vol. III, p. 387.
10. *History of the Church.* Vol. VI, pp. 308-309.
11. *The Bible.* Job, 19:26.

Chapter 22: The Other World

1. Moody, Raymond A. Jr., M.D. *Reflections on Life After Life.* Bantam Books, N.Y., 1978; p. 17.
2. Rawlings, Dr. Maurice. *Beyond Death's Door.* Bantam Books, N.Y., 1979; p. 80.
3. Atwater, P.M.H. *Coming Back to Life.* Ballantine Books, New York, 1988; pp. 45-47.
4. Grey, Margot. *Return from Death.* Arkana, London, New York, 1986; pp. 54,55.
5. Young, Brigham. *Journal of Discourses,* 14:231.
6. *The Pearl of Great Price.* Moses, 3:5.
7. *The Doctrine and Covenants.* 138.
8. Ballard, Melvin J. *The Three Degrees of Glory.* Deseret Book Company, Salt Lake City, Utah.
9. Taylor, John. "In White Rainment." *Journal of Discourses*, Vol. 18, pp. 166-170.
10. Storm, Howard. Taped experience recorded in 1989 at The NDE Research Institute, 702 North Fort Thomas Avenue, Fort Thomas, Kentucky 41705.

Chapter 23: Evil Spirits

1. Grey, *op. cit.*, pp. 63-64.
2. Ritchie, George G. with Sherrill, Elizabeth. *Return from Tomorrow.* Spire Books, Fleming H. Revell Co., Old Tappan, New Jersey, 1978, pp. 59-61.
3. Ritchie, *op. cit.*, pp. 63, 64.
4. Storm, *op. cit.*
5. *The Bible.* Mark, 5:1-13.
6. *The Bible.* Matthew, 4:1-11.
7. Kimball, Heber C. *Journal of Discourses,* 3:229-230.
8. *Doctrine and Covenants.* 29:36-39.
9. *Doctrine and Covenants.* 76:25-39.
10. *The Book of Mormon.* Alma 40:11-14.

11. *The Book of Mormon.* 2 Nephi, 2:25-27.
12. *Doctrine and Covenants.* 76:103-106.
13. *The Book of Mormon.* Mormon, 9:3-5.
14. Gibson, Arvin S. *In Search of Angels.* Horizon Publishers and Distributors, Inc., Bountiful, Utah 84011, 1990, pp. 180-181.
15. Storm, *op. cit.*, Question and Answer period.
16. *The Bible.* Colossians, 3:8-10.
17. *The Bible.* Matthew, 6:33.
18. *The Bible.* Matthew, 22:34-40.

Chapter 24: The Power of God

1. *The Bible.* John, 14:27.
2. *Doctrine and Covenants.* 121:7.
3. Storm, *op. cit.*
4. *Doctrine and Covenants.* 121:9.
5. Serdahely, William J., Ph.D., and Walker, Barbara A., Ph.D. "The Near-Death Experience of a Nonverbal Person with Congenital Quadriplegia." Journal of Near-Death Studies, Vol. 9, No. 2, Winter 1990, Human Sciences Press, 233 Spring St., N.Y., N.Y., pp. 91-96.
6. *Doctrine and Covenants.* 47:19-21.
7. *The Bible.* Mark, 16:16.
8. *The Book of Mormon.* Moroni 8:10-22.
9. *The Bible.* I Corinthians 15:29.
10. *Doctrine and Covenants.* 27:12, 13.
11. *Doctrine and Covenants.* 128:18.

Chapter 25: Judgment and Revelation

1. *The Bible.* Luke, 6:36-38.
2. *Doctrine and Covenants.* 58:42-43.
3. *The Book of Mormon.* Alma, 42:15, 17, 21-23.
4. *The Pearl of Great Price.* Abraham 3:22-25.
5. *The Book of Mormon.* Moroni, 10:3-5.
6. Barker, James L. *The Divine Church; (Course of Study for Melchizedek Priesthood Quorums for 1952)*, Pub. by Deseret News, Salt Lake City, Utah. p. 122.

Chapter 26: Deity

1. The Book of Mormon. Ether, 3:15,16.
2. *The Bible.* John, 20:24-29.
3. *The Bible.* Acts, 7:55-56.
4. *The Bible.* Acts, 22:68.
5. *The Book of Mormon.* 3 Nephi, 11:3,6-11.
6. *The Pearl of Great Price.* Joseph Smith, 2:15-19.
7. *Doctrine and Covenants.* 110:1-4, 7.
8. *Pearl of Great Price.* Joseph Smith, 2: Note at end by Oliver Cowdery.
9. Arrington, Leonard J., and Swinton, Heidi S. *The Presidents of the Church.* "Lorenzo Snow." Deseret Book Company, Salt Lake City, Utah, 1986. p. 173.
10. *Improvement Era,* 4:228; (Burton, Alma P., "Doctrines from the Prophets," Bookcraft Inc., Salt Lake City, Utah. pp. 204-205).
11. *The Bible.* John, 17:3-5.

Chapter 27: Human Destiny

1. Madsen, Truman G. *Eternal Man.* Deseret Book Company, Salt Lake City, Utah, 1966; pp. 29-30.
2. *History of the Church.* Vol. II, pp. 306-307.
3. Stevenson, Ian, M.D. *Twenty Cases Suggestive of Reincarnation.* University of Virginia Press, Charlottesville; 1974 (Reprinted 1978).

   Murphet, Howard. *Beyond Death.* Quest Books, The Theosophocial Publishing House, Wheaton, Ill. 1990, pp. 111-112.

   Almeder, Robert, Ph.D. *Beyond Death.* Charles C. Thomas, Publisher, Springfield, Ill. 1987, pp. 3-21.
4. Wilson, Ian. *The After Death Experience.* William Morrow and Company, Inc., N.Y., 1987, pp. 27-37.
5. Wilson, *op. cit.*, pp. 38-39.
6. Wilson, *op. cit.*, pp. 41-47.
7. Wilson, *op. cit.*, pp. 49-50.
8. Ring, Kenneth. *Heading Toward Omega.* Quill, William Morrow, N.Y., p. 158.
9. Ludwig, Arnold M. *Principles of Clinical Psychiatry.* The Free Press, Macmillan, Inc., N.Y., 1986, pp. 626-627.

   Gregory, Richard L. *The Oxford Companion to the Mind.* Oxford University Press, N.Y., 1988, pp. 328-333.

10. Moody, Raymond A. Jr. *Coming Back-A Psychiatrist Explores Past-Life Journeys.* Bantam Books, N.Y., London, 1991.
11. Moody, *op. cit.*, pp. 187-190.
12. Moody, *op. cit.*, p. 43.
13. Zilbergeld, B. "Hypnosis Questions and Answers," *The Validity of Memories Retrieved in Hypnosis*. W. W. Norton and Co., N.Y., 1986, pp. 45-46.
14. Orne, Martin T.; Whitehouse, Wayne G.; Dinges, David F.; Orne, Emily Carota. "Reconstructing Memory through Hypnosis." University of Pennsylvania School of Medicine; from "Hypnosis and Memory," Edited by Pettinati, Helen M., The Guilford Press, N.Y., 1988, p. 47.
15. Ganaway, George K. *Historical vs. Narrative Truth: Clarifying the Role of Exogenous Trauma in the Etiology of MPD and its Variants.* December, 1989, p. 209; for Reprints write George K. Ganaway, M.D., Program Director, Ridgeview Center for Dissociative Disorders, Ridgeview Institute, 3995 South Cobb Drive, Smyrna, Georgia 30080.
16. *The Bible.* Hebrews, 9:27.
17. *The Book of Mormon.* Alma 11:45.
18. *The Book of Mormon.* Alma 34:32.
19. *The Bible.* I Corinthians, 16:40-43.
20. *Doctrine and Covenants.* 76:50-60, 92-95.
21. *The Bible.* John, 14:2.
22. Snow, Leroi C. "Devotion to a Divine Inspiration," *The Improvement Era*, Vol 22, June, 1919, pp. 653-662.

Select Bibliography

Latter-day Saint Scriptures

The Book of Mormon-Another Testament of Jesus Christ. Translated by Joseph Smith, Junior. Published by The Church of Jesus Christ of Latter-day Saints, Salt Lake City, Utah, 1989.

The Doctrine and Covenants of The Church of Jesus Christ of Latter-day Saints. Published by The Church of Jesus Christ of Latter-day Saints, Salt Lake City, Utah, 1989.

The Holy Bible. Authorized King James Version. Published by The Church of Jesus Christ of Latter-day Saints, Salt Lake City, Utah, 1979.

The Pearl of Great Price. Published by The Church of Jesus Christ of Latter-day Saints, Salt Lake City, Utah, 1989.

Latter-day Saint Historical and Doctrinal Books and Periodicals

Arrington, Leonard J., and Swinton, Heidi S. *The Presidents of the Church*. Deseret Book Company, Salt Lake City, Utah, 1986.

Ballard, Melvin J. *The Three Degrees of Glory*. Deseret Book Company, Salt Lake City, Utah.

Barker, James L. *The Divine Church; (Course of Study for Melchizedek Priesthood Quorums for 1952)*, Pub. by Deseret News, Salt Lake City, Utah.

Burton, Alma P. *Doctrines From the Prophets*. Bookcraft, Inc., Salt Lake City, Utah, 1970.

Crowther, Duane S. *Life Everlasting*. Bookcraft, Inc., Salt Lake City, Utah, 1967.

Draper, Richard D. *Opening the Seven Seals—The Visions of John the Revelator*, Deseret Book Company, Salt Lake City, Utah, 1991.

Evans, John Henry. *Joseph Smith an American Prophet*. Deseret Book, Salt Lake City, Utah, 1963.

History of the Church of Jesus Christ of Latter-day Saints, 7 volumes plus Index. Deseret Book Company, Salt Lake City, Utah, 1970.

Journal of Discourses, 26 volumes. Los Angeles: General Printing and Lithograph Co., 1961.

Madsen, Truman G. *Eternal Man*. Deseret Book Company, Salt Lake City, Utah, 1966.

Roberts, B. H. *The Improvement Era*, Vol. 13, Nov., 1909. Snow, Leroi C. *The Improvement Era*, Vol. 22, June, 1919.

Near-Death Literature

Almeder, Robert, *Beyond Death*. Publisher, Charles C. Thomas, Springfield, Ill., 1987.

Atwater, P.M.H. "Coming Back to Life." Ballantine Books, New York, 1988.

Babb, Raymond C. *Hypnotic Induction of Experiences* (Letter to the Editor) *Journal of Near-Death Studies*, Vol 8, Number 1, Fall 1989, Human Sciences Press, Inc., 233 Spring Street, N.Y. 10013-1578.

Crowther, Duane S. *Life Everlasting*. Bookcraft, Inc., Salt Lake City, Utah, 1967.

Gallup, G., Jr. *Adventures in Immortality*. McGraw Hill, N.Y., 1982.

Grey, Margot. *Return from Death*. Arkana, London and New York, 1987.

Grosso, Michael. *The Final Choice*. Stillpoint Publishing, Walpose, New Hampshire, 1985.

Harris, Barbara. *Full Circle*. Pocket Books, 1991.

Lundahl, Craig R. *A Collection of Near-Death Research Readings*. Nelson-Hall Publishers, Chicago, Ill., 1982.

Millett, Larry R. *A Touch of Here and Beyond*. Hawkes Publishing, Inc., Salt Lake City, Utah 84115.

Moody, Raymond A., Jr. *Life After Life*. Bantam Books, New York, N.Y., 1988.

Moody, Raymond A., Jr. *The Light Beyond*. Bantam Books, New York, N.Y., 1988.

Moody, Raymond A. Jr., M.D. *Reflections on Life After Life*, Bantam Books, N.Y., 1983.

Morse, Melvin with Perry, Paul. *Closer to the Light*. Villard Books, New York, N.Y., 1990

Murphet, Howard. *Beyond Death*. Quest Books, The Theosophocial Publishing House, Wheaton, Ill. 1990.

Nelson, Lee. *Beyond the Veil-Volume I*. Cedar Fort Inc., Orem, Utah 84057, 1988.

Nelson, Lee. *Beyond the Veil-Volume II*. Cedar Fort Inc., Orem, Utah 84057, 1989.

Rawlings, Maurice. *Beyond Death's Door*. Bantam Books, N.Y., 1979.

Ring, Kenneth. *Heading Toward Omega*. William Morrow, Inc. N.Y., 1985.

Ring, Kenneth. *Life at Death*. Quill, New York, N.Y., 1982.

Ritchie, George G. with Sherrill, Elizabeth. *Return from Tomorrow.* Spire Books, Fleming H. Revell Co., Old Tappan, New Jersey, 1978.

Siegel, Ronald K. *Anti-matter—Remembering Rogo*. Omni Magazine, Jan. 1991.

Sorensen, Michele R.; Willmore, David R. *The Journey Beyond Life, Vol. One*. Family Affair Books, Orem, Utah 84057, 1988.

Storm, Howard. Unpublished document in possession of author; transcribed from taped experience recorded in 1989 at The NDE Reasearch Institute, 702 North Fort Thomas Ave., Fort Thomas, KY 41705.

Serdahely, William J., and Walker, Barbara A. *The Near-Death Experience of a Non-verbal Person with Congenital Quadriplegia*. Journal of Near-Death Studies, Vol. 9, No. 2, Winter 1990, Human Sciences Press, 233 Spring St., N.Y., N.Y.

Wilson, Ian. *The After Death Experience*, William Morrow and Company, Inc., N.Y., 1987.

Zaleski, Carol. *Otherworld Journeys*. Oxford University Press, N.Y. and Oxford, 1987.

Other Literature

Ganaway, George K. *Historical vs. Narrative Truth: Clarifying the Role of Exogenous Trauma in the Etiology of MPD and its Variants*, Dissociation, Vol. II, No. 4: December, 1989.

Gibson, Arvin S. *In Search of Angels*. Horizon Publishers and Distributors, Inc., Bountiful, Utah 84011, 1990.

Gregory, Richard L. *The Oxford Companion to the Mind*. Oxford University Press, N.Y., 1988.

Moody, Raymond A. Jr. *Coming Back-A Psychiatrist Explores Past-Life Journeys*, Bantam Books, N.Y., London, 1991.

Ludwig, Arnold M. *Principles of Clinical Psychiatry.* The Free Press, Macmillan, Inc., N.Y., 1986.

Orne, Martin T.; Whitehouse, Wayne G.; Dubges, David F.; Orne, Emily Carota. *Reconstructing Memory through Hypnosis*; University of Pennsylvania School of Medicine; from Hypnosis and Memory, Edited by Pettinati, Helen M., The Guilford Press, N.Y., 1988.

Stevenson, Ian. *Twenty Cases Suggestive of Reincarnation*. University of Virginia Press, Charlottesville; 1974 (Reprinted 1978).

Zilbergeld, B. *Hypnosis Questions and Answers*, The Validity of Memories Retrieved in Hypnosis, W. W. Norton and Co., N.Y., 1986.

Index

I

J

K

N

O

P

R

S

T

U

V

W

Y

Z